REFLECTIONS FOR

DAILY PRAYER

ADVENT **2017** TO
EVE OF ADVENT **2018**

CHRISTOPHER COCKSWORTH
GILLIAN COOPER
STEPHEN COTTRELL
STEVEN CROFT
MAGGI DAWN
MALCOLM GUITE
CHRISTOPHER HERBERT
JOHN KIDDLE
BARBARA MOSSE
MARK OAKLEY
MARTYN PERCY
JOHN PRITCHARD
BEN QUASH
ANGELA TILBY
CATHERINE WILLIAMS
JANE WILLIAMS
LUCY WINKETT
CHRISTOPHER WOODS
JEREMY WORTHEN

Church House Publishing
Church House
Great Smith Street
London SW1P 3AZ

ISBN 978 1 78140 019 7

Published 2017 by Church House Publishing
Copyright © The Archbishops' Council 2017

The opinions expressed in this book are those of the
authors and do not necessarily reflect the official policy of
the General Synod or The Archbishops' Council of the
Church of England.

Liturgical editor: Peter Moger
Series editor: Hugh Hillyard-Parker
Designed and typeset by Hugh Hillyard-Parker
Copy edited by Ros Connelly
Printed and bound by CPI Group (UK) Ltd, Croydon, CR0 4YY

What do you think of *Reflections for Daily Prayer*?

We'd love to hear from you – simply email us at

publishing@churchofengland.org

or write to us at

Church House Publishing, Church House,
Great Smith Street, London SW1P 3AZ.

Visit **www.dailyprayer.org.uk** for more
information on the *Reflections* series, ordering
and subscriptions.

Contents

Table of contributors

About the authors

Christopher Cocksworth is the Bishop of Coventry. He read Theology at the University of Manchester. After teaching in secondary education, he trained for ordination and pursued doctoral studies, serving in parochial and chaplaincy ministry and in theological education, latterly as Principal of Ridley Hall, Cambridge.

Gillian Cooper is a writer who has previously worked as a theological educator, a cathedral verger, and an administrator. After many years of helping Christians read the Bible, she remains committed to exploring how the Old Testament speaks to life and faith.

Stephen Cottrell is the Bishop of Chelmsford. He is a well-known writer and speaker on evangelism, spirituality and catechesis. He is one of the team that produced *Pilgrim*, the popular course for the Christian Journey.

Steven Croft is the Bishop of Oxford. He was previously Bishop of Sheffield and team leader of Fresh Expressions. He is the author of a number of books including *Leadership: according to the Scriptures* and *The Advent Calendar*, a novel for children and adults.

Maggi Dawn is Associate Professor of Theology and Literature, and Dean of Marquand Chapel, at Yale Divinity School in the USA. Trained in both music and theology, she was ordained in the Diocese of Ely and holds a PhD from the University of Cambridge.

Malcolm Guite is the Chaplain of Girton College, Cambridge, a poet and author of *What do Christians Believe?; Faith, Hope and Poetry; Sounding the Seasons: Seventy Sonnets for the Christian Year; The Singing Bowl; Word in the Wilderness* and *Mariner: A voyage with Samuel Taylor Coleridge*.

Christopher Herbert was ordained in Hereford in 1967, becoming a curate and then Diocesan Director of Education. He was an incumbent in Surrey and later, Archdeacon of Dorking. Appointed Bishop of St Albans, he retired in 2009.

John Kiddle is Archdeacon of Wandsworth and was previously Director of Mission in St Albans Diocese. Before that, while in parish ministry in Watford, he led the congregation in a project to build a new church and parish centre. He served his curacy and was a vicar in Liverpool Diocese.

Barbara Mosse is a writer and retired Anglican priest. Prior to retirement she was a lecturer on the MA in Christian Spirituality at Sarum College, Salisbury. Earlier ministerial posts included some parish work, alongside chaplaincy experience in prison, university, community mental health and hospital. She is the author of *The Treasures of Darkness, Encircling the Christian Year* and *Welcoming the Way of the Cross*.

Mark Oakley is Canon Chancellor of St Paul's Cathedral. A former Chaplain to the Bishop of London and Rector of St Paul's, Covent Garden, he is also the author of *The Collage of God* (2001) and *The Splash of Words: Believing in Poetry* (2016), as well as articles and reviews, usually in the areas of faith, poetry and literature. He is Visiting Lecturer in the department of Theology and Religious Studies at King's College London.

Martyn Percy is the Dean of Christ Church, Oxford, one of the University of Oxford's largest colleges, as well as the Cathedral Church of the Diocese of Oxford. From 2004 to 2014 he was Principal of Ripon College, Cuddesdon. Prior to that he was Director of the Lincoln Theological Institute and has also been Chaplain and Director of Studies at Christ's College, Cambridge.

John Pritchard was Bishop of Oxford from 2007 to 2014. Prior to that he was Bishop of Jarrow, Archdeacon of Canterbury and Warden of Cranmer Hall, Durham. His only ambition was to be a vicar, which he was in Taunton for eight happy years. He enjoys armchair sport, walking, reading, music, theatre and recovering.

Ben Quash has been Professor of Christianity and the Arts at King's College London since 2007, and is Director of the Centre for Arts and the Sacred at King's (ASK). Prior to that he was Dean and Fellow of Peterhouse, Cambridge. He runs a collaborative MA in Christianity and the Arts with the National Gallery in London, and is also Canon Theologian of both Coventry and Bradford Cathedrals.

Angela Tilby is a Canon Emeritus of Christ Church Cathedral Oxford. Prior to that she served in the Diocese of Oxford following a period in Cambridge, where she was at Westcott House and St Bene't's Church. Before ordination she was a producer for the BBC, and she still broadcasts regularly.

Rachel Treweek is the Bishop of Gloucester and the first female diocesan bishop in England. She served in two parishes in London and was Archdeacon of Northolt and later Hackney. Prior to ordination she was a speech and language therapist and is a trained practitioner in conflict transformation.

Catherine Williams is an Anglican priest working as a Selection Secretary for the Ministry Division of the Archbishops' Council. Her ministerial priorities are vocational discernment, prayer and spiritual direction. She lives in Tewkesbury and is passionate about poetry, music, theatre and butterflies.

Jane Williams is Assistant Dean and Tutor in Theology at St Mellitus College and is a Visiting Lecturer at King's College London. She is the author of a number of books, her most recent being *Why Did Jesus Have to Die?* (2016).

Lucy Winkett is Rector of St James's Church, Piccadilly. She contributes regularly to Radio 4's 'Thought for the Day' and is the author of *Our Sound is our Wound*. She is a Governor of The Queen's Theological Foundation Birmingham and is on the board of The National Churches Trust. Until 2010, she was Canon Precentor of St Paul's Cathedral, and in 2012 was awarded an honorary doctorate from Winchester University.

Christopher Woods is a vicar in Stepney, East London, also working in the Stepney Training and Development office. Before that he was Secretary to the Church of England's Liturgical Commission and National Worship Adviser.

Jeremy Worthen is a priest in the Church of England and is currently the Secretary for Ecumenical Relations and Theology at the Council for Christian Unity. He previously worked in theological education and has written on a range of subjects, including Jewish–Christian relations. His publications include *Responding to God's Call* (2012).

About Reflections for Daily Prayer

Based on the *Common Worship Lectionary* readings for Morning Prayer, these daily reflections are designed to refresh and inspire times of personal prayer. The aim is to provide rich, contemporary and engaging insights into Scripture.

Each page lists the Lectionary readings for the day, with the main psalms for that day highlighted in **bold**. The Collect of the day – either the *Common Worship* collect or the shorter additional Collect – is also included.

For those using this book in conjunction with a service of Morning Prayer, the following conventions apply: a psalm printed in parentheses is omitted if it has been used as the opening canticle at that office; a psalm marked with an asterisk may be shortened if desired.

A short reflection is provided on either the Old or New Testament reading. Popular writers, experienced ministers, biblical scholars and theologians will be contributing to this series. They all bring their own emphases, enthusiasms and approaches to biblical interpretation to bear.

Regular users of Morning Prayer and *Time to Pray* (from *Common Worship: Daily Prayer*) and anyone who follows the Lectionary for their regular Bible reading will benefit from the rich variety of traditions represented in these stimulating and accessible pieces.

This volume also includes both a simple form of *Common Worship: Morning Prayer* (see inside front and back covers) and a short form of Night Prayer – also known as Compline – (see pp. 326–7), particularly for the benefit of those readers who are new to the habit of the Daily Office or for any reader while travelling.

Building daily prayer into daily life

In our morning routines there are many tasks we do without giving much thought to them, and others that we do with careful attention. Daily prayer and Bible reading is a strange mixture of these. These are disciplines (and gifts) that we as Christians should have in our daily pattern, but they are not tasks to be ticked off. Rather they are a key component of our developing relationship with God. In them is *life* – for the fruits of this time are to be lived out by us – and to be most fruitful, the task requires both purpose and letting go.

In saying a daily office of prayer, we make the deliberate decision to say 'yes' to spending time with God – the God who is always with us. In prayer and attentive reading of the Scriptures, there is both a conscious entering into God's presence and a 'letting go' of all we strive to control: both are our acknowledgement that it is God who is God.

> *... come before his presence with a song...*
>
> *Know that the Lord is God;*
> *it is he that has made us and we are his;*
> *we are his people and the sheep of his pasture.*
>
> *Enter his gates with thanksgiving...*
>
> *(Psalm 100, a traditional Canticle at Morning Prayer)*

If we want a relationship with someone to deepen and grow, we need to spend time with that person. It can be no surprise that the same is true between us and God.

In our daily routines, I suspect that most of us intentionally look in the mirror; occasionally we might see beyond the surface of our external reflection and catch a glimpse of who we truly are. For me, a regular pattern of daily prayer and Bible reading is like a hard look in a clean mirror: it gives a clear reflection of myself, my life and the world in which I live. But it is more than that, for in it I can also see the reflection of God who is most clearly revealed in Jesus Christ and present with us now in the Holy Spirit.

This commitment to daily prayer is about our relationship with the God who is love. St Paul, in his great passage about love, speaks of now seeing 'in a mirror, dimly' but one day seeing face to face: 'Now I know only in part; then I will know fully, even as I have been fully known' (1 Corinthians 13.12). Our daily prayer is part of that seeing in a mirror dimly, and it is also part of our deep yearning for an ever-clearer vision of our God. As we read Scripture, the past and the future converge in the present moment. We hear words from long ago – some of which can appear strange and confusing – and yet, the Holy Spirit is living and active in the present. In this place of relationship and revelation, we open ourselves to the possibility of being changed, of being reshaped in a way that is good for us and all creation.

It is important that the words of prayer and scripture should penetrate deep within rather than be a mere veneer. A quiet location is therefore a helpful starting point. For some, domestic circumstances or daily schedule make that difficult, but it is never impossible to become more fully present to God. The depths of our being can still be accessed no matter the world's clamour and activity. An awareness of this is all part of our journey from a false sense of control to a place of letting go, to a place where there is an opportunity for transformation.

Sometimes in our attention to Scripture there will be connection with places of joy or pain; we might be encouraged or provoked or both. As we look and see and encounter God more deeply, there will be thanksgiving and repentance; the cries of our heart will surface as we acknowledge our needs and desires for ourselves and the world. The liturgy of Morning Prayer gives this voice and space.

I find it helpful to begin Morning Prayer by lighting a candle. This marks my sense of purpose and my acknowledgement of Christ's presence with me. It is also a silent prayer for illumination as I prepare to be attentive to what I see in the mirror, both of myself and of God. Amid the revelation of Scripture and the cries of my heart, the constancy of the tiny flame bears witness to the hope and light of Christ in all that is and will be.

When the candle is extinguished, I try to be still as I watch the smoke disappear. For me, it is symbolic of my prayers merging with the day. I know that my prayer and the reading of Scripture are not the smoke and mirrors of delusion. Rather, they are about encounter and discovery as I seek to venture into the day to love and serve the Lord as a disciple of Jesus Christ.

+ Rachel Treweek

Monday 4 December

Psalms **50**, 54 *or* 1, 2, 3
Isaiah 25.1-9
Matthew 12.1-21

Matthew 12.1-21

'Something greater ...' (v.6)

It's little wonder that the Pharisees 'went out' and set about getting rid of him. Jesus had entered *their* synagogue – and on the *sabbath* – searching out someone on whom he could prove his point – that he, Jesus, was Lord of the sabbath.

Jesus' dangerously controversial claim was made worse by his defence of the law-breaking activity of his disciples. They were simply not permitted to reap and thresh on the sabbath, no matter how small-scale their actions or whatever their apparent hunger.

Yet even though the law was abundantly clear and the interpreters agreed on its meaning, perhaps the Pharisees could have tolerated a sensible discussion within the terms of rabbinic argument. What they couldn't bear was the blasphemous basis of Jesus' argument that with him something greater than David, the temple and the sabbath had come among them.

Controversy about such fundamental symbols of national identity and religious significance – matters on which ethnic survival and promised salvation were seen to depend – was bound to lead to confrontation, and worse was to come. Now, though, Jesus withdraws from the fray. He departs in order to define the sort of greatness to be found in him, and the way he will exercise it. Jesus is God's servant, the bearer of God's Spirit. He brings justice for the nations and he does so gently, neither breaking nor quenching but healing and giving hope. Hence our Advent cry: 'Amen. Come, Lord Jesus!'.

COLLECT

Almighty God,
give us grace to cast away the works of darkness
and to put on the armour of light,
now in the time of this mortal life,
in which your Son Jesus Christ came to us in great humility;
that on the last day,
when he shall come again in his glorious majesty
    to judge the living and the dead,
we may rise to the life immortal;
through him who is alive and reigns with you,
in the unity of the Holy Spirit,
one God, now and for ever.

Reflection by **Christopher Cocksworth**

Psalms **80**, 82 *or* **5**, 6 (8)
Isaiah 26.1-13
Matthew 12.22-37

Tuesday 5 December

Matthew 12.22-37

'... then the kingdom of God has come to you' (v.28)

Yesterday's reading faced us with questions about Jesus' identity – could he really be greater than David, the temple and the sabbath? Today's reading takes us deeper into the identity of Jesus by forcing us to analyse the source of his activity. In so doing we face stark questions about our own identity, and where we stand in relation to the source of all that is good.

Jesus brings speech and sight to a man deprived of both – not through natural disease but by demonic power. On whose authority does Jesus act: the ruler of the demons or the God of Israel? Jesus is not shy of logical argument. It is nonsense, he says, for Satan to cast out Satan. In fact, his case rests on an even more reasoned argument. There is evidence that the strong man has been tied up and his house plundered because those once held in captivity – the blind and the mute among them – are now set free. You decide, he says: is this abundantly good work a sign of God at work among you, God's hand reaching out to heal you and lift you up, or is it the mark of evil in your midst? On your answer depends your destiny, eternally.

Yet to answer well, you will need more than reasoned argument and discerning observation. You will need the Son of David to open your eyes and reset your speech to see and to confess that the child of Mary is truly the Son of Man – and that the Son of Man really is Emmanuel: God with us.

Almighty God,
as your kingdom dawns,
turn us from the darkness of sin to the
light of holiness,
that we may be ready to meet you
in our Lord and Saviour, Jesus Christ.

COLLECT

Wednesday 6 December

Psalms 5, **7** *or* **119.1-32**
Isaiah 28.1-13
Matthew 12.38-end

Matthew 12.38-end

'Teacher, we wish to see a sign from you' (v.38)

If Jesus really was the Servant of the Lord, full of God's Spirit and, thereby, the promised Son of Man who is Lord of the sabbath, then it wasn't unreasonable for the religious authorities to ask for some sort of sign to back up these momentous claims. It wasn't that Jesus objected to the request for evidence of spiritual credibility. After all, the great figures of old – Moses, Gideon, Elijah among them – had been supported by signs that reinforced their words. It was just that he knew that the sort of indicators of God's blessing on his ministry – healings, exorcisms, even a stilled storm – that had been clearly evident would not convince those whose hearts were hard.

Another sign would come, though, greater even than the sign of Jonah because something greater than Jonah and all the prophets had come with Jesus. This is the sign that will bring deliverance from the strongest grip of the monster that stalks humanity, release from the inexorable clutch of death. It won't just cause life to return to how it was. It will recreate life, raising it into life with God, for ever.

Although even this greatest sign will be dismissed by the hard of heart, for the new community of Jesus – those who are truly his mother, brothers and sisters – it will be more than a sign. It will be the reality of resurrection life, the lived experience of the will of Jesus' Father.

Waiting for the light of the child in the manger through the darkness of Advent is like waiting in Lent for the brilliance of resurrection dawn after the shadow of the tomb, for the light of Christ is the light of life.

COLLECT

Almighty God,
give us grace to cast away the works of darkness
and to put on the armour of light,
now in the time of this mortal life,
in which your Son Jesus Christ came to us in great humility;
that on the last day,
when he shall come again in his glorious majesty
    to judge the living and the dead,
we may rise to the life immortal;
through him who is alive and reigns with you,
in the unity of the Holy Spirit,
one God, now and for ever.

Reflection by **Christopher Cocksworth**

Psalms **42**, 43 *or* 14, **15**, 16
Isaiah 28.14-end
Matthew 13.1-23

Thursday 7 December

Matthew 13.1-23

*'... many prophets and righteous people longed to see
what you see' (v.17)*

'That same day', writes Matthew. He wants to underline the
connection with what has just happened. Earlier in the day, Jesus had
defined his family of disciples as those who do the will of his Father.
They are the people who hear 'the word of the kingdom' and
understand it sufficiently to know that it calls them to follow Jesus and
live in his way. They have seen and heard the parable that is Jesus
himself. They have perceived that in the hidden form of the carpenter's
son, the Servant of the Lord – beloved of God in whom God is well
pleased – has come to bring the reality of the kingdom of heaven to
the peoples of the earth, and they have joined him in that new life.

Jesus, the parable of God's purposes, speaks of God's purposes in
parables – stories and sayings that, like him, bear a deeper meaning
than their surface shows. To those who have responded to 'the word
of the kingdom', Jesus explains the meaning of his parables so that
they become a commentary on the life of the kingdom. For those who
still stand on the outside, the parables are more of a challenge. But it
is one to which they can rise. Jesus' community is not a closed circle. It
is always open to those who are ready to receive the seed of the
kingdom and determined to let it grow deep within them, bearing the
good fruit of God's will on earth as in heaven.

Almighty God,
as your kingdom dawns,
turn us from the darkness of sin to the
light of holiness,
that we may be ready to meet you
in our Lord and Saviour, Jesus Christ.

COLLECT

Friday 8 December

Matthew 13.24-43

'I will proclaim what has been hidden' (v.35)

Parables make known the word of the kingdom. They reveal God's ways in hidden form. We need to search for the word veiled in the story. At first elusive, it becomes clear – slowly but surely.

That's how the kingdom of heaven comes to earth – at first hidden, then, finally, abundantly clear. It's hidden in the smallness of the mustard seed, a tiny speck of life buried in a large field. It's hidden in a little lump of sourdough that's mixed with three measures – about sixty pounds – of flour. The generative capacities of the seed and the leaven are out of all proportion to their begetting form: shrub as large as a tree, enough bread to feed a village.

The Son of Man, who makes known what has been hidden since the foundation of the world, does so as the one hidden in the form of a servant, born, as we shall soon celebrate, in human likeness as the child of Mary. Christmas is the 'day of small things' (Zechariah 4.10), the day of a child born in obscurity. With all those who are truly wise, we will rejoice on that day with exceedingly great joy (Matthew 2.10), not only because we are overwhelmed by the humility of the hidden God, but also because we are humbled before the one who will come with the angels as the judge of the world. For then, as the hidden realities come fully to light, evil will be burnt away and the children of the kingdom will shine with their Father's glory.

COLLECT

Almighty God,
give us grace to cast away the works of darkness
and to put on the armour of light,
now in the time of this mortal life,
in which your Son Jesus Christ came to us in great humility;
that on the last day,
when he shall come again in his glorious majesty
    to judge the living and the dead,
we may rise to the life immortal;
through him who is alive and reigns with you,
in the unity of the Holy Spirit,
one God, now and for ever.

Reflection by **Christopher Cocksworth**

Psalms **9**, (10) *or* 20, 21, **23**   **Saturday 9 December**
Isaiah 29.15-end
Matthew 13.44-end

Matthew 13.44-end

'Where then did this man get all this?' (v.56)

Jesus, travelling through Galilee, arrives at his home town, Nazareth, and teaches in the synagogue where he had been such a familiar figure. Astonishment at his teaching was not unusual, but here it took a nasty turn. How could such wisdom and power come from one they had seen growing up with his brothers and sisters, and who had earned his living in his father's firm of local builders? They were scandalized, Matthew tells us: the very reaction that Jesus had warned against earlier when he set out his case to John the Baptist that he was, as John had dared to hope, 'the one who is to come' (Matthew 11.2-6).

Luke tells us more about the incident, how it led to a riot and came very close to a lynching. For all their apparent piety, the people of Jesus' home town who had gathered in the synagogue to hear God's word, missed the treasure in their midst, the pearl of greatest price that was being put in their hands. They proved the point of the parables that Jesus had been telling. Although the word of the kingdom is scattered with indiscriminate grace, not everyone who hears will believe. The eyes of some will remain closed.

Those who see that this wisdom and these deeds of power come from God will use all their strength to take hold of not only his words and works but Jesus himself, the Saviour of the world found in the son of the carpenter, once wrapped in swaddling clothes and laid in a manger.

Almighty God,
as your kingdom dawns,
turn us from the darkness of sin to the
light of holiness,
that we may be ready to meet you
in our Lord and Saviour, Jesus Christ.

COLLECT

Reflection by **Christopher Cocksworth**   15

Monday 11 December

Matthew 14.1-12

'Herod wanted to put him to death' (v.5)

On first reading, this gory account of John the Baptist's illegal execution seems like a distraction from Matthew's carefully staged narrative of Jesus' ministry, with the unfolding of his works and the unveiling of his ministry. On closer inspection, though, Jesus is woven into the story at every point.

Jesus bookends this flashback to John's death. Herod hears reports about Jesus that worry him. Jesus is told of John's fate, and takes himself out of the limelight. The flashback itself foreshadows the fate of Jesus. As 'they did to him whatever they pleased', so they will do to Jesus (Matthew 17.12). The destructive cameo of Herod Antipas' household is the antithesis of the picture Matthew has been painting of the life of the kingdom of heaven and the Servant of the Lord who brings it.

Yes, Herod senses the spiritual in Jesus but he's overtaken by superstition. Herod has his eyes on a prize – he wants John dead – but it brings him grief, deeply disturbing his spirit. Herod feasts with his family and admirers, but their indulgence descends into hellish debauchery. The feast that Jesus is soon to share with thousands will open a window to heaven.

This tale of Herod's excess is a parable not of the kingdom of heaven but of the kingdom of the enemy, the evil one from whose clutches 'the one who is come' is determined to set us free. Like the parables that Jesus told, it invites us to weave our stories into Jesus' story and not another.

COLLECT

O Lord, raise up, we pray, your power
and come among us,
and with great might succour us;
that whereas, through our sins and wickedness
we are grievously hindered
in running the race that is set before us,
your bountiful grace and mercy
may speedily help and deliver us;
through Jesus Christ your Son our Lord,
to whom with you and the Holy Spirit,
be honour and glory, now and for ever.

16 | *Reflection by* **Christopher Cocksworth**

Tuesday 12 December

Matthew 14.13-end

'We have nothing here but ...' (v.17)

The disciples have some bread and fish, hardly enough to feed themselves after a long day, let alone in excess of 5,000 people. Later, on the lake, they have only fear – fear exacerbated by the sight of a mysterious figure gliding over the waters. The crowds in Gennesaret have little chance of the personal attention Jesus usually gave to those he healed, but they are in such need.

To the disciples who have something in their hands, he tells them to bring what they have to him. Taking that into his hands, he multiplies it. To the disciples in the storm who have nothing in their hearts but fear, he walks towards them, speaking words of peace, transforming their fear into faith. 'Come', he says to Peter, but when Peter's faith fails, he reaches out to save him and lifts the sinking man to safety. To the crowds in Gennesaret, the sick and suffering, so many people in need, pleading with unrealistic expectations, Jesus – as it were – extends himself, and the apparently impossible becomes the actually happening as they touch even the edges of his clothing and are healed.

To those who come to Jesus in every age and every state, he poses the challenge of whether we will rely only on the evidence of our senses, or whether we will trust that his heart truly goes out to us, broken open by the compassion of God for his world, the God whose power is made perfect in our weakness (2 Corinthians 12.9).

COLLECT

Almighty God,
purify our hearts and minds,
that when your Son Jesus Christ comes again as
judge and saviour
we may be ready to receive him,
who is our Lord and our God.

Reflection by **Christopher Cocksworth**

Wednesday 13 December

Matthew 15.1-20

'For out of the heart ...' (v.19)

Jesus' public ministry in Galilee is drawing to a close. The shadow of the long walk to Jerusalem begins to loom. Pharisees and scribes travel north from Jerusalem's seat of authority to interrogate Jesus. Perhaps they expect that this rural rabbi, with no credentials, will be put easily into his place. Not a bit of it. For their criticism of his disciples breaking the tradition of the elders, Jesus charges them with breaking the commandments of God and making void the word of the Lord.

Tensions with the religious establishment are escalating, and Jesus, far from easing them, raises them even higher. He gathers a crowd and implores them to understand that a fundamental principle of God's ways is at stake, a principle undermined by the philosophy and practice of scribal orthodoxy. The heart – that driving seat of human attitude and action – is the defining source of personal purity before the personal God. It is with all the strength of the heart that we are to love the Lord our God. Observance of diet and avoidance of dirt without the obedience of the heart will not protect us from defilement. Keeping our hearts close to God determines our capacity to fulfil his law.

Jesus has made a decisive break with his religious culture, a step that sets him on an unstoppable course to Jerusalem, where the obedience of his heart, and the willing offering of his body, creates in us a clean heart and a steadfast spirit (Psalm 51.10). When 'the secrets of the heart' are disclosed, we know that the Christ who comes to the world is at work, and that 'God is really among us' (1 Corinthians 14.24).

COLLECT

O Lord, raise up, we pray, your power
and come among us,
and with great might succour us;
that whereas, through our sins and wickedness
we are grievously hindered
in running the race that is set before us,
your bountiful grace and mercy
may speedily help and deliver us;
through Jesus Christ your Son our Lord,
to whom with you and the Holy Spirit,
be honour and glory, now and for ever.

| *Reflection by* **Christopher Cocksworth**

Psalms 53, **54**, 60 *or* **37***
Isaiah 32
Matthew 15.21-28

Thursday 14 December

Matthew 15.21-28

'Lord, help me' (v.25)

It's very interesting the way two treasured pieces from the Communion Service come from the mouths of gentiles who turn to Jesus, Israel's Messiah, for help and healing. Inspired by the centurion (Matthew 8.5-13), we say in our own day, 'Lord, I am not worthy to receive you, but only say the word, and I shall be healed'. Or, drawing on the words of the Canaanite woman in this story, we admit that 'we are not worthy to gather up the crumbs' under the table of the Lord, but we affirm that the Lord's nature is 'always to have mercy'. Both liturgical gems combine humility before God with a confidence in the abundance of divine grace for all, outsiders as we were and sinners as we are.

Jesus' encounter with the woman doesn't make for easy reading. His words seem unusually harsh. Perhaps the baldness of the words on a page hides a gesture of the arm, a twinkle of an eye, a tongue in a cheek. Or perhaps Jesus made his words hard so as to test the faith of the woman, to see whether she really understood that the grace of Israel's God abounded for the gentiles as well.

What is clear is that Jesus had already prophesied that many will come from 'east and west' (Matthew 8.11) and that now, when this woman comes from the west and says, 'Lord, help me', he does as she asks, gladly sharing the bread of healing. She is, indeed, sent away, but not before she – like us today – has been fed with manna that comes down from heaven.

Almighty God,
purify our hearts and minds,
that when your Son Jesus Christ comes again as
judge and saviour
we may be ready to receive him,
who is our Lord and our God.

COLLECT

Reflection by **Christopher Cocksworth**   19

Friday 15 December

Matthew 15.29-end

'I do not want to send them away hungry' (v.32)

Having headed west towards Tyre, Jesus turned towards the east, probably the gentile region of Decapolis. Walking clockwise around the Sea of Galilee, Jesus climbed into the Golan Heights, perhaps seeking – as he often did – quiet and solitude for prayer. The gentiles, as the Jews before, did not allow that space for himself and God. They came, searching him out in large numbers, bringing with them the sick and suffering, pressing upon him, jostling for their space, hoping for their share in the God of Israel's power.

Jesus did not disappoint them. He healed with the same extravagance as he had done in Jewish circles. Neither, though, did the gentiles disappoint Jesus. Putting their faith in and offering their praise to the God of Israel, they also stayed for a few days with Jesus in the dangerous terrain of the mountains, even to the point of physical risk.

Jesus' heart goes out to them with the same compassion he had for the Jewish crowds who had come to him hungering for healing and hope, yearning for the bread of heaven. But this time the disciples don't even offer the small amount of food they have between them. Jesus may have healed some Gentiles, surely he is not going to miraculously multiply bread for them as well? Had they not understood that 'many will come from east and west and will eat with Abraham, Isaac and Jacob in the kingdom of heaven' (Matthew 8.11)? Have we grasped that Israel's God, and his Messiah, does not want to send any away hungry? Do we live as those who truly believe that God's Son was born the Saviour for all, and that he 'will appear a second time ... to save those who are eagerly waiting for him' (Hebrews 9.28)?

COLLECT

O Lord, raise up, we pray, your power
and come among us,
and with great might succour us;
that whereas, through our sins and wickedness
we are grievously hindered
in running the race that is set before us,
your bountiful grace and mercy
may speedily help and deliver us;
through Jesus Christ your Son our Lord,
to whom with you and the Holy Spirit,
be honour and glory, now and for ever.

20 | *Reflection by* **Christopher Cocksworth**

Psalm **145** *or* 41, **42**, 43
Isaiah 35
Matthew 16.1-12

Matthew 16.1-12

*'How could you fail to perceive that I was not speaking
about bread?' (v.11)*

Here we go again. Religious authorities arrive from Jerusalem to test
Jesus, demanding a sign from heaven to give unambiguous
authentication of his claims and teaching that caused them so much
concern. But as Jesus had earlier told the local leaders, the only sign
that will be given, will be the sign of Jonah – the sign of death and
resurrection, and even that may fail to convince.

Jesus' exasperation with the Pharisees and Sadducees spills over into an
argument with the disciples. How could they be worried about running
out of bread? They had seen with their eyes the extraordinary powers
at work through him in the feedings of multitudes. Have they not
perceived with their hearts the meaning of the miracles? Have they
swallowed the toxic leaven of the leaders' cynicism and, despite
everything they had seen and heard, still failed to recognize that here,
in Jesus, was Israel's Messiah, the Lord's Servant, the Son of Man – the
Bread of Life that comes down from heaven to feed the world?

Jesus heads toward the north, far from Jerusalem, and there, he will
become the examiner, testing his disciples to see whether he can tease
from them the sort of spiritual perception that they will need if they
are to stand any chance of bearing the load that will come their way
when they walk towards Jerusalem.

Will they finally confess that he is the Messiah, the Son of the living
God; and will they take up their cross and follow him? Will we?

Almighty God,
purify our hearts and minds,
that when your Son Jesus Christ comes again as
judge and saviour
we may be ready to receive him,
who is our Lord and our God.

COLLECT

Monday 18 December

Matthew 16.13-end

'... on this rock' (v.18)

Poor Peter! One minute he's blessed and exalted, and the next he's Satan! One minute he's had a great insight; the next he's made an elementary mistake. Yet right in the middle of this alternation (and altercation!) Peter receives a new name – he becomes 'The Rock', the rock that will be a foundation for others; the rock against which hell shall not prevail. And Jesus is as good as his word: in all Peter's ups and downs, insights and idiocies, affirmations and denials, the one thing that is never in doubt is Christ's rock-solid love for Peter, calling, provoking, almost teasing out his love in return.

And it's the same with us. It's not just that we sometimes have to go from plaudits to brickbats and back again in the blink of an eye – you get used to it, people behave like that. The hardest thing is when it feels as if the Lord himself is wavering – when one day we feel so close, and the next it seems that God is, as the poet Geoffrey Hill said, 'distant, difficult'. That's the Petrine experience. But there's another side to it, as Peter himself discovered. Deep down underneath the current crisis is the Love who is himself our rock and our refuge. Jesus loved Peter even as he fell and loved him into recovery. And in the end it was, as always, the risen Jesus, who set things right – and steadied the rock.

COLLECT

O Lord Jesus Christ,
who at your first coming sent your messenger
to prepare your way before you:
grant that the ministers and stewards of your mysteries
may likewise so prepare and make ready your way
by turning the hearts of the disobedient to the wisdom of the just,
that at your second coming to judge the world
we may be found an acceptable people in your sight;
for you are alive and reign with the Father
in the unity of the Holy Spirit,
one God, now and for ever.

| *Reflection by* **Malcolm Guite**

Psalms 144, **146**
Isaiah 38. 9-20
Matthew 17.1-13

Tuesday 19 December

Matthew 17.1-13

'... he was transfigured before them' (v.2)

I once heard this account of the transfiguration described as 'a misplaced resurrection narrative', as though St Matthew had made a slight error with his laptop's cut and paste feature! There is a real and mysterious way this story is a 'resurrection narrative', but it is certainly not 'misplaced'! As we saw yesterday, Peter had already discerned that Jesus was the true messiah. He had some inkling of Christ's glory, but had no idea what that would mean, or how it must lead to the cross. Now Jesus is turning his face towards Jerusalem, and if his disciples are to sustain the sorrow that awaits them all there, they need this mountaintop moment to sustain them, this glimpse of the true glory, of the joy of the kingdom, the light of the resurrection. The light of mount Tabor is there to accompany them through the darkness and eclipse of Good Friday, and it is indeed a resurrection light, a premonition of Easter dawn. My sonnet on the transfiguration is set on Good Friday and voiced for Peter:

> *A sudden blaze of long-extinguished hope*
> *Trembled and tingled through the tender skin.*
> *Nor can this this blackened sky, this darkened scar,*
> *Eclipse that glimpse of how things really are.* *

Maybe it is also good for us, and no 'misplaced narrative', to visit this scene in the dark days of December, days before the light and glory will be veiled in the flesh of the baby at Bethlehem.

*Malcolm Guite, *Sounding the Seasons*, Canterbury Press 2012

God for whom we watch and wait,
you sent John the Baptist to prepare the way of your Son:
give us courage to speak the truth,
to hunger for justice,
and to suffer for the cause of right,
with Jesus Christ our Lord.

COLLECT

Wednesday 20 December

Matthew 17.14-21

'How much longer ...?' (v.17)

'How much longer must I put up with you?' It is at once shocking and comforting to hear these words on the lips of Jesus. Shocking because we have constructed such a safe and sanitized idea of his perfection that we assume that a sinless person would never be exasperated – or at least never give voice to their exasperation. Yet here is Jesus, perfect God and perfect man, utterly exasperated by his own disciples and letting them know! The experience of having delegated a task, only to find it hasn't been done and you have to do it yourself after all is almost universal, so it's good to know that God has been through it too. And here is the comfort: perhaps we needn't be so hard on ourselves when patience wears thin and we sometimes lose our cool, and think – or even say, as Jesus did: 'How much longer must I put up with you?'

But there is more of course, and, as with so many stories of Jesus, a twist in the tail. Jesus may lose *patience* with the disciples and with us, but he never loses *faith*. He turns to them and to us and says: 'Don't ask for more faith; the faith you already have, however tiny it may be, is already more than enough, provided you understand that it is not a strength, or an achievement, it is a seed; not something to hold on to for yourselves, but something to give away so that it grows elsewhere.'

O Lord Jesus Christ,
who at your first coming sent your messenger
to prepare your way before you:
grant that the ministers and stewards of your mysteries
may likewise so prepare and make ready your way
by turning the hearts of the disobedient to the wisdom of the just,
that at your second coming to judge the world
we may be found an acceptable people in your sight;
for you are alive and reign with the Father
in the unity of the Holy Spirit,
one God, now and for ever.

Reflection by **Malcolm Guite**

Thursday 21 December

Matthew 17.22-end

'... cast a hook' (v.27)

I love this story. It's so improper. In the midst of a solemn discussion of tax and tribute, of the mixture of necessity and oppression that goes into funding religion, suddenly comes this magical tale; a tale that feels like it's come from folklore and fairyland; a tale that's full of sheer, delightful, creative serendipity. The context is sombre, indeed, sinister: 'Does your teacher not pay the temple tax?' That is a loaded question! We have just heard Jesus say that he is going to be betrayed. The authorities are looking for any hook they can use to reel Jesus in, and failure to pay a controversial tax might just be the one. After all they try the same ruse again in the temple with the question about Ceasar, which Jesus also answers with a coin.

Here Jesus does something wonderful. In the distinction between children and subjects, he not only affirms what Paul later called 'the glorious liberty of the children of God' (Romans 8.21, KJV), but he also discloses the heart of the gospel: that we are not God's oppressed subjects but his beloved children. However, having established the point in principle, Jesus graciously concedes to paying the tax, so as not to cause unnecessary offence over a small thing (if only his followers also avoided giving unnecessary offence!). And then, with his wonderful searching irony and humour, Jesus suggests that Peter should drop a hook into the sea and reel in something to satisfy those who had hoped to hook and reel him in instead.

God for whom we watch and wait,
you sent John the Baptist to prepare the way of your Son:
give us courage to speak the truth,
to hunger for justice,
and to suffer for the cause of right,
with Jesus Christ our Lord.

COLLECT

Friday 22 December

Psalms **124**, 125, 126, 127
Zephaniah 3.1-13
Matthew 18.1-20

Matthew 18.1-20

'Who is the greatest ...?' (v.1)

There is so much that is rich and challenging in this reading, but perhaps in these days before Christmas, it is this powerful image of the child in the midst that most calls and draws us. It is the worldly desire amongst the disciples to be 'the greatest' that leads Jesus to place in their midst 'the least', not only the smallest in stature but one of the least regarded, most marginalized, most powerless group in that culture: a child.

Jesus then begins another of his great and creative reversals. He calls the grown-ups to learn a lesson from the children; calls the disciples to change and become child-like again. It is no small thing he is asking: that humility, that willing self-diminishment, setting aside power and privilege, refusing to tower over people. But Jesus never asks of us anything he does not do himself. We read this story on the brink of Christmas, approaching the day when we remember that the king of heaven himself did indeed change and become like a little child – indeed more than just *like* a child, for the God of heaven came down and became a child, that he might find, redeem and enthrone the child in us, and that we in turn might welcome, and find our welcome in, the lowest and the least, rather than wasting our breath on the heart-withering question: 'Who is the greatest?'

COLLECT

O Lord Jesus Christ,
who at your first coming sent your messenger
to prepare your way before you:
grant that the ministers and stewards of your mysteries
may likewise so prepare and make ready your way
by turning the hearts of the disobedient to the wisdom of the just,
that at your second coming to judge the world
we may be found an acceptable people in your sight;
for you are alive and reign with the Father
in the unity of the Holy Spirit,
one God, now and for ever.

Reflection by **Malcolm Guite**

Psalms 128, 129, **130**, 131
Zephaniah 3.14-end
Matthew 18.21-end

Matthew 18.21-end

'... seventy-seven times' (v.22)

C. S. Lewis has a nice take on this call to forgive 77 times. He says it may not be that we have to forgive 77 separate offences; it's that it may take us 77 attempts to forgive someone fully even once. We forgive them. We say 'I've let it go'. Then that night we remember the offence again. It rankles. We get cross. We suddenly realize we haven't really forgiven them, so we sigh and forgive again, saying 'Now that's done'. But then, something else reminds us and we have to start again. We may only have said 'I forgive' out loud once, but there's been a lot more unspoken forgiving to do.

If that is so, if it is so hard to forgive, if we find ourselves trapped in a repetitive loop of resentment, then Jesus' outrageous parable of the two debtors might reframe everything for us and break the cycle. In this story we are invited to give up playing the tiresome role of the magnanimous (but secretly resentful) forgiver and suddenly remember that we are also the unexpectedly, utterly, forgiven. Then, instead of the effort to muster up a feeling we may not have, we can let sheer gratitude for our own undeserved release from guilt flow out naturally into release and peace for others.

God for whom we watch and wait,
you sent John the Baptist to prepare the way of your Son:
give us courage to speak the truth,
to hunger for justice,
and to suffer for the cause of right,
with Jesus Christ our Lord.

COLLECT

Reflection by **Malcolm Guite**

Monday 25 December
Christmas Day

Psalms 110, 117
Isaiah 62.1-5
Matthew 1.18-end

Matthew 1.18-end
'... do not be afraid' (v.20)

If there was immense courage in Mary's 'yes' to God, then there is also quiet courage in Joseph's 'yes' to Mary here. Courage to go through with a commitment he thought had been betrayed; courage to take the extraordinary adventure as it came; courage to step aside, to set himself and his rights aside, to make room for Mary and the baby.

Now her 'yes', and his, have made way and room for God's most gracious and beautiful 'yes' to all of us, in the birth of Jesus Christ in whom 'every one of God's promises is a "Yes"' (2 Corinthians 1.20).

His name, the promise hidden in 'Emmanuel', is fulfilled not only on this day of his birth but throughout his life and ministry: he is with us and for us, from the first sign of his glory in the wedding at Cana, to his last words in Matthew's Gospel 'I am with you always, to the end of the age'. He is with us from the cradle to the grave – from our cradles and his, as this day he shares our infancy, to our graves and his, as he goes through the grave and gate for us and wins for us a way through that shadowed valley so that he might bring us to the day of resurrection – his and ours.

He was born to be with us on earth, with us in and through all things, so that, at the end of all things, we might be with him in heaven.

COLLECT

Almighty God,
you have given us your only-begotten Son
to take our nature upon him
and as at this time to be born of a pure virgin:
grant that we, who have been born again
and made your children by adoption and grace,
may daily be renewed by your Holy Spirit;
through Jesus Christ your Son our Lord,
who is alive and reigns with you,
in the unity of the Holy Spirit,
one God, now and for ever.

| *Reflection by* **Malcolm Guite**

Psalms 13, 31.1-8, 150
Jeremiah 26.12-15
Acts 6

Tuesday 26 December

Stephen, deacon, first martyr

Jeremiah 26.12-15

'... innocent blood' (v.15)

What a difference a testament makes! This Old Testament reading, about a prophet ready for martyrdom, is set for St Stephen's day because in the speech that led to his own martyrdom Stephen mentioned the suffering of the prophets: 'Which of the prophets did your ancestors not persecute?' (Acts 7.52)

But if that is continuity with the Old Testament, it is the difference between the Old and the New that we should note: Jeremiah unsparingly calls down the condemnation of blood-guilt on his persecutors: 'if you put me to death, you will be bringing innocent blood upon yourselves and upon this city'. By contrast, Stephen ends his life with these words: 'Lord do not hold this sin against them' (Acts 7.60), words that echo Christ's own 'Father forgive them' (Luke 23.34).

This testament of Stephen's, this New Testament witness, proved more than fruitful. If the blood of the martyrs is the seed of the church, then the first fruit of Stephen's sowing was nothing less than the conversion of St Paul. The odious young Saul, who held the coats at Stephen's stoning, rode out of the Damascus gate, the scene of that martyrdom, perhaps remembering, as he passed the spot, the light in Stephen's face and the last words on his lips. But Paul was to meet on that road the same light and love that had shone from Stephen's face in his dying. Jeremiah said 'you will be bringing innocent blood upon yourselves' as a curse; Paul and Stephen knew whose innocent blood it was, and knew it for a blessing.

Gracious Father,
who gave the first martyr Stephen
grace to pray for those who took up stones against him:
grant that in all our sufferings for the truth
we may learn to love even our enemies
and to seek forgiveness for those who desire our hurt,
looking up to heaven to him who was crucified for us,
Jesus Christ, our mediator and advocate,
who is alive and reigns with you,
in the unity of the Holy Spirit,
one God, now and for ever.

COLLECT

Reflection by **Malcolm Guite**   29

Wednesday 27 December

John, Apostle and Evangelist

Psalms **21**, 147.13-end
Exodus 33.12-end
1 John 2.1-11

1 John 2.1-11

'Whoever loves a brother or sister ...' (v.10)

John may be the most mystical of the evangelists, but he is also the most clear and practical, and here he couldn't be clearer – if you are hating, you are still in the darkness; if you are loving, you are already in the light. The light in the darkness, the light that darkness never overcomes, is a strong theme in his Gospel, but that Gospel is sometimes read so cerebrally, so 'spiritually', that, irony of ironies, light and life end up only as words and not as words made flesh.

It's good in this Christmas season to receive a letter from the evangelist who told us at the midnight mass that the Word was made flesh, reminding us that all our good words – 'love', 'light', 'truth', all God's good words to us – must also be made flesh. If heaven is made visible in Jesus, then Jesus must be made visible in us, walking just as he walked.

Today's reading gives us the extraordinary words 'a new commandment that is true in him and in you'. All that is true in Jesus, all that he does and is, comes to dwell in and with us. Jesus comes so close to us in John that we are invited with the beloved disciple to lean on his bosom and listen to his heart. Now John invites us to keep that intimate pulse of love beating in the world.

COLLECT

Merciful Lord,
cast your bright beams of light upon the Church:
that, being enlightened by the teaching
of your blessed apostle and evangelist Saint John,
we may so walk in the light of your truth
that we may at last attain to the light of everlasting life;
through Jesus Christ your incarnate Son our Lord,
who is alive and reigns with you,
in the unity of the Holy Spirit,
one God, now and for ever.

Reflection by **Malcolm Guite**

Psalms **36**, 146
Baruch 4.21-27
or Genesis 37.13-20
Matthew 18.1-10

Thursday 28 December
The Holy Innocents

Genesis 37.13-20

'... they conspired to kill him' (v.18)

It's always hard, Holy Innocents day coming so swiftly after Christmas. Yet almost inevitably the news seems to mirror the lectionary, so that right in the midst of the Christmas season, surrounded by family and safe ourselves, images of children dying in war pour into our homes. As we reel from, and wrestle with, these horrors, at least we know that our faith is not a stranger to pain and betrayal, that others who share our almost impossible hope in the gospel, hope in the light that shines in darkness, have wrestled with these things too. Genesis reminds us of the fratricidal conspiracy of Joseph's brothers, but will go on to tell us of how the persecution of 'this dreamer' Joseph led in a strange way to the salvation of his whole people, his brothers included.

Last week we reflected on another Joseph, another dreamer, who also left Israel for Egypt; today we contemplate the appalling massacre that triggered that second Joseph's flight with his family. But we do so in the knowledge that, just as Joseph's brothers came in the end to stand in humility before their victim, so every Herod too will stand before the lamb, as I wrote in my sonnet 'Refugee':

> *'Whilst Herod rages still from his dark tower*
> *Christ clings to Mary, fingers tightly curled,*
> *The lambs are slaughtered by the men of power,*
> *And death squads spread their curse across the world.*
> *But every Herod dies, and comes alone*
> *To stand before the Lamb upon the throne.'*

*Malcolm Guite, Sounding the Seasons, Canterbury Press 2012

COLLECT

Heavenly Father,
whose children suffered at the hands of Herod,
though they had done no wrong:
by the suffering of your Son
and by the innocence of our lives
frustrate all evil designs
and establish your reign of justice and peace;
through Jesus Christ your Son our Lord,
who is alive and reigns with you,
in the unity of the Holy Spirit,
one God, now and for ever.

Reflection by **Malcolm Guite** | 31

Friday 29 December

Psalms 19, 20
Jonah 1
Colossians 1.1-14

Colossians 1.1-14

'... as you bear fruit' (v.10)

This great prayer of Saint Paul's takes root in us and bears fruit because, rooted and growing in the prayer itself, is the hidden image of a fruitful tree. Paul speaks of 'the hope' of 'the gospel that has come to you' as something that 'is bearing fruit and growing in the whole world'. Having evoked the image of the gospel hope as a tree, he goes on to see each of us also, in our own way, as a tree. So he prays 'as you bear fruit in every good work and as you grow ... May you be made strong'.

The seed of this fruitful image in surely sown in the gospel itself: in Christ's teaching that a sound tree cannot bear bad fruit (Matthew 7.18); in his parable of the mustard seed that becomes a tree whose branches are so hospitable (Matthew 13.31-2); in his mysterious 'I am' saying about the vine whose branches we are, whose fruit we bear (John 15.5).

Colossians is a letter that reminds us that we are rooted in Christ, that we can both be and bear his fruit, and that Christ himself is the root and ground of all existence, the tree that joins heaven and earth, the one in whom and through whom all things hold together. Over the Christmas season we may have sung 'Jesus Christ the Apple Tree', that mystic and prophetic poem; today's reading reminds us that we belong to that tree whose leaves are for the healing of the nations.

COLLECT

Almighty God,
you have given us your only-begotten Son
to take our nature upon him
and as at this time to be born of a pure virgin:
grant that we, who have been born again
and made your children by adoption and grace,
may daily be renewed by your Holy Spirit;
through Jesus Christ your Son our Lord,
who is alive and reigns with you,
in the unity of the Holy Spirit,
one God, now and for ever.

| *Reflection by* **Malcolm Guite**

Psalms 111, 112, **113**
Jonah 2
Colossians 1.15-23

Saturday 30 December

Colossians 1.15-23

'... in him all things hold together' (v.17)

This great hymn to Christ in Colossians has the same cosmic resonance – indeed hints at the same final coherence – as the prologue to John's Gospel. It lifts us out of our littleness. The next time your PCC is bogged down in a discussion of stationery, or the minutiae of the coffee rota seems to loom larger than it should, it would be well to recite, in awe-struck tones these verses of Colossians: all-inclusive, and all-transforming, that great phrase 'all things' is repeated again and again. Nothing and no one is beyond God's presence, or the reach and scope of his concern.

But there is more: this passage is not only about presence and coherence, about all things holding together in Christ; it is also about peace and reconciliation. It is not only that Christ reconciles things on a cosmic scale, bringing together, as he does, the very things we contrast and oppose – heaven and earth, time and eternity, truth and grace – but he is also reconciling us, individually and collectively, on a detailed, difficult, nitty-gritty level, so that we who have been 'estranged and hostile in mind' can be reconciled and make 'peace through the blood of this cross'.

Maybe that's worth sharing with the PCC too!

Lord Jesus Christ,
your birth at Bethlehem
draws us to kneel in wonder at heaven touching earth:
accept our heartfelt praise
as we worship you,
our Saviour and our eternal God.

COLLECT

Reflection by **Malcolm Guite** | 33

Monday 1 January

Naming and Circumcision of Jesus

Psalms **103**, 150
Genesis 17.1-13
Romans 2.17-end

Romans 2.17-end

'... a matter of the heart' (v.29)

This is a day and a week for reflection and resolutions, for new beginnings. Paul takes us right to the heart of the matter. We read this passage today because we remember the circumcision of Jesus. These verses form part of Paul's great argument in Romans that all of us can be set right with God only through faith in Jesus Christ and not through outward observance of the law. Our salvation does not depend on us but on the one whose name means 'Saviour'.

Paul encourages us to look deeper than our outward keeping of the commandments and our boasting. Paul directs us to look within, at our own desires and motives and actions; true circumcision (being set right with God) is a matter of the heart.

And if we look within, we will find that God has so much more still to do in our long journey to holiness. We are a long way from the good people we would like to be. Our motives are mixed; our minds are confused. Goodness is an elusive and a lifelong calling.

It may not feel like it, but this is good news. God is patient and kind and draws near not to condemn but to encourage and to transform us. We offer God our hearts at the beginning of a new year in faith and trust that Jesus comes to dwell in them not because we are perfect but because we need his presence.

COLLECT

Almighty God,
whose blessed Son was circumcised
in obedience to the law for our sake
and given the Name that is above every name:
give us grace faithfully to bear his Name,
to worship him in the freedom of the Spirit,
and to proclaim him as the Saviour of the world;
who is alive and reigns with you,
in the unity of the Holy Spirit,
one God, now and for ever.

Reflection by **Steven Croft**

Psalm **18.1-30**
Ruth I
Colossians 2.8-end

Tuesday 2 January

Colossians 2.8-end

'Do not let anyone disqualify you' (v.18)

Jesus Christ is the golden thread running through Colossians. In chapter 1, Paul presents Christ as the image of the invisible God, the one who holds the universe together. In chapter 2, he begins to answer the question, 'How then shall we live as the body of Christ?' The headline answer is in verse 6: 'As you therefore have received Christ Jesus the Lord, continue to live your lives in him, rooted and built up in him and established in the faith ...' The rest of the epistle unpacks what it means to go on as we began.

Colossians gives us first a negative vision, then a positive one. The negative vision is in two parts: first the ideas we must avoid and then the practices. It's a great letter to read in the first week of a new year, as we examine our lives and strip out what has crept in and make new resolutions for the future.

What are the ideas we must avoid then? Basically anything that makes the Christian life more complicated and adds to our obligations. The gospel is remarkably simple and very good news. There has been a constant temptation to add to its simplicity a range of other obligations about worship or diet or special knowledge. Whenever this happens, Christ moves out of the central focus of our lives and we easily fall back from freedom to captivity again.

Take stock at the beginning of the year. What have you mentally added to the core of your Christian faith? Make your return, once again, to mere Chrsitianity, to the heart of the gospel.

COLLECT

Almighty God,
who wonderfully created us in your own image
and yet more wonderfully restored us
through your Son Jesus Christ:
grant that, as he came to share in our humanity,
so we may share the life of his divinity;
who is alive and reigns with you,
in the unity of the Holy Spirit,
one God, now and for ever.

Reflection by **Steven Croft**

Wednesday 3 January

Colossians 3.1-11

'... you have stripped off the old self' (v.9)

There are two images woven through this passage, both rooted in the baptism service. The first is the theme of death and resurrection. At baptism, the disciple goes down into the waters of death and rises to new life in Christ. This death is a once and for all event ('for you have died') but also a continual call to holiness ('Put to death, therefore, whatever in you is earthly').

In a similar way, resurrection and new life have already begun. The new self 'is being renewed in knowledge according to the image of its creator'. We look forward to the day when we will 'be revealed with him in glory'.

The second image from baptism is taking off one set of clothes and putting on another. At baptism, the disciple comes out of the water, strips off their old garments and is given a new white robe. This profound image is taken deeper. According to Colossians, 'you have stripped off the old self with its practices and have clothed yourselves with the new self'. It is one thing to take off your soiled old clothes. Christ's love penetrates even to peeling back layers of our very self so that we might be healed and renewed.

Each Christian is baptized only once, but the power and the symbolism of our baptism affects us every day as we seek to live our lives in Christ. Every day means death to the old self and awaking to new life. Every day means putting aside our old, soiled clothes and putting on the new self.

COLLECT

Almighty God,
who wonderfully created us in your own image
and yet more wonderfully restored us
through your Son Jesus Christ:
grant that, as he came to share in our humanity,
so we may share the life of his divinity;
who is alive and reigns with you,
in the unity of the Holy Spirit,
one God, now and for ever.

| *Reflection by* **Steven Croft**

Psalm **89.1-37**
Ruth 3
Colossians 3.12 – 4.1

Thursday 4 January

Colossians 3.12 – 4.1

'... clothe yourselves with compassion, kindness, humility, meekness and patience' (3.12)

New clothes are a great event in many families. In parts of Yorkshire and elsewhere, there is still a memory of the annual Whit walks at Pentecost when children would be given their annual new sets of clothes and come together in great festivals.

Paul continues here the image of the new clothes of our baptism. Here is a list of things we should put on, similar to the picture of the whole armour of God in Ephesians 6. Here there are six virtues: compassion, kindness, humility, meekness, patience and love. The sense of the Greek is that we should put on this character in our inmost being: our foundation garments, as it were. These qualities, the qualities of Christ, should be underneath and flow through all we do.

As we read this passage, we should remember that it is addressed primarily not to you or me as individuals but to the whole Church. These virtues lead immediately to forbearance and forgiveness in the body of Christ. From these in turn come peace and thanksgiving, wisdom, worship and glory.

The practical outworking of these qualities will be different in every household and at every life stage. But for today, whatever you are facing, reflect on these six core virtues. How are you called to put them on and live them out where you live and where you work?

God in Trinity,
eternal unity of perfect love:
gather the nations to be one family,
and draw us into your holy life
through the birth of Emmanuel,
our Lord Jesus Christ.

COLLECT

Reflection by **Steven Croft**   37

Friday 5 January

Colossians 4.2-end

'Remember my chains' (v.18)

In the final verse of a beautiful letter, Paul reminds us of the context from which he writes. He is confined and in prison, devoting himself to prayer and to the wellbeing of the Church.

In this chapter, however, Paul is constructing a different set of chains: chains of love to bind together the early Christian community across the distances that separate them. Paul is consciously growing a network, a living community. The body of Christ is more than an abstract idea; it is a lived reality across the cities of the Roman world. This community is not to be dependent on its pastor alone but interdependent, growing to maturity in Christ.

So we read of the connections between individuals, of the bearers of the letter, of Paul's fellow prisoners, of growing connections between Colossae and Laodicea. The Church is more than local: more than my small parish or home group.

Paul had only pen and parchment and faithful companions to connect people together. Today we have printed books, letters, emails and social media. Every communication is the opportunity to build careful connections between different people, to make introductions, to build the Church and the kingdom.

This work of connection is rooted in the prayer of intercession, whether giving thanks or wrestling in prayer on others' behalf. Out of this prayer flows great care in communication: let your speech today be seasoned with salt.

COLLECT | Almighty God,
who wonderfully created us in your own image
and yet more wonderfully restored us
through your Son Jesus Christ:
grant that, as he came to share in our humanity,
so we may share the life of his divinity;
who is alive and reigns with you,
in the unity of the Holy Spirit,
one God, now and for ever.

| *Reflection by* **Steven Croft**

Psalms **132**, 113
Jeremiah 31.7-14
John 1.29-34

Saturday 6 January
Epiphany

John 1.29-34

'I myself did not know him' (vv.31,33)

John's Gospel introduces Jesus with a great fanfare in the first 18 verses. We know that Jesus is the Word become flesh. We know that in him is light, that he is God's Son, that grace and truth come through him.

And then, in the very first scene of the Gospel proper, Jesus is hidden from view. He is in the midst of the crowd as the priests and Levites come from Jerusalem, looking for the Messiah. He watches the drama unfold.

There will be many echoes of this first scene as we read through the Gospel. Jesus is hidden and unseen before he is revealed. He is hidden at the wedding in Cana, working a miracle through Mary. He is hidden to the woman at the well. He hides from the crowd by the lake. He goes in secret to the festival. He is hidden from the man born blind.

Epiphany is about learning to see who Jesus is: about discovering the glory that at first is hidden. John invites us by his irony and riddles to ponder this. The crowd are in the same place as the Messiah they long for, yet they cannot see him or receive him. What are we missing still about Jesus and his glory? Come deeper. Look for longer. Where will you find him in this day and in this season?

O God,
who by the leading of a star
manifested your only Son to the peoples of the earth:
mercifully grant that we,
who know you now by faith,
may at last behold your glory face to face;
through Jesus Christ your Son our Lord,
who is alive and reigns with you,
in the unity of the Holy Spirit,
one God, now and for ever.

COLLECT

Reflection by **Steven Croft**   39

Monday 8 January

Psalms **2**, 110 or **71**
Genesis 1.1-19
Matthew 21.1-17

Matthew 21.1-17

'Who is this?' (v.10)

We return to our reading of Matthew's Gospel, which we began in early November. The story of the triumphal entry begins Matthew's passion narrative. The passage contains four solemn quotations from the Scriptures (echoing the birth narratives in Matthew 1). We are re-introduced to Jesus, as it were, at this point in the Gospel. We no longer see him through the eyes of the disciples. Now our perspective is that of the long years of waiting, of the crowds and the chief priests. There will be hard questions and conflict in the coming days.

At the centre of the passage is the question asked by the whole city: 'Who is this?'. This question has been asked and answered by the disciples at Caesarea Philippi. We return to it from the viewpoint of the crowds and of the long history of Israel. Here is a prophet but more than a prophet: here is the king who has come, the long-awaited one, the Messiah.

What does this king do first as he enters his city? Where does he begin the work of renewal? In the temple, the place of prayer. He clears the space of those who have corrupted its purpose. He establishes again the place of prayer and healing.

Be prepared for your picture of Jesus to grow wider and deeper as we read Matthew this week. Begin with the cleansing of the place and time for prayer as you go forward into this still new year.

COLLECT

Eternal Father,
who at the baptism of Jesus
revealed him to be your Son,
anointing him with the Holy Spirit:
grant to us, who are born again by water and the Spirit,
that we may be faithful to our calling as your adopted children;
through Jesus Christ your Son our Lord,
who is alive and reigns with you,
in the unity of the Holy Spirit,
one God, now and for ever.

Reflection by **Steven Croft**

Psalms 8, **9** or **73**
Genesis 1.20 – 2.3
Matthew 21.18-32

Tuesday 9 January

Matthew 21.18-32

'... if you have faith and do not doubt' (v.21)

The theme of prayer continues in the story of the fig tree. We are often at pains to teach that prayer is much more than asking for things; it is about our relationship with God. However, prayer *is* also about asking for things: both prayer for ourselves and prayer for others. Jesus teaches his disciples a lesson by the roadside: to be bold and full of faith in our prayers of intercession. Prayer is about asking for the impossible, about having big visions, about mustard-seed faith casting mountains into the sea (Matthew 17.20).

The second half of the passage is about authority. Jesus will not tell the chief priests and the elders where his authority comes from. But he will tell the disciples at the very end of the Gospel, that 'all authority in heaven and earth has been given to me' (Matthew 28.18).

Take a moment this day to ponder your vision for your work and life in the coming year. What fruit are you hoping to bear for God? What are the obstacles to that vision? What are the mountains standing in the way? Is your vision wide and deep enough for God's kingdom?

Make a note and begin to pray, in faith and with authority for that vision to come about, for those mountains to be moved.

Heavenly Father,
at the Jordan you revealed Jesus as your Son:
may we recognize him as our Lord
and know ourselves to be your beloved children;
through Jesus Christ our Saviour.

COLLECT

Wednesday 10 January

Matthew 21.33-end

'Finally he sent his son ...' (v.37)

Matthew now offers us three parables, then three questions asked by the Pharisees, and finally a single question and response asked by Jesus. The whole of this teaching and dialogue is set in the courts of the temple, in the presence of the crowd and of the priests and elders.

Matthew is helping us to grapple with a central question for the Gospel writers. If Jesus is the Messiah, why did the leaders of the people reject him? Was his death simply an accident or does it have a deeper meaning?

The parable of the wicked tenants is a brilliant summary of the entire history of Israel. It is rooted in Isaiah's song of the vineyard (Isaiah 5). At the end of Isaiah's parable, the owner of the vineyard promises judgement. Instead of judgement, the owner in Jesus' parable sends messengers again and again, and finally sends his son.

The rejection of Jesus, the Son of God, by the leaders of the people is both the outworking of the whole history of Israel and itself part of the history of salvation. God turns an impossible situation around; Jesus himself is the stone who is rejected but he will become the cornerstone of a new community, a new people 'that produces the fruits of the kingdom'.

Give thanks today for the shape of salvation history and for God's mercy, which triumphs even over rejection.

COLLECT

Eternal Father,
who at the baptism of Jesus
revealed him to be your Son,
anointing him with the Holy Spirit:
grant to us, who are born again by water and the Spirit,
that we may be faithful to our calling as your adopted children;
through Jesus Christ your Son our Lord,
who is alive and reigns with you,
in the unity of the Holy Spirit,
one God, now and for ever.

Reflection by **Steven Croft**

Psalms **21**, 24 *or* **78.1-39***
Genesis 3
Matthew 22.1-14

Thursday 11 January

Matthew 22.1-14

'... but they would not come' (v.3)

There is a seriousness about Matthew's Gospel. Contrast his parable of the wedding banquet with Luke's parable of the great dinner (Luke 14.15-24). In Luke there is almost a sense of comedy in the excuses and the outcome. In Matthew the picture is bleaker. The guests maltreat the servants. The king takes his revenge. The parable ends not with the banquet but with the rejected guest in outer darkness.

Matthew's Church, like much of the Church worldwide today, has lived through persecution and deep suffering. That suffering shapes the tone of the Gospel story and also the sense that our discipleship demands everything. We are responding to God's grace but our response must be the best that we can offer.

Through this sober tone, Matthew is also telling us that salvation is a weighty matter, a serious subject for reflection. The guests 'make light' of their invitation; their lives, like chaff, fly upwards. The people of God are called to be more serious and more substantial.

In a world and a culture that prizes humour, it is easy to laugh but not so easy to be serious and sober. But in the face of the grief and suffering in this world, that is what our faith – and Christian maturity – demand.

Heavenly Father,
at the Jordan you revealed Jesus as your Son:
may we recognize him as our Lord
and know ourselves to be your beloved children;
through Jesus Christ our Saviour.

COLLECT

Friday 12 January

Matthew 22.15-33

'... they were astounded at his teaching' (v.33)

Jesus is very good at controversy. Here are two riddles, two questions designed to entrap him. There is a serious and deadly purpose at work. The first at least is asked with both flattery and malice (v.18).

Jesus demonstrates his wisdom. In his first answer he settles the question of loyalty to the state and loyalty to God once and for all. They are not incompatible. One fits inside the other. There is to be no fanatical rejection of this world or of political reality by the disciples. A judgement can be made about what is due to Caesar. But the greater challenge is to discern what is due to God.

In his second answer, Jesus settles an even more fundamental controversy: will our lives continue beyond death? Is there to be a resurrection? The Sadducees argue that our lives here cannot continue. There will be too many contradictions and complexities. Jesus agrees. However, there is and there will be resurrection, but our lives will be of a different order.

Argument and controversy are a vital part of any teaching ministry. If we would lead others to truth, we cannot agree with everyone. Argument is part of the dialogue between the Church and the world. Controversy in every generation has been part of the life of the Church.

Take time to pray today for areas of controversy in the Church – international, national and local – and for those involved. Pray for sharp wits, for deep wisdom, for courage.

COLLECT

Eternal Father,
who at the baptism of Jesus
revealed him to be your Son,
anointing him with the Holy Spirit:
grant to us, who are born again by water and the Spirit,
that we may be faithful to our calling as your adopted children;
through Jesus Christ your Son our Lord,
who is alive and reigns with you,
in the unity of the Holy Spirit,
one God, now and for ever.

Reflection by **Steven Croft**

Psalms 29, **33** *or* **76**, 79
Genesis 6.1-10
Matthew 22.34-end

Saturday 13 January

Matthew 22.34-end

*'... nor from that day did anyone dare to ask him
any more questions' (v.46)*

Christian disciples are not to be single minded in this sense. It is impossible to separate the priorities of love of God and love of neighbour. Jesus is invited to offer one commandment to top his list. He subverts the question and instead offers two, on which 'hang all the law and the prophets'.

The Church lives in the rhythm set by these commandments. We draw together in worship and prayer, to love God with all our heart and soul and mind and strength. We bring into our worship our love for our neighbour as ourselves, our compassion for the world. We are sent out from worship to love and serve God in the whole of our lives, dedicating ourselves afresh to be a living sacrifice.

The final question returns to the beginning of this section of the Gospel. As Jesus rode into Jerusalem the crowd shouted 'Hosanna to the Son of David!' (Matthew 21.9). Then they asked, 'Who is this?' (Matthew 21.10).

Jesus received their acclamation, but tells them clearly now that they have more still to learn about the Messiah who is to come. He is greater still than David's son, carrying the hopes of the royal line of Israel. As Paul writes, he is David's son according to the flesh but the Son of God according to the Holy Spirit (Romans 1.4).

'Who is this?' Matthew asks the one who dares to read the Gospels today.

> Heavenly Father,
> at the Jordan you revealed Jesus as your Son:
> may we recognize him as our Lord
> and know ourselves to be your beloved children;
> through Jesus Christ our Saviour.

COLLECT

Monday 15 January

Psalms 145, **146** *or* **80**, 82
Genesis 6.11 – 7.10
Matthew 24.1-14

Matthew 24.1-14

'Truly I tell you, not one stone will be left here upon another' (v.2)

Throughout history, human beings have repeatedly tried to predict the date of Christ's return, despite Jesus' warnings not to do so (Matthew 25.13). Repeated failure seems to be no discouragement! As I write, we have survived two recent predictions reported in the press: that the earth was on collision course with a giant meteorite and that we were all about to be obliterated by a sudden flipping of the Earth's poles.

At first glance, today's reading could be seen to be encouraging this kind of speculation. Our passage opens a sequence known as Matthew's 'Little Apocalypse', and in it, Jesus responds to his disciples' admiration of the splendour of the temple buildings by foretelling their total destruction. Despite the disciples' immediately asking for a confirmatory sign, the author seems to focus more on the community's need to be ready for Christ's return wherever and whenever it occurs, rather than waste time and energy in useless speculation.

Jesus' blunt words about the temple offer his disciples a bracing lesson in the spiritual attitude of detachment. Resist the temptation to become attached to 'things', however good and noble. Value the good gifts of God's world, but realise and accept they have no lasting permanence. 'Set your minds on things that are above, not on things that are on earth, for you have died, and your life is hidden with Christ in God' (Colossians 3.2-3).

COLLECT

Almighty God,
in Christ you make all things new:
transform the poverty of our nature by the riches of your grace,
and in the renewal of our lives
make known your heavenly glory;
through Jesus Christ your Son our Lord,
who is alive and reigns with you,
in the unity of the Holy Spirit,
one God, now and for ever.

Psalms **132**, 147.1-12 *or* 87, **89.1-18**   **Tuesday 16 January**
Genesis 7.11-end
Matthew 24.15-28

Matthew 24.15-28

'For false messiahs ... will appear and produce great signs' (v.24)

The Little Apocalypse continues with the description of a situation of great insecurity and danger. The 'desolating sacrilege' standing in the holy place referred originally to the desecration of the temple in 167 BC by the Seleucid king Antiochus IV Epiphanes, an apocalyptic image that became a subject of repeated interpretation. In Matthew it carries the added significance of the destruction of the Temple in AD 70, which may have been obvious to Jesus from the terms of God's original warning to Solomon when the first temple was built: 'If you turn aside from following me ... This house will become a heap of ruins' (1 Kings 9.6,8).

The old certainties have vanished; the atmosphere is tense and the threat real. Jesus warns again about the temptation to look for signs, knowing that in times of great fear and uncertainty, false prophets and leaders will be only too ready to step into the security vacuum. These false prophets may be so convincing that even the 'elect' may be in danger of being deceived by them.

Despite the increase in the narrative's dramatic tension, the lesson here is contiguous with Jesus' earlier teaching. Don't become attached to either place or possessions, because you may have to leave them at a moment's notice. The New Testament scholar Eugene Boring states that 'the community scattered and fleeing is the community in a missionary mode'.* The re-gathering of the community, and the timing of that event, is God's promise and responsibility.

*New Interpreter's Bible, Volume 8, p. 443

Eternal Lord,
our beginning and our end:
bring us with the whole creation
to your glory, hidden through past ages
and made known
in Jesus Christ our Lord.

COLLECT

Wednesday 17 January

Psalms **81**, 147.13-end *or*
119.105-128
Genesis 8.1-14
Matthew 24.29-end

Matthew 24.29-end

'But about that day and hour no one knows ...' (v.36)

As Matthew's Little Apocalypse continues with the signs of the coming cataclysm, today's passage presents us with an apparent paradox. Jesus assures his hearers that these events will soon be fulfilled, but then immediately states that no one knows the timing, not even the Son. Some commentators believe that what we have here are two events: an imminent catastrophe – the Fall of Jerusalem in AD 70 – conflated with more general warnings about signs of the end time.

The challenge for us is to hold the paradox: to accept, and live with, *both* these apparently contradictory pieces of advice. Human nature leans towards an attempt to dissolve the paradox by retreating to one or other of its poles. We find the tension difficult and do our utmost to resolve it into something that feels clear and unambiguous. So some will read the signs of the times and confidently set dates, again and again, on which the end is to come (see 15 January); others carry on 'eating and drinking, marrying and giving in marriage' as if there was never going to be an 'end' at all.

The Lord who urges us to 'be ready' is the same Lord who created more wine for the wedding feast at Cana (John 2.1-11). We need to be ready, but this readiness was never intended to exclude joyful and thankful living. Our task is to walk the tightrope and keep our balance!

COLLECT

Almighty God,
in Christ you make all things new:
transform the poverty of our nature by the riches of your grace,
and in the renewal of our lives
make known your heavenly glory;
through Jesus Christ your Son our Lord,
who is alive and reigns with you,
in the unity of the Holy Spirit,
one God, now and for ever.

Reflection by **Barbara Mosse**

Psalms **76**, 148 *or* 90, **92**   **Thursday 18 January**
Genesis 8.15 – 9.7
Matthew 25.1-13

Matthew 25.1-13

'Truly I tell you, I do not know you' (v.12)

The theme of watching and waiting continues with the parable of the ten bridesmaids. One commentator has remarked that, although we are told at the outset that five of the bridesmaids are wise and five foolish, from outward appearances it is not possible to say which are which. All are eager and dressed for their role, lamps trimmed, and waiting. The difference between the two groups only becomes evident when the arrival of the bridegroom is delayed. The oil for the bridesmaids' lamps runs out, and the foolish ones have not thought to bring a spare supply.

Inevitably, we perhaps feel, the bridegroom arrives while the foolish bridesmaids have left their post to buy more oil. The bridegroom's reply to the latecomers when they return and ask to be admitted may seem harsh, but Jesus' teaching here is echoed many centuries later in a different context: 'the readiness is all' (*Hamlet*, Act 5, Scene 2). It is a teaching Jesus repeats many times, disguised in different parables. If a person wants to build a tower, they should first make sure they have enough resources to complete it (Luke 14.28-30); a king going to war needs first to reckon whether he has sufficient troops to win (Luke 14.31-33). And the parable of the sower tells us that, though many may start out on the Christian journey with enthusiasm, not all will have the resources to see the journey through (Matthew 13.1-8).

Eternal Lord,
our beginning and our end:
bring us with the whole creation
to your glory, hidden through past ages
and made known
in Jesus Christ our Lord.

COLLECT

Reflection by **Barbara Mosse**   49

Friday 19 January

Matthew 25.14-30

'For to all those who have, more will be given ...' (v.29)

Here we have another of Jesus' 'hard sayings', one that, on the surface at least, seems manifestly unfair. Is our Lord *really* endorsing the way our unjust society so often seems to work, with the rich getting richer and the poor, poorer? But of course there is more to it than that, and the message offered here is one of hope, not despair.

As with this week's earlier reflections, the context is again one of waiting, but this time the master gives his slaves personal responsibility for his money while they await his return. There are no precise instructions as to how they are to exercise this responsibility. The first two slaves work steadily and conscientiously, and are praised by their master for doubling the value of what they were given. The master's response to the fearful slave does seem severe, but perhaps its meaning is revealed in part when we remember that earlier in Matthew's Gospel, Jesus told his disciples that no one 'after lighting a lamp puts it under the bushel basket, but on the lampstand' (Matthew 5.15). Disciples are to let their light – their talents – shine out, not bury them in the ground where no one can see them.

Everyone has talents, but inevitably some will have more than others. What matters though is not *how* talented we may happen to be, but the ways in which, before God, we choose to put our own particular talents to use.

COLLECT

Almighty God,
in Christ you make all things new:
transform the poverty of our nature by the riches of your grace,
and in the renewal of our lives
make known your heavenly glory;
through Jesus Christ your Son our Lord,
who is alive and reigns with you,
in the unity of the Holy Spirit,
one God, now and for ever.

| *Reflection by* **Barbara Mosse**

Saturday 20 January

Matthew 25.31-end

'... inherit the kingdom prepared for you from the foundation of the world' (v.34)

When I became a committed Christian many years ago, one of the things that appealed to me most during that time was the clear-cut nature of the teaching I was receiving. People at my church were very clear who was 'in' and who was 'out' regarding Christ and the salvation he offers; but it was this very certainty that I became less comfortable with as time went on.

Jesus' discourse on the Last Judgement seems to challenge our tendency to formulate clear-cut certainties. To those whose Christian pathway has followed a 'faith not works' emphasis, Jesus' illustration may come as something of a shock. The 'sheep' are characterized, not by their faith, but by their *works*. And this kingdom of God where the hungry are fed, the naked clothed and prisoners visited is set against the negative counter-kingdom where the 'goats' – whose destination is 'the eternal fire prepared for the devil and his angels'– do none of these things.

There is a disorienting feel to this teaching, as even the sheep and goats seem unaware of their true status – 'Lord, when was it...?'. If Jesus' words seem harsh, we would do well to look for the underlying problem being held up for judgement. For the 'goats', it is far more than a simple failure of charity; rather there has been a repeated failure to appreciate that in denying the needy, they are denying Christ himself.

COLLECT

Eternal Lord,
our beginning and our end:
bring us with the whole creation
to your glory, hidden through past ages
and made known
in Jesus Christ our Lord.

Reflection by **Barbara Mosse**

Monday 22 January

Psalms 40, **108** *or* **98**, 99, 101
Genesis 11.27 – 12.9
Matthew 26.1-16

Matthew 26.1-16

'Why this waste?' (v.8)

Unlike the parallel accounts of this incident elsewhere in the Gospels, Matthew neither names the woman (as in John 12.1-8), nor does he give any information about her social or moral standing in the community (as in Luke 7.36-50). She is simply 'a woman' who enters Simon's house at Bethany, and pours a jar of expensive perfume over Jesus' head. The disciples' angry reaction may indicate various levels of discomfort: the intimate proximity of the woman to Jesus, perhaps, along with a genuine concern over such apparent 'waste' given Jesus' known concern for the poor and the outcast. Jesus' response will have wrong-footed his followers. There is indeed a reckless extravagance about the woman's behaviour, and she may not have been consciously aware of the reasons for her actions. But Jesus is unequivocal: she has 'performed a good service' for him by anointing his body for burial – and the disciples are to leave her alone.

The passage poses challenging questions as we consider our own relationship to Christ. Do we value God's abundant outpouring of love upon us, and offer him in return the best of our time and attention, our love and commitment? Or are we so distracted that only the dregs are left? Are we ready to 'strive first for the kingdom of God' (Matthew 6.33), and willing for our lives to be so re-ordered that they reflect God's priorities and perspective, rather than our own?

COLLECT

Almighty God,
whose Son revealed in signs and miracles
the wonder of your saving presence:
renew your people with your heavenly grace,
and in all our weakness
sustain us by your mighty power;
through Jesus Christ your Son our Lord,
who is alive and reigns with you,
in the unity of the Holy Spirit,
one God, now and for ever.

Reflection by **Barbara Mosse**

Psalms 34, **36** *or* **106*** (*or* 103)
Genesis 13.2-end
Matthew 26.17-35

Tuesday 23 January

Matthew 26.17-35

*'"Even though I must die with you, I will not deny you."
And so said all the disciples.' (v.35)*

Not for the first time, Peter's heroic intentions are destined to fall short of their mark. Jesus has just made the startling pronouncement that all the disciples would desert him that night. Peter responds instantly and impulsively in the way we have come to expect of him – and the others all agree. The Greek word *skandalizō*, translated here as 'to desert', is an interesting one. Sometimes it is rendered as 'to be offended' – 'And blessed is anyone who takes no offence at me' (Matthew 11.6) – and in Matthew tends to carry the sense of people 'stumbling' when confronted with the truth of Jesus and the kingdom of God. Jesus is here warning his disciples that even they, his closest friends, will 'stumble' as events move towards their inevitable end.

We have here an uncomfortable reminder of our own human tendency to overestimate our strength and courage. We like to believe that our deepest selves are automatically in tune with our intended bravery, and that we will always have the courage to stand firm in the face of danger. But when critically challenged we may find, as did Peter and the other disciples, that an unbridgeable gap exists between our stated intentions and our ability to actually stand by them. We repeatedly fall short; our only hope lies in the realization that God knows us better than we know ourselves, and yet continues to love and forgive us

God of all mercy,
your Son proclaimed good news to the poor,
release to the captives,
and freedom to the oppressed:
anoint us with your Holy Spirit
and set all your people free
to praise you in Christ our Lord.

COLLECT

Wednesday 24 January

Psalms 45, **46** or 110, **111**, 112
Genesis 14
Matthew 26.36-46

Matthew 26.36-46

'... remain here, and stay awake with me' (v.38)

Events move rapidly towards their climax as Jesus and his disciples enter the garden of Gethsemane. Leaving most of the disciples to wait while he prays, Jesus moves further into the garden with Peter, James and John – the privileged trio who were earlier witnesses of his glory at the transfiguration.

For this group, the experience is intended to be more than simply waiting: they are instructed to stay awake and in the process witness something of the agony of Jesus' inner suffering. This is the flip-side of what they experienced on the mountain. There, they saw Jesus' glory; so wonderful that Peter wanted to make it permanent – 'I will make three dwellings...' (Matthew 17.4). Here, however, the mood is altogether darker, and their instinct is to shut out the pain by repeatedly falling asleep.

Writing to his many friends and correspondents, writer and mystic Thomas Merton acknowledged the resistance the human heart encounters when dealing with pain, and its tendency to resort to 'mental tranquillizers'. These aren't of much help, writes Merton, stating that faith needs to go deeper, and to be 'rooted in the unknown and in the abyss of darkness that is the ground of our being'.* In practical terms this means that if we learn how to have a deep inner patience, 'things solve themselves, or God solves them if you prefer: but do not expect to see how. Just learn to wait ...'

*Thomas Merton, *Christmas Letter*, 1966

COLLECT

Almighty God,
whose Son revealed in signs and miracles
the wonder of your saving presence:
renew your people with your heavenly grace,
and in all our weakness
sustain us by your mighty power;
through Jesus Christ your Son our Lord,
who is alive and reigns with you,
in the unity of the Holy Spirit,
one God, now and for ever.

| *Reflection by **Barbara Mosse***

Psalms 66, 147.13-end
Ezekiel 3.22-end
Philippians 3.1-14

Thursday 25 January
The Conversion of Paul

Philippians 3.1-14

'Yet whatever gains I had, these I have come to regard as loss because of Christ' (v.7)

Today's passage from Philippians begins with a warning couched in strong and derogatory language: 'Beware of the dogs, beware of the evil workers, beware of those who mutilate the flesh!'. How does the bitter language expressed here represent the 'good news'?

Context is vital. Here, Paul is denouncing a poisonous attitude that is beginning to threaten the young Church community: the insistence that circumcision was still necessary for the Christian believer. For Paul, circumcision itself becomes representative of a more wide-ranging problem: a tendency to exclusivity that was beginning to infect the Church. All too readily, people began to rely on their own credentials within the community; this then began to act as a means of excluding those who didn't conform, rather than including them.

Paul's response to this dilemma is to turn the whole issue on its head. If credentials are important, then nobody can top Paul's claim! But all this means nothing. Boasting is valid, he states, in one form only: when our boasting is of our fellowship *in Christ* rather than in the supposed priority of our own position. Paul counts his own good standing as loss 'because of the surpassing value of knowing Christ Jesus my Lord'. Our human claims to status tend to exalt some at the expense of others. But to boast of – to acknowledge and own – our mutual belonging in Christ does not create human distinctions; it abolishes them.

COLLECT

Almighty God,
who caused the light of the gospel
to shine throughout the world
through the preaching of your servant Saint Paul:
grant that we who celebrate his wonderful conversion
may follow him in bearing witness to your truth;
through Jesus Christ your Son our Lord,
who is alive and reigns with you,
in the unity of the Holy Spirit,
one God, now and for ever.

Reflection by **Barbara Mosse** | 55

Friday 26 January

Matthew 26.57-end

'You also were with Jesus the Galilean' (v.69)

Peter's earlier protestations of courage and faithfulness to Jesus are soon put to the test. Peter followed the arresting party 'at a distance' to the courtyard of the high priest. Once there, he sat down with the guards 'in order to see how this would end'. Already we see the weakening of his resolve to die with Jesus, if need be; the words of the text paint a skilful and graphic picture of someone concerned to know what happens, but even more concerned to preserve his own skin. Two servant-girls in succession and then a group of bystanders identify Peter as one of Jesus' companions, leading him to deny his association with Jesus with a curse. And then the cock crew...

It could be argued that nothing was to be gained by Peter holding to his resolve. Indeed, the long-term plan outlined earlier by Jesus would have been thwarted had he done so (Matthew 16.18). But we should not, on this account, let Peter – or ourselves – off the hook. It is all too easy for us to gloss over questionable behaviour on the grounds that the eventual outcome was good. When the cock crew, Peter realized immediately the depth of his treachery and cowardice, and it opened up a wound that needed the post-resurrection healing and forgiveness of Christ. We, too, need to recognize our own need for such deep healing.

COLLECT

Almighty God,
whose Son revealed in signs and miracles
the wonder of your saving presence:
renew your people with your heavenly grace,
and in all our weakness
sustain us by your mighty power;
through Jesus Christ your Son our Lord,
who is alive and reigns with you,
in the unity of the Holy Spirit,
one God, now and for ever.

| *Reflection by* **Barbara Mosse**

Psalms **68** *or* 120, **121**, 122
Genesis 17.1-22
Matthew 27.1-10

Saturday 27 January

Matthew 27.1-10

*'When Judas, his betrayer, saw that Jesus was condemned,
he repented ...' (v.3)*

Why did Judas betray Jesus? Over the centuries, history and Church tradition have heaped guilt upon guilt on Judas. Some scholars have suggested, however, that he never actually believed Jesus to be guilty – that his 'betrayal' was nothing more than a disastrously misguided attempt to force Jesus' hand and make him fight back. Verse 3 of today's passage could be read as offering some support to this more compassionate view. When Judas saw the tragic outcome of his actions, he repented and did the best he could to make restitution.

Why did Judas hang himself, rather than go back to the disciples? As we saw in yesterday's reading, Peter too had failed, in his denial of Jesus, while all the other disciples 'deserted him and fled' (Mark 14.50). None of them had behaved well. But the utterly disastrous outcome of Judas' actions may have led the other disciples to view their own disloyalty in a less serious light.

Judas' situation poses difficult questions, and we are not going to resolve the centuries-old arguments over his role within the scope of this short reflection. We can, however, allow the dilemma of Judas' situation, and the Church's subsequent reaction to it, to shed a spotlight on our own tendency to make scapegoats. How often do we point the finger at others in order to lessen our own sense of guilt, enabling us to cling to the illusion that *our* behaviour is somehow less blameworthy?

God of all mercy,
your Son proclaimed good news to the poor,
release to the captives,
and freedom to the oppressed:
anoint us with your Holy Spirit
and set all your people free
to praise you in Christ our Lord.

COLLECT

Reflection by **Barbara Mosse** | 57

Monday 29 January　　　Psalms **57**, 96 *or* 123, 124, 125, **126**
Genesis 18.1-15
Matthew 27.11-26

Matthew 27.11-26

'His blood be on us and on our children!' (v.25)

It is a terrible cry; a cry not just from a crowd but, as Matthew implies, from the whole Jewish nation; a cry that has reverberated down the centuries. We know, with the benefit of hindsight, that that shout twisted medieval Christian thinking about the Jews and led to appalling anti-Semitism in England, Russia and across Europe. We realize, almost 2,000 years after the event, that that cry played a part in the warped thinking that led to the evil of the Holocaust.

There was no way, of course, that Matthew could have foreseen the wicked uses to which his narrative would be put. Nevertheless, we need to ask why he included it in his Gospel.

Perhaps he was reporting what he regarded as an historical fact: that the self-immolating cry had indeed been made on that bleak morning in Jerusalem. Perhaps, for political, theological or cultural reasons, he wanted to demonstrate that it was the Jewish people who were to blame for Jesus' crucifixion, whereas the Romans were morally innocent in the grim affair. Perhaps, at the time he was writing, relations between Jews and Christians were fraught and he wanted to create a kind of *cordon sanitaire* between the young churches and their (possibly hostile) Jewish neighbours.

When you read today's passage, please pray that your own heart and mind might be free of prejudice, and then consider what you might do to ensure that such stereotyping never returns to sully the earth.

COLLECT | God our creator,
who in the beginning
commanded the light to shine out of darkness:
we pray that the light of the glorious gospel of Christ
may dispel the darkness of ignorance and unbelief,
shine into the hearts of all your people,
and reveal the knowledge of your glory
　　in the face of Jesus Christ your Son our Lord,
who is alive and reigns with you,
in the unity of the Holy Spirit,
one God, now and for ever.

| *Reflection by* **Christopher Herbert**

Psalms **93**, 97 *or* **132**, 133
Genesis 18.16-end
Matthew 27.27-44

Matthew 27.27-44

'... and they gathered the whole cohort around him' (v.27)

It is the sounds of the passion we so rarely think about: the banging of the soldiers' hobnailed marching boots on the paving stones; the scrape and swish of the short swords drawn from their scabbards; the cacophony of leather-covered wooden shields being placed on the ground; the bored and restive murmurings of the 480 confused but battle-hardened soldiers; the shouts of their commanding officers echoing off the walls; the slamming of doors; the muffled noises from the street outside ... and at the centre of all of this noise the silent, blood-spattered and exhausted figure of Jesus.

There were worse sounds still to come, but for the moment it was the sounds made by the barely-under-control cohort of soldiers that were dominant.

It is not difficult to imagine. It is relatively easy for us to dwell on the horrors of that early morning encounter between the might of an imperial army and the vulnerability of a single man. But we also need to recall the hard creative task that Matthew set himself when he wrote his account of Christ's last hours on earth. He did not over-emphasize the horrors (he left that to his readers' imaginations); instead, drawing on previous accounts he had seen or heard, he tried to create a narrative that would echo his earlier chapters about Jesus as Emmanuel, God with us.

This is not only a human story; it is also a story at whose very heart is heard the holy sound of the Name of God.

God of heaven,
you send the gospel to the ends of the earth
and your messengers to every nation:
send your Holy Spirit to transform us
by the good news of everlasting life
in Jesus Christ our Lord.

COLLECT

Wednesday 31 January

Psalms **95**, 98 *or* **119.153-end**
Genesis 19.1-3, 12-29
Matthew 27.45-56

Matthew 27.45-56

*'At that moment the curtain of the temple was torn in two,
from top to bottom' (v.51)*

The curtain in the temple separated the Holy of Holies from the Holy Place. Once each year, on the Day of Atonement, the High Priest entered through the curtain into the Holy of Holies. The curtain symbolized the *absolute* distance that existed between God and humankind.

With his vivid picture of the temple curtain being torn in two at the moment of Christ's death, Matthew has asserted that the distance between God and humankind has now been abolished. It's an idea that is radically dramatic. Through Christ's sacrificial death, argues Matthew, humankind has entered an entirely new relationship with God. Nothing can ever be the same again.

It is an astonishing claim, not least because it seems so presumptuous on our part to behave as though the distance between us and God has been eliminated. And yet, in spite of Matthew's daring assertion, we still experience from time to time not just a distance between us and God but the searing *absence* of God. He appears not to be there. We feel as though we are entirely alone on the surface of our planet careering through empty and meaningless space. At such times it isn't as though there is a great gulf fixed between us and God; it's as if God does not exist at all. The anguish is profound and intense.

What can we do at such moments? Simply hang on by our fingertips and wait in faith, believing that the curtain really has been destroyed for ever.

COLLECT

God our creator,
who in the beginning
commanded the light to shine out of darkness:
we pray that the light of the glorious gospel of Christ
may dispel the darkness of ignorance and unbelief,
shine into the hearts of all your people,
and reveal the knowledge of your glory
in the face of Jesus Christ your Son our Lord,
who is alive and reigns with you,
in the unity of the Holy Spirit,
one God, now and for ever.

Reflection by **Christopher Herbert**

Psalms 99, **110** *or* **143**, 146
Genesis 21.1-21
Matthew 27.57-end

Thursday 1 February

Matthew 27.57-end

'Joseph took the body and ... laid it in his own new tomb,
which he had hewn in the rock' (vv.59–60)

The pickaxe rose into the air and swinging through its arc was brought down with intense force on to a natural fissure in the face of the rock. Splinters of stone flew in all directions. The man raised the pickaxe again and again, and each time he split the rock further asunder. He worked with tireless energy until he had made a large hole. He came back the next day and the next, working in the early morning's coolness to create his own cave-like tomb ... It was an honest, slightly obsessive task he had set himself. But in the holy city of Jerusalem he wanted to stake his claim to a place that he had created with his own strong hands, and which would be his and his alone when he died.

It was not to be. Joseph of Arimathea, out of compassion, allowed the grave he had so painstakingly created for himself to become the resting place of the body of Jesus.

That act of generosity has caught the imagination of people ever since and has led to the weaving of delightful legends about him. It is somehow the wrapping of the body so tenderly in linen contrasted with the hardness of the rock-hewn tomb that sets up a creative dissonance in our minds and sends us winging away on flights of imagination.

Even when reading of the degradation of Christ's last moments on earth, our imaginations should be allowed to play their creative part in nourishing our souls.

God of heaven,
you send the gospel to the ends of the earth
and your messengers to every nation:
send your Holy Spirit to transform us
by the good news of everlasting life
in Jesus Christ our Lord.

Reflection by **Christopher Herbert**   61

Friday 2 February
Presentation of Christ
in the Temple

Psalms **48**, 146
Exodus 13.1-16
Romans 12.1-5

Romans 12.1-5

'... present your bodies as a living sacrifice' (v.1)

When Rembrandt was about 25 years of age, he painted a great scene: a towering set of steps going up into the darkness. On the steps are crowds of people. At the foot of the steps is Simeon holding the Christ child. The scene is dramatic, carefully lit, thronged with onlookers. Close to the end of his life Rembrandt reprised the event but this time he concentrated on Simeon and the child Jesus held in Simeon's outstretched arms. Rembrandt has moved his focus from the theatrically grandiose and resplendent to the human and poignant. In his own old age he has contrasted the elderly Simeon and the new life being held with such tender awe. Both paintings are immensely powerful.

The original offering of Jesus in the temple in fulfilment of the law's demands was made by Mary and Joseph. The Christ-child had no say in the matter, but in the child's passivity Simeon foresees the present and the future when God's salvation will be given to all – 'a light for revelation to the Gentiles and for glory to your people Israel' (Luke 2.32). It is our human task simply to receive it with thankful hearts.

Paul continues to explore the theme of offering. He implies that there is reciprocity in it: as Jesus offers himself to us, so we are called to offer ourselves to him. It's a kind of universal dance, a giving and receiving in which our humanity is encircled by the loving arms of God.

COLLECT

Almighty and ever-living God,
clothed in majesty,
whose beloved Son was this day presented in the Temple,
in substance of our flesh:
grant that we may be presented to you
with pure and clean hearts,
by your Son Jesus Christ our Lord,
who is alive and reigns with you,
in the unity of the Holy Spirit,
one God, now and for ever.

| *Reflection by* **Christopher Herbert**

Saturday 3 February

Matthew 28.16-end

'When they saw him, they worshipped him; but some doubted' (v.17)

It's the humanity of the disciples that is so encouraging. There they are: they have received from Mary Magdalene the news of Jesus' resurrection and following her instructions they have gone to a mountain in Galilee. There the risen Jesus himself meets them ... and still some of the disciples are doubtful.

What did they doubt? The evidence of their own senses? The whole resurrection thing? Were they still so traumatized by the Crucifixion that nothing could shake them from their feelings of confused and broken-hearted disbelief?

But it was not just the believing ones who were then commissioned by Jesus, so too were the doubtful ones. Both groups were commanded to go out into all the world and make disciples. Yet again the whole gamut of humanity is taken into the heart and purpose of God. It isn't simply a job for the elite. Doubters and believers are in God's new dispensation together.

If only we Christians could stop trying to decide who is 'in' and who is 'out'. Making decisions of that kind seems to be our primary default setting. And why? Because we fail to trust the merciful bounty of God who takes us as we are, doubts and all, and by grace uses us in his service. Doubters are not discarded as failures.

That surely is a matter for huge thankfulness; we are allowed to be fallible, allowed to be doubtful knowing that God in his merciful goodness is always with us, even to the end of time.

Almighty God,
by whose grace alone we are accepted
and called to your service:
strengthen us by your Holy Spirit
and make us worthy of our calling;
through Jesus Christ your Son our Lord,
who is alive and reigns with you,
in the unity of the Holy Spirit,
one God, now and for ever.

COLLECT

Reflection by **Christopher Herbert**   63

Monday 5 February

Genesis 29.31 – 30.24

*'When Rachel saw that she bore Jacob no children,
she envied her sister' (30.1)*

Those of us who enjoy family history will know the pleasure of trying to trace our ancestors. We hope for stories, for the discovery perhaps of a Duke or Duchess, a rogue or a villain, anything that will add a bit of flavour to the mix. Sometimes we strike lucky; other times a promising lead runs into the sand. The desire to make some sense of where we have come from – and therefore who we are now – is very powerful.

So it was with the people of Israel. They created, or perhaps remembered, some of their folk myths and rehearsed their genealogies with salty delight. Names of clan leaders from the distant past, for instance, Dan or Asher or Reuben, gave them a sense of who they were. But they added to the stories an emotional set of spices: jealousy, betrayal, double-dealing, love. These were not simple genealogical researches; they were stories that encompassed our human foibles and failings. Yet running through the stories is also a sense that this collection of clans was not a chance political creation; somewhere in this muddle there was God who was working out his purposes through them.

Of course, the historians who composed these stories had their own motives for doing so and we must not leap simplistically from the clan story to the conditions of our own age, but if God be God then is not entering the muddle of who we are and bringing pattern and purpose to it, what God does?

COLLECT

Almighty God,
you have created the heavens and the earth
and made us in your own image:
teach us to discern your hand in all your works
and your likeness in all your children;
through Jesus Christ your Son our Lord,
who with you and the Holy Spirit reigns supreme over all things,
now and for ever.

| *Reflection by* **Christopher Herbert**

Psalms **5**, 6 (8)
Genesis 31.1-24
2 Timothy 4.9-end

Tuesday 6 February

Genesis 31.1-24

*'And Jacob saw that Laban did not regard him as favourably
as he did before' (v.2)*

The phrase 'a week is a long time in politics' has entered the standard vocabulary of political analysts. It was originally coined by the British Prime Minister, Harold Wilson, and was his way of saying that politics is an unpredictable game. So it was in the relationship between Jacob and his father-in-law, Laban. Jacob regarded himself as having served and worked with Laban faithfully for many years, but Laban's sons became jealous of Jacob's wealth and wanted him out of the way.

According to the composer of this chapter in Genesis, God now enters the story as a significant character, telling Jacob to leave Laban and to return to the land of his ancestors. For the author this is not an entirely surprising development. He has an over-all story that he has plotted out; he needs to portray Jacob not only as the highly successful father of twelve sons, who will be the founders of the twelve tribes, but also as one who was faithful to God's commands. The story is developing at a cracking pace.

For the moment, however, the author needs us to understand that, notwithstanding the duplicitous politics, God is actually in charge. Things will work out. And the women in the story, who have been treated as chattels thus far, now have a crucial role to play. They tell Jacob that he must do whatever God has commanded.

Is this an authorial trick or does it actually tell us something of the nature of God?

Almighty God,
give us reverence for all creation
and respect for every person,
that we may mirror your likeness
in Jesus Christ our Lord.

COLLECT

Wednesday 7 February

Genesis 31.25 – 32.2

'"Come now, let us make a covenant, you and I ..."
So Jacob took a stone, and set it up as a pillar' (31.44,45)

The marking of boundaries is an important human activity. In this episode Jacob and Laban build pillars and cairns to indicate their respective territories. But they were also metaphorical markers on that spiritual journey that Jacob was making as he was guided by God towards what would eventually become his own promised domain. It is mysterious: Jacob is unaware of the eventual outcome of his trek. In that sense, he is following in the footsteps of his ancestor Abraham, who also set out on a life-changing journey not knowing where it would lead.

And so perhaps with us?

It is a strange and intriguing feature of our thinking that as we look back across our lives, we can see things happening whose significance we did not recognize at the time, but which in retrospect we sense were part of the providential guidance of God. While that might be true as we look in the rear-view mirror, it is much less clear looking forwards. It is very rare to sense the distinctive outlines of what God might have in store for us on the road ahead. It is perhaps why we use the word 'vocation' to describe this experience. It's a way of saying that we know that God is moving us onwards, though we have no real clue what that will involve. We have to move on in faith, trusting that as God has been with us in the past, so he will be with us in the future.

COLLECT

Almighty God,
you have created the heavens and the earth
and made us in your own image:
teach us to discern your hand in all your works
and your likeness in all your children;
through Jesus Christ your Son our Lord,
who with you and the Holy Spirit reigns supreme over all things,
now and for ever.

Reflection by **Christopher Herbert**

Psalms 14, **15**, 16
Genesis 32.3-30
Titus 2

Thursday 8 February

Genesis 32.3-30

'Jacob was left alone; and a man wrestled with him until daybreak'
(v.24)

In 1940 the sculptor Jacob Epstein was faced in his studio with an enormous block of alabaster weighing over two and a half tons. He must have gazed at it for many, many weeks before he set to work with hammer and chisel. Going with the grain of the material, rather than against it, and after expending huge amounts of physical energy (you can still see the chiselled gouges in the sculpture) the outline of two figures gradually emerged. They were locked in a wrestling embrace. It was Jacob and the angel.

Epstein himself had spent a good deal of time in the previous decade reading the Book of Genesis and, perhaps because of his own name, was particularly moved by the story. The resulting work is stupendous. Jacob rests, apparently defeated, in the arms of the angel whose bulging thighs and biceps strain to hold Jacob upright. Will the weight of Jacob drag the angel to earth or will the power of the angel lift Jacob to heaven? Which of the two forces, gravity or grace, will win? The sculpture does not tell us: it is poised, held in balance between the two.

Part of the message of the sculpture is about the dogged resistance of the materials with which Epstein was so strenuously working and part of the message is autobiographical, but part is spiritual – that with effort, discipline and concentrated attention, beauty and meaning can emerge out of recalcitrance.

Almighty God,
give us reverence for all creation
and respect for every person,
that we may mirror your likeness
in Jesus Christ our Lord.

COLLECT

Friday 9 February

Psalms 17, **19**
Genesis 33.1-17
Titus 3

Genesis 33.1-17

'Jacob looked up and saw Esau coming, and four hundred men with him' (v.1)

The relationship between the twin brothers, Jacob and Esau, had been difficult for many years. The elder, Esau, claimed that his birthright had been 'stolen' from him when he was in extremis. Jacob's defence was that he had not stolen it; rather Esau had sold it to him. Then, after some duplicitous scheming by their mother Rebecca (who favoured Jacob), Esau's primacy had been usurped by Jacob. And so, unsurprisingly, when Jacob returned home after a 20-year stay with his uncle, Laban, he was very uncertain about the welcome he would receive from his twin brother.

Of course the author of this saga has written it from a particular perspective. He wants his readers to believe that Jacob was indeed favoured by God. He explains that God had said to Jacob that he would prosper and that his descendants would be as numerous as the sand of the sea. But he also has a political scenario in mind; the story provides an explanation for the tensions that existed between two rival nations: the Edomites descended from Esau and the Israelites descended from Jacob. This Jacob saga is certainly theological, but it is also strongly political. The two elements are not separable.

All nations have their founding myths and Israel was no exception. The Jacob myth is foundational for the self-understanding and the identity of Israel and its sense that it has been 'chosen'.

This was Jesus' religious and cultural heritage. He cherished it but also broke out of its confines ...

COLLECT

> Almighty God,
> you have created the heavens and the earth
> and made us in your own image:
> teach us to discern your hand in all your works
> and your likeness in all your children;
> through Jesus Christ your Son our Lord,
> who with you and the Holy Spirit reigns supreme over all things,
> now and for ever.

| *Reflection by* **Christopher Herbert**

Saturday 10 February

Genesis 35

'... no longer shall you be called Jacob, but Israel shall be your name' (v.10)

Here is the turning-point, that moment when God's purposes have become crystal clear. Jacob is re-named 'Israel' by God himself, and thus the author of the saga takes us into a new and powerful part of the founding story.

As all parents know, to name someone is a powerful act, but biblically the act of 'naming' has an extra dimension. The 'name' was regarded as somehow revealing the very nature of the person, and therefore to know someone's name was to have insight about their inner being. Renaming, as happened in the Jacob story, is even more powerful because it is not only about that person's inner being; it is also a symbolic statement about their destiny. Think, for example, of that moment when Jesus renamed Peter and called him the 'Rock' on which the Church would be founded.

So it is here. The renaming is immediately followed by God foretelling the foundation of a great nation and the giving of a special territory in which that nation can flourish. At long last, the hidden processes of God have been revealed.

At this point we find ourselves in a real intellectual and spiritual quandary. Do we accept and believe that founding story with all its religious and political implications, or do we see it as just one foundation myth amongst many others, a device for the creation and sustenance of personal and national identity? Or is it possible that both interpretations could be true?

Almighty God,
give us reverence for all creation
and respect for every person,
that we may mirror your likeness
in Jesus Christ our Lord.

COLLECT

Reflection by **Christopher Herbert** | 69

Monday 12 February

Psalms 27, **30**
Genesis 37.1-11
Galatians 1

Genesis 37.1-11

'This is the story of the family of Jacob' (v.2)

The story of Joseph seems to stand apart from the earlier patriarchal narratives. It has a coherence and integrity that mean that we tend to read it alone, forgetting that, however it may have started life, it is now part of the story of the patriarchs, the story of God's relationship with a particular people and a particular land. Chapters 37–50 take us off on what may seem like a meander from the main themes of Genesis, but actually open out into the defining act of God's faithfulness to the covenants in Genesis: the exodus from Egypt. The Joseph episode leads the whole enterprise into danger, as Jacob's descendants settle in the wrong land and begin to lose touch with the promise to Abraham. But then, the whole of God's commitment to us is fraught with the dangers we bring through misunderstanding and thinking we're in charge of our own history.

Here, at the beginning of the story of Joseph, we see again that God does not wait until he has perfect people to work with. All the patriarchs come from and produce dysfunctional families, but Jacob and Esau perhaps more so than any. So now we see Jacob reaping the rewards of his own earlier disregard of family hierarchy, as his son, Joseph, annoys first his older brothers and then Jacob himself.

COLLECT

Almighty Father,
whose Son was revealed in majesty
before he suffered death upon the cross:
give us grace to perceive his glory,
that we may be strengthened to suffer with him
and be changed into his likeness, from glory to glory;
who is alive and reigns with you,
in the unity of the Holy Spirit,
one God, now and for ever.

| *Reflection by* **Jane Williams**

Psalms 32, **36**
Genesis 37.12-end
Galatians 2.1-10

Tuesday 13 February

Genesis 37.12-end

'Here comes this dreamer' (v.19)

The repercussions of family strife continue to echo through this story. The understated tone of the narrative shows us, without comment, the violent hatred between the brothers. It is hard not to hold Jacob to account for this: in our passage today, his dealings with his sons are inconsistent in the extreme. To begin with, we have to wonder why Joseph was not out with the other brothers, pasturing the flocks. If he is old enough to be sent off on his own to look for them, he is surely old enough to help with the work. But having allowed Joseph to stay at home in the first place, Jacob then manufactures what he hopes will be a bonding occasion between the brothers. It was never a good plan – to send the spoiled younger brother to check up on the older ones who are doing all the hard work – but Jacob can have had no idea quite how badly wrong it was going to go.

When he receives the news of Joseph's presumed death, Jacob, in his grief, makes all his other children feel irrelevant: he speaks of Joseph as 'my son', as though he had no others; without Joseph, he says, life is not worth living. Jacob did not force his sons to hate their brother, but he did little to help them love him.

Holy God,
you know the disorder of our sinful lives:
set straight our crooked hearts,
and bend our wills to love your goodness
and your glory
in Jesus Christ our Lord.

COLLECT

Wednesday 14 February

Ash Wednesday

Psalm **38**
Daniel 9.3-6, 17-19
I Timothy 6.6-19

Daniel 9.3-6, 17-19

'Lord, great and awesome God,
keeping covenant and steadfast love' (v.4)

This is both a high point and a low point in the book of Daniel, as it is in the Christian year. Daniel, according to the narrative, has been surprisingly successful. Admittedly, he is in exile, but he has found favour with the king, been allowed to be faithful to his religion, and has been given divine guidance in interpreting dreams.

But now Daniel has hit something he cannot understand. He had been waiting, faithfully, for God to end the exile, as the prophet Jeremiah had foretold, but nothing is happening. Daniel has reached the end of what human intelligence, even with the gift of angelic interpretation, can cope with.

If that is the low point, the high point is Daniel's response: he abandons attempts to read the signs of the times and casts himself on what he knows of God, the God who keeps covenant with faithful love (v.4). Daniel repents, not for his own faults, but for the world that is no longer transparent to God, where we can no longer read the purposes of God, not because God has changed, but because we have lost our way.

Daniel's great insight is that our best hope is that God is always God. Whether we understand what is happening or not, we know that God is faithful and loving. We are dust, but God has breathed life into us.

COLLECT

Almighty and everlasting God,
you hate nothing that you have made
and forgive the sins of all those who are penitent:
create and make in us new and contrite hearts
that we, worthily lamenting our sins
and acknowledging our wretchedness,
may receive from you, the God of all mercy,
perfect remission and forgiveness;
through Jesus Christ your Son our Lord,
who is alive and reigns with you,
in the unity of the Holy Spirit,
one God, now and for ever.

| *Reflection by* **Jane Williams**

Thursday 15 February

Genesis 39
'The Lord was with him' (v.23)

This is the first time we encounter the Lord in the story of Joseph. Whereas with Abraham, Isaac and Jacob, God appeared and spoke to them, with Joseph, God works behind the scenes and we need the narrator's help to read the divine actions. God enables Joseph to prosper at work, for example, but does not protect him from the advances of Potiphar's wife: there are bigger things at stake here than just Joseph's well-being.

Without his father's fond protection, Joseph is growing up fast. There was no indication, when he lived at home and teased his brothers, that he had a gift for leadership and management, but alone, enslaved, he proves a successful steward. Unlike Jacob, God is not cossetting Joseph but training him for the next step. The old Joseph is not entirely gone: the boy who boasted that he was more important than all his brothers – and even his father – now boasts that he is as great as his master. Joseph still stirs up strong emotions wherever he goes, and Potiphar and his wife react with passion, with anger, with jealousy – all emotions Joseph has provoked before. Only the Lord does not over-react to Joseph, acting only in response to his own nature, not Joseph's. The Lord shows Joseph the steadfast love he has never known before, and so Joseph continues to grow towards his destiny.

Holy God,
our lives are laid open before you:
rescue us from the chaos of sin
and through the death of your Son
bring us healing and make us whole
in Jesus Christ our Lord.

COLLECT

Friday 16 February

Genesis 40

'Do not interpretations belong to God?' (v.8)

There is a glimpse today of the arbitrary world that slaves inhabit. Joseph is in prison because of the lies and jealousy of his employers, and is joined by Pharaoh's baker and cupbearer, who are equally here at the whim of someone more powerful than themselves. But there is hierarchy even among imprisoned slaves, and so Joseph, no longer anyone's spoilt darling, is a servant to the servants of Pharaoh. They treat him as they have been treated: they use him when it suits them, and forget him when it doesn't; they have little interest in his story of abduction and wrongful arrest, and when the cupbearer is duly restored to his place of favour, as Joseph predicted, he forgets him instantly.

What hard lessons Joseph is learning about himself and his value in the world. They are lessons that will stand him in good stead when he finally comes to power, and they will enable him to value his family properly when he meets them again, but alone, forgotten, in prison, Joseph does not know this.

We are not told if Joseph feels God's presence. Certainly, for the first time, Joseph acknowledges God's role in dreams and their interpretation – something he didn't mention when crowing over his brothers. From the safety of narrative omniscience, we know that God is with him, and perhaps we can be comforted, too, by the knowledge that a hidden God is not an absent one.

COLLECT

Almighty and everlasting God,
you hate nothing that you have made
and forgive the sins of all those who are penitent:
create and make in us new and contrite hearts
that we, worthily lamenting our sins
and acknowledging our wretchedness,
may receive from you, the God of all mercy,
perfect remission and forgiveness;
through Jesus Christ your Son our Lord,
who is alive and reigns with you,
in the unity of the Holy Spirit,
one God, now and for ever.

Reflection by **Jane Williams**

Psalm **71** *or* 41, **42**, 43
Genesis 41.1-24
Galatians 3.15-22

Genesis 41.1-24

'It is not I; God will give Pharaoh a favourable answer' (v.16)

There is a kind of gentle humour at work in this story. Joseph's interest in dreams is what got him into trouble in the first place, and now God is going to use that interest to get him out of it again. But the humour also points up a theological assumption: human action and God's action work in different ways and are not in competition. Joseph could tell his story, at this point, as one of hardship, of being abandoned by his family and his God: he has now been in prison, apparently forgotten, for two years. That perspective would not be untruthful, in terms of the human actions so far, but it leaves out God's actions. Even though God does not speak directly to Joseph, that does not mean that God has left himself without ways to communicate.

Most cultures are fascinated by dreams and the powerful sense of profound but hidden meaning they carry. As a king, Pharaoh would expect his dreams to be of great significance – an obvious channel from the divine realm to the divine ruler on earth. His dreams in this case are fairly self-explanatory, so much so, that his own interpreters must either have been useless or too scared to explain what was coming. But Joseph seizes the chance that God has given him, with all the confidence of a favourite son, confidence still somewhere in him, after all this time.

Holy God,
our lives are laid open before you:
rescue us from the chaos of sin
and through the death of your Son
bring us healing and make us whole
in Jesus Christ our Lord.

COLLECT

Reflection by **Jane Williams**

Monday 19 February

Psalms 10, 11 *or* 44
Genesis 41.25-45
Galatians 3.23 – 4.7

Genesis 41.25-45

*'Since God has shown you all this,
there is no one so discerning and wise as you' (v.39)*

Pharaoh's dream is terrible and clear. Egypt's economy is based on cattle and agriculture, fed by the fertile waters of the Nile. The thin cows and the empty ears of grain are a nightmarish foretaste of what is to come. We hear the dream three times in this chapter: twice from Pharaoh and once as Joseph interprets it, so there can be no mistake about its grim portent, or its divine origin. No wonder Pharaoh's own interpreters did not want to tell him what it meant.

But Joseph is not a professional court interpreter, and he feels no need to stop at explaining what the dream means. Just hauled out of prison, clean, properly dressed and shaved for the first time in two years, Joseph has the courage to tell Pharaoh what to do. The narrator lets Pharaoh show us how this is possible: it is Pharaoh who points out that Joseph speaks with the authority of God (vv.38-39).

Instantly, Joseph's world is different. Instantly, he becomes Pharaoh's representative in the land, with people bowing before him, a new name, a new wife, a new world. The spare narration of this story does not tell us how Joseph the interpreter read his own circumstances, whether he thought this was God acting on his behalf, of whether he knew that he was part of something bigger. Not that those two are mutually exclusive, of course.

COLLECT

Almighty God,
whose Son Jesus Christ fasted forty days in the wilderness,
and was tempted as we are, yet without sin:
give us grace to discipline ourselves in obedience to your Spirit;
and, as you know our weakness,
so may we know your power to save;
through Jesus Christ your Son our Lord,
who is alive and reigns with you,
in the unity of the Holy Spirit,
one God, now and for ever.

| *Reflection by* **Jane Williams**

Tuesday 20 February

Genesis 41.46 – 42.5

*'God has made me forget all my hardship
and all my father's house' (v.51)*

Pharaoh and Joseph are showing extraordinary confidence in God. Joseph is given absolute authority to go through all the cities of Egypt and commandeer grain and food and put it away in storage. For seven whole years of plentiful harvests, this foreigner is given permission to take away the fruits of the labour of the local farmers who must, surely, have been sceptical about the so-called famine that was meant to be coming. There must have been muttering and anger against Joseph, suspicions that he was just lining his own pockets. But Joseph and Pharaoh have shared that moment of certainty about God's presence and meaning, and neither questions at all.

While Joseph is unswervingly obeying God and his new master, Pharaoh, he is also trying to convince himself that he is happy and settled, free of the past. But the names he gives his children suggest otherwise: they are family names, not Egyptian ones, and the very fact that they speak of forgetting and contentment suggests that Joseph does not yet have either.

And now the past that he thinks he has dismissed is about to return, as the famine begins to bite beyond the borders of Egypt and the narrative swings back from Joseph's changed life to the unchanged tension between Jacob and his remaining sons. Jacob is still nagging his older sons and still favouring his younger son. Time, that has transformed Joseph, has done little for Jacob.

Heavenly Father,
your Son battled with the powers of darkness,
and grew closer to you in the desert:
help us to use these days to grow in wisdom and prayer
that we may witness to your saving love
in Jesus Christ our Lord.

COLLECT

Wednesday 21 February

Psalms **6**, 17 *or* **119.57-80**
Genesis 42.6-17
Galatians 4.21 – 5.1

Genesis 42.6-17

*'Joseph's brothers came and bowed themselves before him with
their faces to the ground' (v.6)*

The author of the Joseph story has already trained us to see what is
going on from more than one perspective: how it might be viewed if
we didn't know God was at work, and how we view it, knowing that
God is. Now this layering technique is going to switch back and forth,
from Joseph to his brothers and then back to us, as we see with the
narrator's knowledge.

So we, and Joseph, see the irony as Joseph's brothers come back on
the scene, bowing to him, calling themselves his servants, thinking that
they are describing only themselves as 'sons of one man', little realizing
that they are also describing the great official in front of them. We
and Joseph remember Joseph's dream, and see it fulfilled, though the
brothers do not. We and Joseph understand why Joseph does not
immediately reveal himself to the brothers who sold him into slavery.
We and Joseph see that three days in prison is not a lot, compared with
the years that Joseph spent there. And we understand why Joseph
needs to find out whether fraternal love and loyalty have grown in
his absence.

We, with the narrator, see how much Joseph has changed, from the
brat who would certainly have used his new position to boast to his
brothers, to the statesman, but also to the man who longs to know if
anything can be saved from his own bitter past.

COLLECT

Almighty God,
whose Son Jesus Christ fasted forty days in the wilderness,
and was tempted as we are, yet without sin:
give us grace to discipline ourselves in obedience to your Spirit;
and, as you know our weakness,
so may we know your power to save;
through Jesus Christ your Son our Lord,
who is alive and reigns with you,
in the unity of the Holy Spirit,
one God, now and for ever.

Reflection by **Jane Williams**

Psalms **42**, 43 *or* 56, **57** (63*)
Genesis 42.18-28
Galatians 5.2-15

Thursday 22 February

Genesis 42.18-28

'He turned away from them and wept' (v.24)

While we, the readers, have been following Joseph's story, his brothers have been left behind, dealing with the consequences of their actions. Now we get a glimpse into the tortured years the brothers have suffered. Their guilt has bitten deep: it is as though they have been waiting, ever since, for this moment when they will have to pay. Reuben's anguished, 'I told you so!' gets no response because it has been said so often between the brothers. They are wholly turned in on their shared burden, utterly unaware that the foreign official can understand them.

Very briefly, the focus shifts back to Joseph, weeping. This is what he has longed to hear: that he is not forgotten, that he is regretted, that his brothers have not just carried on, happy and unconcerned. Joseph's power, grandeur, new wife, new children are not enough to make him a new identity; for that, he needs his brothers' love.

It's hard to tell whether it is a desire for revenge or a residual insecurity that prolongs the anguish, postpones the moment when Joseph reveals himself. But the test he sets his brothers suggests the latter: will they abandon Simeon, now that they have what they came for? Will they treat him as they treated Joseph, as expendable? Or have they learned loyalty the hard way?

Heavenly Father,
your Son battled with the powers of darkness,
and grew closer to you in the desert:
help us to use these days to grow in wisdom and prayer
that we may witness to your saving love
in Jesus Christ our Lord.

COLLECT

Reflection by **Jane Williams**   79

Friday 23 February

Genesis 42.29-end

*'I am the one you have bereaved of children ...
All this has happened to me!' (v.36)*

In this final section of chapter 42, we see the world that Joseph's brothers have been living in. Jacob is one of the least lovable characters in stories of the patriarchs, with his underhanded plot to get his brother's birth right. The trickster is tricked in his turn, marries the wrong wife and has to wait for the right one, and that legacy of duplicity and favouritism is what we see played out in this narrative of Joseph. Jacob is also, of course, a mystic and seer, one who encounters God in vivid and intimate ways. But it is surely no accident that Jacob the cheat is left with a permanent limp when he wrestles with the angel.

The brothers may have been changed by remorse, but it seems that Jacob has not. He may or may not have his suspicions about how Joseph disappeared, but it is clear that he has made his sons pay every day for the fact that they are not Joseph. He is still making Leah's children feel that they are not truly his, as though the fault of their birth is theirs. It is terrible to hear how Reuben has absorbed that message, so that he is willing to offer his own children as surety against Benjamin's safety.

There is no hint from the narrator here that this is God at work. God will deal with what happens, but our choices are real, as are those of Jacob and his sons.

COLLECT

Almighty God,
whose Son Jesus Christ fasted forty days in the wilderness,
and was tempted as we are, yet without sin:
give us grace to discipline ourselves in obedience to your Spirit;
and, as you know our weakness,
so may we know your power to save;
through Jesus Christ your Son our Lord,
who is alive and reigns with you,
in the unity of the Holy Spirit,
one God, now and for ever.

Reflection by **Jane Williams**

Saturday 24 February

Genesis 43.1-15

'Why did you treat me so badly as to tell the man that you had another brother?' (v.6)

Hunger finally drives Jacob to give in. He has been willing to manage without Simeon, left imprisoned in Egypt, rather than risk Benjamin, but now crisis has come: Benjamin or Jacob? Inevitably, Jacob chooses himself. This time, it is Judah, not Reuben, who bargains with Jacob, but there is a kind of hypocrisy about the bargain. Reuben had offered his own sons if he failed to bring Benjamin safely home, but Judah just says, trust me, and stop fussing. Judah, it seems, is the practical one. It was his idea to sell Joseph into slavery, rather than leaving him in the pit to die, whereas Reuben had been planning to save Joseph behind his brothers' back.

Jacob gives in, with as much bad grace as he can. 'Bring back your other brother (whose name I can't be bothered with) and Benjamin', he says.

Leah's children always seem to have to act as a single entity in Jacob's eyes. They may have wives and children of their own, but for Jacob, they are the expendable sons, whose job it is to work for him and to look after Joseph and Benjamin, Rachel's children. The subsequent history of Israel suggests that that is not how God sees them: God chooses the twelve tribes, and Jesus chooses twelve to help him reconstitute the kingdom of love.

Heavenly Father,
your Son battled with the powers of darkness,
and grew closer to you in the desert:
help us to use these days to grow in wisdom and prayer
that we may witness to your saving love
in Jesus Christ our Lord.

COLLECT

Monday 26 February

Genesis 43.16-end

'So they drank and were merry with him' (v.34)

It was a very different affair, the last time the brothers ate when Joseph was with them. They weren't in a house in Egypt with various attendants, but alone in the fields at Dothan. Joseph wasn't sitting with them then either, but that's because they had thrown him in a pit, without even water (Genesis 37.16-25). Now they are enjoying the portions he sends down from his table. Then the big topic of conversation was how to get rid of him; we're not told what they're talking about here, but they seem to be having a good time. Joseph's lavish hospitality has dulled the jumpiness and bad conscience that have marked their expedition so far.

A meal is an occasion to celebrate the goodness of God in creation, and the particular blessing of human relationships. Yet it can also show up the shadows of sin and of human tragedy. At the meals we will be part of this week, will there be people, like Joseph, with a secret that could change everything, but which they fear – perhaps with good reason – to declare? Will there be people, like the brothers in Egypt, trying to block out feelings of guilt and shame by throwing themselves into the party? Will there even be people like the brothers in Dothan, heedless of suffering they are inflicting on others, wishing them out of sight and mind? And will any of those people be us?

COLLECT

Almighty God,
you show to those who are in error the light of your truth,
that they may return to the way of righteousness:
grant to all those who are admitted
    into the fellowship of Christ's religion,
that they may reject those things
    that are contrary to their profession,
and follow all such things as are agreeable to the same;
through our Lord Jesus Christ,
who is alive and reigns with you,
in the unity of the Holy Spirit,
one God, now and for ever.

Reflection by **Jeremy Worthen**

Psalm **50** *or* **73**
Genesis 44.1-17
Hebrews 2.1-9

Tuesday 27 February

Genesis 44.1-17

'Joseph said to his steward, "Go, follow after the men"' (v.4)

It is taking a while, this story about the brothers meeting Joseph in Egypt. Old Testament narrative can sketch out the most profound events in a few elliptical sentences, but here we have detail on detail as the plot twists this way and that.

It is taking a while, because Joseph is taking his time. He knows who they are the moment he sees them – and what they did to him. He also knows how deeply he longs to be with Benjamin, his brother, with Jacob, his father, and with his whole family, together. But this is not something that can be quickly resolved.

Joseph is taking his time, because reconciliation takes time. Whenever it happens, it is a kind of miracle, an event of grace, but also a long and difficult journey, the slow work of healing and restoration of trust. The fear is always that the script will just run again: those who harmed, those who abused, will harm and abuse again as soon as the circumstances are right. So Joseph sets a test. Once more, the favourite son, the youngest son, is away from the protection of his father. The other brothers can walk out of trouble and back into freedom if they would only dump Benjamin, make up a lie and forget him too.

Reconciliation takes time. Those who are called to the ministry of reconciliation must therefore be willing to wait, with prayer and compassion, for the journey to unfold and the miracle to come.

Almighty God,
by the prayer and discipline of Lent
may we enter into the mystery of Christ's sufferings,
and by following in his Way
come to share in his glory;
through Jesus Christ our Lord.

COLLECT

Reflection by **Jeremy Worthen** | 83

Wednesday 28 February

Psalm **35** *or* **77**
Genesis 44.18-end
Hebrews 2.10-end

Genesis 44.18-end

'... a slave to my lord in place of the boy' (v.33)

Judah has changed. In chapter 42, Reuben, the eldest, spoke for the brothers, but it was Judah who persuaded Jacob to let them return to Egypt with Benjamin, and it is Judah who, at this critical juncture of the story, turns its shifting direction decisively towards reconciliation.

Judah has changed. The one who persuaded the others to sell their youngest brother into slavery (Genesis 37.26-27) offers to become a slave himself so that the youngest can go free. Yet this is not a case of conversion to philosophical altruism. What comes across most strongly in Judah's speech – the longest speech in the book of Genesis – is his love for his father, his willingness to lay down his own life for the sake of the happiness of his father's final days. Did he not love his father before? Yes, in a way, but a way that made him so resentful of the love Jacob had for Joseph that he wanted to make sure that the father would lose the beloved son forever. Now again, 'his life is bound up in the boy's life', but there is no resentment, no jealousy, no hatred. Instead, his love for his father means he will protect at any cost the brother his father loves.

May our hearts be so full of love for God that our only care is the salvation of that which God loves, God's life bound up in it, the world for which the Father gave the only-begotten Son.

COLLECT

Almighty God,
you show to those who are in error the light of your truth,
that they may return to the way of righteousness:
grant to all those who are admitted
into the fellowship of Christ's religion,
that they may reject those things
that are contrary to their profession,
and follow all such things as are agreeable to the same;
through our Lord Jesus Christ,
who is alive and reigns with you,
in the unity of the Holy Spirit,
one God, now and for ever.

Reflection by **Jeremy Worthen**

Thursday 1 March

Genesis 45.1-15

'God sent me before you to preserve life' (v.5)

The tension that has been building finally breaks. Joseph reveals himself to his brothers, accepting that this means undergoing a loss of control, as he lets the grief that had been frozen in his heart and the joy for which he had not dared to hope course through him and overwhelm him.

Surely there would have been so very many things he wanted to say to them. But there is really only one thing he tells them in this first, momentous encounter: God sent me here. He knows they are frightened, bewildered, confused, so he wisely tells them not once but three times, in verses 5–8: God sent me here. And the word for 'send' he uses is the same one that resonates through the many stories of vocation in the Old Testament and that stands behind those that follow from them in the New.

Joseph is not naïve about what happened, and the man running the imperial economy can hardly be characterized as otherworldly. He sees the complexities of human agency, yet beneath and above it all he discerns God's agency. He sees the sin mixed up with human action, which flared up in his brothers' wicked deed, but he perceives that God is always working for life (the Hebrew word for which appears in verses 5 and 7), faithful to the promise. And he knows that he has a part in that promise: he has been called, he has been sent. The strong root of his wisdom.

Almighty God,
by the prayer and discipline of Lent
may we enter into the mystery of Christ's sufferings,
and by following in his Way
come to share in his glory;
through Jesus Christ our Lord.

COLLECT

Friday 2 March

Psalms 40, **41** *or* **55**
Genesis 45.16-end
Hebrews 3.7-end

Genesis 45.16-end

'... the spirit of their father Jacob revived' (v.27)

The Hebrew term for 'revived' used here is the same word that was key to the first part of the chapter: the verb whose basic meaning is 'to live'. Jacob's spirit 'lives' or 'comes alive' as he comes to believe the unbelievable good news that Joseph is still living. As the switching between the names 'Jacob' and 'Israel' in this section reminds us, the one person represents the people, and the people cannot live incomplete, the life of the whole without the life of all.

Not every story of fraternal jealousy, or human trafficking, or false accusation, ends as happily as the story of Joseph, of course. Sometimes there is no reconciliation or end to grief. Sometimes people die of violence or neglect. Sometimes those who do wicked deeds live on in prosperity and apparent peace, indifferent to what they have done.

Luke says of the disciples meeting the risen Jesus that at first 'in their joy they were disbelieving' (Luke 24.41). Like Jacob, they cannot believe that what they thought was lost has been restored and transformed in a way they could never have imagined. The good news of Christ is that death does not triumph, and that no loss, no failure, no evil and no tragedy can deal death to the spirit of those who are alive in Christ Jesus. In him, we are called to share in the story of Israel, as people of hope, people who do not give up.

COLLECT

Almighty God,
you show to those who are in error the light of your truth,
that they may return to the way of righteousness:
grant to all those who are admitted
    into the fellowship of Christ's religion,
that they may reject those things
    that are contrary to their profession,
and follow all such things as are agreeable to the same;
through our Lord Jesus Christ,
who is alive and reigns with you,
in the unity of the Holy Spirit,
one God, now and for ever.

| *Reflection by* **Jeremy Worthen**

Psalms 3, **25** *or* **76**, 79
Genesis 46.1-7, 28-end
Hebrews 4.1-13

Saturday 3 March

Genesis 46.1-7, 28-end

'I myself will go down with you' (v.4)

The case for emigration is very clear: starvation in Canaan, with no one to help, versus a stable supply of food in Egypt, administered by Jacob's beloved son, sent there by God to provide for them all. Yet all the same, Jacob hesitates. He is leaving the land of God's promise to enter alien territory. Can this really be part of the plan?

This is the only time in the Joseph story that God speaks directly, with a promise of presence and of restoration. Verse 4 twice uses the emphatic pronoun for 'I' in Hebrew where it is not required grammatically: 'I myself will go down with you to Egypt, and I [myself] will also bring you up again.' This is, at it were, a detour, to a place that is not and cannot be home: but God will be there. At the same time, the God who goes with him and whose presence he will not lose is also the one who will restore the body of Jacob and the life of Israel to their true, abiding home.

Not every place to which God calls us to go is somewhere we should stay, or put down deep roots of attachment. We can be confident that if God calls us, then God goes with us, and however strange and hard the road may be, we will not lose God's presence. But we also need to remember where home is, the place prepared for us, the promise that awaits us.

Almighty God,
by the prayer and discipline of Lent
may we enter into the mystery of Christ's sufferings,
and by following in his Way
come to share in his glory;
through Jesus Christ our Lord.

COLLECT

Reflection by **Jeremy Worthen**   87

Monday 5 March

Genesis 47.1-27

'Jacob blessed Pharaoh' (v.7)

Jacob blesses Pharaoh; Israel blesses Egypt – not once but twice (vv. 7 and 10). It could be argued that this denotes no more than a formal greeting and then leave taking, yet it seems unlikely that the resonance of the word in this context should be treated entirely casually. Jacob is a frail old man, reliant on his famous son, a suppliant seeking a place to live, indeed the basic means to live, from the most powerful person on earth, so far as he is aware. And Jacob blesses Pharaoh; Israel blesses Egypt – not once but twice.

Jacob also has a word for Pharaoh. The inquiry about his age is no more than formal politeness. For us, to ask someone their age is seen as rudeness, as if length of years were a thing to be ashamed of; here, it is the opposite. Jacob initially responds in conventional fashion, underlining the span of his life with suitable modesty, but then draws attention to the case of his ancestors, whose election was marked with even greater abundance. Yet for them as for him, this is all a 'sojourn' – a dwelling in a land that is not one's final home, whether in Ur or in Canaan or in Egypt. 'They confessed that they were strangers and foreigners on the earth, for people who speak in this way make it clear that they are seeking a homeland' (Hebrews 11.13*b*–14).

A subtle word, and an unobtrusive blessing; who can say with what effect?

COLLECT

Almighty God,
whose most dear Son went not up to joy but first he suffered pain,
and entered not into glory before he was crucified:
mercifully grant that we, walking in the way of the cross,
may find it none other than the way of life and peace;
through Jesus Christ your Son our Lord,
who is alive and reigns with you,
in the unity of the Holy Spirit,
one God, now and for ever.

| *Reflection by* **Jeremy Worthen**

Tuesday 6 March

Genesis 47.28 – 48.end

'I buried her there on the way to Ephrath' (48.7)

Jacob is ill and dying, but he must pass on his blessing to Joseph and his sons. To do that, he begins by remembering how he was blessed by God, many years previously. That memory causes him to mention two names that have been more or less absent from Genesis since the focus moved to Joseph and his brothers in chapter 37.

The first is Rachel. Though she appears in the genealogical list in chapter 46, and her death in childbirth, recorded in Genesis 35.16–21, colours everything that follows, only now is she spoken of directly. Her death follows immediately after God's appearing to Jacob, so it seems that to recall God's blessing moves him to speak also of his loss.

The second is Abraham. God who blesses Jacob in Genesis 35.9–15 names Abraham along with Isaac, and now Jacob mentions Abraham and Isaac twice in his blessing of Joseph and his sons. To share in the blessing is to stand in the line of Abraham; the story that begins with his call goes on, because the promise of God does not fail.

We want to bring blessing to others. To do that, we need to remember how we have received the blessing of God, for we have no other to pass on. That means that our blessing of others will be marked by what has happened to us, our old scars and open wounds, to draw them also into the one story of God's promise, God's steadfast love.

Eternal God,
give us insight
to discern your will for us,
to give up what harms us,
and to seek the perfection we are promised
in Jesus Christ our Lord.

COLLECT

Wednesday 7 March

Psalm **38** *or* **119.105-128**
Genesis 49.1-32
Hebrews 6.13-end

Genesis 49.1-32

'I wait for your salvation, O Lord' (v.18)

Jacob's parting words to his sons form the first extended poem in the Bible. Full of Hebrew word play and obscure expressions, it is very difficult to translate. It is also hard to know what we are to make of it. A kind of prophecy? Perhaps. Some of the sayings in this collection seem to refer to events that have already happened to the characters (e.g. vv.4 and 6), others to the future fortunes of the tribes once they have returned to Canaan (e.g. vv.13 and 19). For centuries, Jewish and Christian interpreters saw messianic meaning in verse 10, though disagreeing passionately about what exactly it might be.

Confronted by so many puzzles, we might be tempted to imagine that verse 18 was despairingly inserted by a similarly perplexed ancient scribe, whose standard for sacred poetry was the psalms. But this poem, this prophecy, is an act of faithful waiting. Jacob senses there is a long road ahead, and that it will not be simple or straightforward. His descendants will return to the land of God's promise, but that will not be the end of history but only a further chapter, in which sin, struggle and suffering will still feature heavily. There remains, however, a horizon beyond that, a horizon that looms darkly, obscurely, in the blessing of Joseph in verses 24–26: unbreakable blessing, powerful beyond all the powers of creation, from one who provides for us, saves us and cares for us like a shepherd.

COLLECT

Almighty God,
whose most dear Son went not up to joy but first he suffered pain,
and entered not into glory before he was crucified:
mercifully grant that we, walking in the way of the cross,
may find it none other than the way of life and peace;
through Jesus Christ your Son our Lord,
who is alive and reigns with you,
in the unity of the Holy Spirit,
one God, now and for ever.

| *Reflection by* **Jeremy Worthen**

Psalms **56**, 57 *or* 90, **92**
Genesis 49.33 – 50.end
Hebrews 7.1-10

Thursday 8 March

Genesis 49.33 – 50.end

'... forgive the crime of your brothers' (50.17)

Perhaps only in fiction or at a distance are repentance and forgiveness simple, instantaneous events. Are the brothers truly sorry for what they did to Joseph, or merely afraid of the possible consequences with their father no longer around? Fear leads them once again to lie, as they lied to Jacob for decades about Joseph, yet in their deceit they nonetheless speak a kind of truth. They use the words 'wrong' and 'crime' for the first time in the narrative to refer to what they did, and it is in their own name, and not that of their father, that they finally ask to be forgiven.

If their repentance is not straightforward, neither perhaps is Joseph's forgiveness. He never says to them, 'I forgive you.' Indeed, his rhetorical question to them, 'Am I in the place of God?', might be taken as a refusal to offer a forgiveness only God can grant, as well as to enact a judgement only God can determine. But what Joseph does is refrain from seeking vengeance, and, more than that, he continues to do good to those who had wronged him, both through material provision and through the moral quality of his communication with them. He has come to see what happened in the light of God's unshakeable purpose for good; he will not let their 'crime' – which he acknowledges – define his or their existence.

Without grace drawing repentance and forgiveness together into the deepening mystery of reconciliation, the Bible would have ended here.

COLLECT

Eternal God,
give us insight
to discern your will for us,
to give up what harms us,
and to seek the perfection we are promised
in Jesus Christ our Lord.

Reflection by **Jeremy Worthen** | 91

Friday 9 March

Exodus 1.1-14

'Come, let us deal shrewdly with them' (v.10)

If fascination can be a compound of fear, attraction and control, then the new Pharaoh and his people are fascinated by the Israelites. They are intimidated by their numbers and their strength, strength that could make them a military threat if their loyalty cannot be guaranteed. Yet the obvious solution to that – that they relocate back to Canaan – appears only as the final stage in Pharaoh's worst-case scenario in verse 10. No, they want to keep them near. And the way to stay close to what is dangerous is to control it, pressure it relentlessly into submission, break its power.

Ultimately, this fascination proves self-destructive. The energy pulsing through the children of Israel cannot be contained by human means, no matter how shrewd or ruthless those means may be. Fascination leads to escalating, damaging conflict, preventing Pharaoh from acceding to the request that would have been liberation for him, as well as for the Hebrews: 'Let my people go' (Exodus 9.1). It only ends with the drowning of his army, his power, in the waters of the Red Sea.

Fascination of this kind is the distortion of desire, to which the only true antidote is love, which casts out fear and seeks the release of the beloved from all that blocks its flourishing. It is perhaps easy to persuade ourselves that fascination with what is good is itself a kind of goodness, when it may turn out to be a creeping paralysis that shuts us off from the path of life.

COLLECT
| Almighty God,
whose most dear Son went not up to joy but first he suffered pain,
and entered not into glory before he was crucified:
mercifully grant that we, walking in the way of the cross,
may find it none other than the way of life and peace;
through Jesus Christ your Son our Lord,
who is alive and reigns with you,
in the unity of the Holy Spirit,
one God, now and for ever.

| *Reflection by* **Jeremy Worthen**

Psalm **31** *or* 96, **97**, 100
Exodus 1.22 – 2.10
Hebrews 8

Saturday 10 March

Exodus 1.22 – 2.10

'He was crying, and she took pity on him' (2.6)

However high the walls may rise between communities, there are likely to be occasions when encounter still happens, so that common humanity can become the exceptional ground for communication and cracks may even begin to appear across them. The decision of Moses' mother to put him in a papyrus basket has nothing to do with wanting to attract the attention of Egyptians: a pragmatic hiding place away from living quarters, and literalistic (even parodic?) compliance with Pharaoh's chilling command. Yet the basket becomes the place where Egyptian meets Hebrew, suffering evokes pity, pity leads to care, and care brings lasting interchange between the two communities, focused on a single person but with effects that will change them both irrevocably.

Pharaoh's daughter's life would have been carefully designed to ensure she never heard the cries of the oppressed Israelites. But somehow, those cries impinge on her world, and she responds with a simple act of compassion. Moreover, she recognizes immediately that she does not possess by herself, for all her riches, the means to provide the care that is required: help for the Hebrew must involve the Hebrews, without her just walking away and leaving the situation to them.

Are there people around you who are suffering, but whose cries you never hear? Are there cries you are hearing today, and call on your compassion? Might you be called to act and take a share of responsibility, not alone but with others, including those whose cries these are?

Eternal God,
give us insight
to discern your will for us,
to give up what harms us,
and to seek the perfection we are promised
in Jesus Christ our Lord.

COLLECT

Reflection by **Jeremy Worthen** |

Monday 12 March

Exodus 2.11-22

'... an alien residing in a foreign land' (v.22)

God's big plan is in tatters. The descendants of Abraham, chosen by God to be his own people in a land of their own, are slaves in Egypt. Worse, they are victims of attempted genocide. One baby boy miraculously survives – but through his own stupidity and violence has to run away from his family and home. We need to forget we have read this story before, and recognize a hopeless situation. These people seem capable of destroying themselves if Pharaoh does not do it first.

Yet there are perhaps signs of hope. Moses' fighting skills are put to better use when they help him acquire a new family. He is also learning the hard way what it means to be a Hebrew. We assume he now knows his true identity, but this is the first time he has felt what it is like to be in danger and to live in exile. The boy brought up in a royal palace is being hardened into the man he is destined to be.

The story told by Exodus is one of God's infinite persistence. Even on occasions when God's patience seems to run out, a way is found for the plan to go forward. Promises have been made, and God will not break them, however badly his people behave. It is good news for Israel, and good news for us, unworthy recipients of God's promises that we are.

COLLECT

Merciful Lord,
absolve your people from their offences,
that through your bountiful goodness
we may all be delivered from the chains of those sins
which by our frailty we have committed;
grant this, heavenly Father,
for Jesus Christ's sake, our blessed Lord and Saviour,
who is alive and reigns with you,
in the unity of the Holy Spirit,
one God, now and for ever.

| *Reflection by* **Gillian Cooper**

Psalms 54, **79** *or* **106*** *(or* 103)
Exodus 2.23 – 3.20
Hebrews 9.15-end

Tuesday 13 March

Exodus 2.23 – 3.20

'God remembered his covenant' (2.24)

Who is this God, who remembers his promises? Moses needs to know, he thinks, if he is to be believed. He demands a name. God's answer is enigmatic in the extreme. For all the best efforts of scholars, we do not know what to make of 'I am who I am'. We are not helped by the nature of tenses in Hebrew verbs. Is it 'I will be who I will be'? Or perhaps 'I am who I will be'?

Moses needs to listen more carefully. Three times he is told who this God is: 'the God of Abraham, the God of Isaac, and the God of Jacob'. Other gods have names: lesser gods, members of divine families. The God of Israel needs no name to pin him down. He is defined by something much more dynamic. He has been active in the lives of the ancestors of the Hebrews. He has made promises. He has paid attention to their plight. He has been preparing to act. He has analysed the difficulties. He has chosen and prepared his messenger and given him a message. A land is waiting.

Past, present or future – this God is who he is in every tense. Israel will call him Yahweh, but avoid saying the name by replacing it with 'Lord'. No name, no graven image, nothing fixed, but a living, moving force in the life of Israel and of his people for all time.

Merciful Lord,
you know our struggle to serve you:
when sin spoils our lives
and overshadows our hearts,
come to our aid
and turn us back to you again;
through Jesus Christ our Lord.

COLLECT

Reflection by **Gillian Cooper**   95

Wednesday 14 March

Psalms 63, **90** *or* 110, **111**, 112
Exodus 4.1-23
Hebrews 10.1-18

Exodus 4.1-23

'O my Lord, please send someone else' (v.13)

Moses is not as inspired as he should be, and we wonder whether God has made the right choice. Not that we do not feel a certain sympathy alongside our impatience. After all, the task seems suicidal, although we might expect that having seen the burning bush, Moses would have more grasp of God's power to achieve the impossible.

We all know the temptation of making excuses when we know we have to do something hard. In Moses' case, it is the talking he is particularly worried about. This is the first we hear about a brother, but Aaron is literally an answer to prayer. Moses runs out of arguments, and sets off back to Egypt.

Verses 21 to 23 contain a little theological interlude that seems to interrupt the story. We are heading for the account of a marathon battle of wills and magic between God and Moses on one side and Pharaoh on the other. So why is it not all over before it starts? Surely God cannot lose?

The writer explains. It is God who hardens Pharaoh's heart, to make the victory all the more emphatic when it comes. It is a question for us too. If God is omnipotent, how can human beings resist him? We have been given free will, we believe. Our writer however offers us an alternative answer, that God can sometimes create his own difficulties. It is something for us to ponder.

COLLECT

Merciful Lord,
absolve your people from their offences,
that through your bountiful goodness
we may all be delivered from the chains of those sins
which by our frailty we have committed;
grant this, heavenly Father,
for Jesus Christ's sake, our blessed Lord and Saviour,
who is alive and reigns with you,
in the unity of the Holy Spirit,
one God, now and for ever.

Reflection by **Gillian Cooper**

Thursday 15 March

Exodus 4.27 – 6.1

'... you have done nothing at all' (5.23)

The first part is easy. Moses and Aaron follow instructions and are recognized by the Israelites as messengers from the God of their ancestors. They will soon discover the fickleness of public opinion.

The battle begins. Moses and Aaron invent a threat in order to persuade Pharaoh that the people are only going into the desert for a religious observance. Pharaoh, however, is not fooled, and he has no intention of losing his workforce. His answer, like that of many tyrants after him, is to ensure that his slaves are even more firmly under his thumb by making impossible demands and ruthlessly punishing their failure. Predictably, the people's leaders turn on Moses and Aaron, who have made matters much worse with their stupid demand. Equally predictably, Moses then turns on the Lord. The journey to freedom has not begun well. The main characters in the drama are behaving in a typically human way. Fortunately, God is willing to make allowances. His plan is not going to be derailed by the complaining that will become such a theme throughout Exodus.

We are near the beginning of the Old Testament's great story of salvation. It is already clear that if freedom comes, it will be entirely God's doing. Moses and Aaron are God's agents, but what happens does not depend on them. In the complaining Israelites we see ourselves, saved not by our own merits but by God alone.

Merciful Lord,
you know our struggle to serve you:
when sin spoils our lives
and overshadows our hearts,
come to our aid
and turn us back to you again;
through Jesus Christ our Lord.

COLLECT

Reflection by **Gillian Cooper**   97

Friday 16 March

Psalm **102** *or* **139**
Exodus 6.2-13
Hebrews 10.26-end

Exodus 6.2-13

'I will redeem you' (v.6)

Exodus is the Old Testament book that shows most clearly the hallmarks of being a compilation of traditions. The story sometimes seems disjointed, names vary, and there are differing theological emphases. We could tease apart the various strands, with the help of the scholars, but better perhaps to live with the inconsistencies and appreciate the power of the whole with its many layers of meaning. So let us treat this alternative version of the call of Moses as a clarification of the major themes of the early chapters of Exodus.

God's identity is once more at the centre. This God is Yahweh (the Lord in our English translations). His name is newly revealed, but he has been there all along, since the choice of Abraham and his family. The Lord has promised a land, and will deliver it.

Once again the Israelites do not play their part and 'know that I am the Lord your God', but it has now become irrelevant. Their cooperation is not required. Moses and Aaron are sent straight to Pharaoh to get on with the job of salvation anyway.

Here we see an emphasis on the power of the God of Exodus who is also our God. Resistance is futile, whether it comes from doubtful Israelites, a despotic Pharaoh, or the powers of sin and death. The 'outstretched arm and mighty acts of judgement' will bring redemption.

COLLECT

Merciful Lord,
absolve your people from their offences,
that through your bountiful goodness
we may all be delivered from the chains of those sins
which by our frailty we have committed;
grant this, heavenly Father,
for Jesus Christ's sake, our blessed Lord and Saviour,
who is alive and reigns with you,
in the unity of the Holy Spirit,
one God, now and for ever.

| *Reflection by* **Gillian Cooper**

Saturday 17 March

Exodus 7.8-end

'... until now you have not listened' (v.16)

So the battle begins in earnest. Who can perform the best tricks? Today it is a draw.

The story of the plagues is difficult for today's readers. It seems a very primitive way for God to operate. Why not just cut to the end and get the people out? Who needs this display of magic? Then there is the issue of the blood in the Nile, and similarly unpleasant things to come. It is the ordinary people of Egypt who suffer.

Let us try to think ourselves into the mind of the writers of Exodus. They know all the stories; everyone knows the stories – they have been told and retold down the centuries, embellished no doubt, their order confused, and there is no hope of reconstructing events as they happened. The final authors/editors attempt to make sense of it all. They describe a dramatic battle. On the one side is the tyrant, the Pharaoh, who imagines himself to have ultimate power over the land of Egypt. On the other are Moses and Aaron. What Pharaoh so far fails to realize is that Moses and Aaron are not alone. Behind them, calling the shots, is Yahweh their God. Prolonging the agony for Egypt makes the achievement of freedom all the greater. 'Look what God did for us!' we imagine the first readers exclaiming.

'Look what God did for us!' we exclaim as we look at a cross.

Merciful Lord,
you know our struggle to serve you:
when sin spoils our lives
and overshadows our hearts,
come to our aid
and turn us back to you again;
through Jesus Christ our Lord.

COLLECT

Reflection by **Gillian Cooper**   99

Monday 19 March
Joseph of Nazareth

Isaiah 11.1-10

'... the root of Jesse shall stand as a signal to the peoples' (v.10)

In a welcome respite from the Egyptian plagues, we miss frogs and gnats in order to celebrate St Joseph with Isaiah's beautiful vision of peace.

It is through Joseph that Matthew's Gospel traces Jesus' ancestry. Jesus is a descendant of Jesse, a new David, a king of the Jews. Throughout their history the people of Israel had a love/hate relationship with kings. When they crowned their first king, Saul, God disapproved, the Old Testament writers tell us. Kings can turn into tyrants, and will not always make wise choices. So it proved, according to the story told by the biblical historians. The ideal of kingship remained, however, despite the failings of actual kings. There was still the dream of a king who would genuinely represent God's own rule on earth. The result would be an almost unimaginable, impossible peace and prosperity.

Today reminds us that the prophecy has been fulfilled – in part. The king has come, though in a quiet and unexpected way. God's kingdom exists on earth as in heaven – almost. But wolves still kill lambs, and the meek of the earth still suffer. The establishment of the kingdom still has some way to go.

Isaiah's vision is still our vision. We know a little more now about the king's identity: Jesus, son of David, a member of the family of wise Joseph. We still dream of the day when his reign will come on earth.

COLLECT

God our Father,
who from the family of your servant David
raised up Joseph the carpenter
to be the guardian of your incarnate Son
and husband of the Blessed Virgin Mary:
give us grace to follow him
in faithful obedience to your commands;
through Jesus Christ your Son our Lord,
who is alive and reigns with you,
in the unity of the Holy Spirit,
one God, now and for ever.

| *Reflection by* **Gillian Cooper**

Psalms **35**, 123 *or* **132**, 133
Exodus 8.20-end
Hebrews 11.32 – 12.2

Exodus 8.20-end

'Pray for me' (v.28)

The battle continues, but Pharaoh is weakening. His magicians have admitted defeat, whereas there seems no limit to the horrors Moses and Aaron are prepared to inflict on the poor Egyptians. In an uncomfortable episode, Moses lies to Pharaoh about the reason the Israelites need to leave Egypt, and Pharaoh, extraordinarily, gives them permission to go, asking for their prayers. He changes his mind, however, when the plague of flies disappears before their departure, in what looks like a tactical error on the part of Moses. There is much more to come before God's people can leave. The new element here is that the Israelites are protected from the effects of the plague.

The story of the plagues has traditionally been interpreted as a classic account of a battle between good and evil. God fights the forces of darkness to win the victory of salvation for his people. For Christians, of course, this foreshadows an even greater battle and act of salvation. It may be hard to ignore the human elements of the story: Pharaoh is not entirely unsympathetic, with his desire to defend his people and his request for prayer; Moses is manipulative. In the end, though, the pattern of request and refusal, and plagues delivered and removed, heightens the readers' tension. We understand that something unbelievably bad is coming, and we know that if salvation is won, it will be associated with death.

Most merciful God,
who by the death and resurrection of your Son Jesus Christ
delivered and saved the world:
grant that by faith in him who suffered on the cross
we may triumph in the power of his victory;
through Jesus Christ your Son our Lord,
who is alive and reigns with you,
in the unity of the Holy Spirit,
one God, now and for ever.

COLLECT

Reflection by **Gillian Cooper**

101

Wednesday 21 March

Psalms **55**, 124 *or* **119.153-end**
Exodus 9.1-12
Hebrews 12.3-13

Exodus 9.1-12

'But the Lord hardened the heart of Pharaoh' (v.12)

Things are getting serious now. The previous disasters have been bad enough, but now livestock are dying and people are being seriously disabled by boils. The plagues have become life-threatening. Tension is increasing. Surely Pharaoh has to crack soon? But Pharaoh is in essence a tyrant like any other, despite his occasional concessions, and we know from our experience of Pharaoh's contemporary equivalents that it is almost impossible for a tyrant to back down once a stance has been taken.

Life in the Nile delta was precarious in ancient times, and any of the plagues could have happened in the natural course of events. We are not, however, intended to read this story as a history of natural disasters. In some places it has an almost pantomime quality: Yes he will! No he won't! My magic is better than yours! The good hero is destined to win in the end, no matter how powerful the evil king. We can imagine the fun involved in the retelling of the story to children down the years.

Yet the story is, of course, deadly serious. The repetition of the pattern of Pharaoh's agreement and refusal, of the plague imposed and lifted, in the end causes us horror rather than amusement, as we contemplate what may happen next. This is a story about salvation, and we are being told over and over what an extraordinary and difficult matter that is.

COLLECT

Most merciful God,
who by the death and resurrection of your Son Jesus Christ
delivered and saved the world:
grant that by faith in him who suffered on the cross
we may triumph in the power of his victory;
through Jesus Christ your Son our Lord,
who is alive and reigns with you,
in the unity of the Holy Spirit,
one God, now and for ever.

| *Reflection by* **Gillian Cooper**

Psalms **40**, 125 *or* **143**, 146
Exodus 9.13-end
Hebrews 12.14-end

Thursday 22 March

Exodus 9.13-end

'... to show you my power, and to make my name resound through all the earth' (v.16)

So now we know. This is not about punishing the Egyptians. It is not even about freeing the Israelites. It is about God and the world.

The final editors of Exodus knew that their work would be read by the descendants of people who had experienced defeat by a succession of tyrannical emperors, and who had suffered exile from their homeland. They had good reason to doubt their God and his promises. They had lost their land and their kings, and ended up a small corner of a province of an empire, insignificant as far as the world was concerned. What would they think? That God was not very powerful? Or perhaps that God was just not very interested in them?

Remember your history, our writers tell them. Your God defeated Pharaoh and all his magicians with a prolonged demonstration of power. God kept his promises once and will do so again. Resistance to God's plan, however fierce, can only ever be temporary. It took a long time to be freed from Egypt, and even longer to make it to their promised land, but God's promises can only ever be deferred, never cancelled.

We are not yet at the end of the story. Pharaoh is still resisting. But readers then and now are invited to trust that there can only be one winner of this battle, however high the cost proves to be.

Gracious Father,
you gave up your Son
out of love for the world:
lead us to ponder the mysteries of his passion,
that we may know eternal peace
through the shedding of our Saviour's blood,
Jesus Christ our Lord.

COLLECT

Reflection by **Gillian Cooper** | 103

Friday 23 March

Exodus 10

*'... that you may tell your children and grandchildren how I have
made fools of the Egyptians' (v.2)*

It is a story worth telling, and the reason we have this story to read
now is that it was indeed told.

The Old Testament writers place great emphasis on retelling and
remembering. They know that a nation that forgets its history loses its
place in the world. They know too that a nation that forgets how much
it owes to its God is heading for disaster. So our author reminds us that
the story of the plagues is the nation's story for all time. For many
centuries to come, families will re-enact the Passover meal that
heralded the Israelites' final departure from Egypt. They will remember
that their escape was not easy. They will tell a story of powerful
enemies, of danger, and of wavering faith in an uncertain future. But
the story they tell will mostly be about the wonder of their God. They
have a God who faces up to the fiercest opposition with calm planning;
a God who keeps his promises no matter what; a God who cannot be
beaten; a God who saves them even when they do not want to be
saved; and a God who expects much from them in return.

For now, Pharaoh is weakening, but Moses is expanding his demands.
The Israelites must leave all together, with all their belongings. No one
is any longer pretending they will come back. Darkness descends on
Egypt. We are nearing the end-game.

COLLECT

Most merciful God,
who by the death and resurrection of your Son Jesus Christ
delivered and saved the world:
grant that by faith in him who suffered on the cross
we may triumph in the power of his victory;
through Jesus Christ your Son our Lord,
who is alive and reigns with you,
in the unity of the Holy Spirit,
one God, now and for ever.

| *Reflection by* **Gillian Cooper**

Psalms **23**, 127 *or* **147**
Exodus 11
Hebrews 13.17-end

Saturday 24 March

Exodus 11

'Then there will be a loud cry throughout the whole land' (v.6)

This is it, the final act. The Israelites start to get ready. The Egyptians will be glad to see the back of them, so glad that they give them all their disposable wealth to get rid of them. They do not yet know what final horror awaits them.

How high the cost of the Israelites' freedom! How high for his people the cost of Pharaoh's stubbornness! Even as we rejoice with the Israelites, we weep with the Egyptians, to whom the other plagues will soon seem as nothing in the face of their overwhelming grief.

This is a hard story to read. It seriously challenges our moral sensibilities. It has done so from the beginning, as the people of Egypt have suffered, but the slightly pantomime quality of the magic contest has mitigated our distaste. Now, however, there is no escape. Egyptian men, women and children will die, and mourn, so that God's own people can live freely. Any justifications we may create fail before that grief. In the battle between good and evil, these are innocent casualties, collateral damage. The story is what it is. We have to deal with it. We cannot pretend it is all right. Its retelling must surely be full of grief as well as rejoicing.

As we approach Holy Week, death is on our minds. Another first-born will soon die. This time, however, the cost is borne by God himself.

Gracious Father,
you gave up your Son
out of love for the world:
lead us to ponder the mysteries of his passion,
that we may know eternal peace
through the shedding of our Saviour's blood,
Jesus Christ our Lord.

COLLECT

Reflection by **Gillian Cooper**　105

Monday 26 March

Monday of Holy Week

Psalm 41
Lamentations 1.1-12*a*
Luke 22.1-23

Lamentations 1.1-12*a*

'The roads to Zion mourn … all her gates are desolate' (v.4)

I confess that I have a penchant for films that feature dystopias. I think of *Logan's Run*, a wonderful science fiction classic from 1976 starring Jenny Agutter and Michael York. Set a long time in the future, this unlikely couple escape the clutches of their pursuers, only to find that the sanctuary they reach is a 'wasted place' – a city in ruins. Its former glory is there to glimpse – but the city is now an uninhabited wasteland. This is an Aleppo, Palmyra, Benghazi and Tripoli.

The Holy Week readings serve up plenty of paradoxes, and the evocative image of a desolate city is no exception. It prefigures the death and desertion of Good Friday. It is also a metaphor for inner grief, the death and destruction inside our souls. We mourn for the state we are in.

In this lamentation, the writer speaks for his people, but also echoes something of what Jesus' experience of Holy Week and Good Friday must be – abandoned, scorned, an object of vilification and wrath. What has he done to deserve this? 'My God, my God, why have you forsaken me?' (Matthew 27.46).

Yet Holy Week is also about remembering that no matter how deserted we may feel, God never abandons us. We are ultimately raised up from despair and death. That is the paradox of Good Friday. Jesus becomes the desolate one on our behalf, so that we might never be without God again. Jesus becomes forsaken so we might forever have eternity with God.

COLLECT | Almighty and everlasting God,
who in your tender love towards the human race
   sent your Son our Saviour Jesus Christ
to take upon him our flesh
and to suffer death upon the cross:
grant that we may follow the example of his patience and humility,
and also be made partakers of his resurrection;
through Jesus Christ your Son our Lord,
who is alive and reigns with you,
in the unity of the Holy Spirit,
one God, now and for ever.

Psalm 27
Lamentations 3.1-18
Luke 22.[24-38] 39-53

Tuesday 27 March

Tuesday of Holy Week

Lamentations 3.1-18

*'... he has besieged and enveloped me with bitterness
and tribulation' (v.5)*

The writer of Lamentations offers us a meditation of deep despair –
a diminishment of his humanity that is disturbing and disabling, and a
sense that God, no less, is 'afflicting' Jeremiah. But all of it is felt inside
the body of the writer – and keenly so. Jeremiah laments that God will
slowly humiliate and obliterate him. He internalizes this, as a process
of corrosion, wasting and disablement.

Jeremiah's lament is about as dark and depressing as it can get. So
what are we to say of God in all this? Three things, it seems to me.

First, that God will never leave us or forsake us. God does not know
how to be absent in our lives or our world. So even when we think we
experience God's absence, God is there. Second, and to paraphrase
C. S. Lewis, God whispers in our pleasure, but shouts in our pain. God
will yet find a way to shine a light in this darkness of ours. Third, that
'all shall be well', as Julian of Norwich so poignantly expressed it. We
are held by God, and will be held and raised up.

In Holy Week it is Jesus who, in taking on our humanity, must also take
on the darkest hours of isolation and desolation. In his life, they are
fully assumed so we can be fully redeemed. God knows what we feel;
in Jesus, it is known and taken to the heart of the creator, where it is
held, treasured and transformed.

True and humble king,
hailed by the crowd as Messiah:
grant us the faith to know you and love you,
that we may be found beside you
on the way of the cross,
which is the path of glory.

COLLECT

Wednesday 28 March
Wednesday of Holy Week

Psalm 102 [*or* 102.1-18]
Wisdom 1.16 – 2.1; 2.12-22
or Jeremiah 11.18-20
Luke 22.54-end

Jeremiah 11.18-20

'... a gentle lamb led to the slaughter' (v.19)

From the first Easter, Christians have proclaimed that 'the Lamb that was slain' takes away the sins of the world. Here at Christ Church in Oxford, the college has a painting from the 1580s by Annibale Carracci known as *The Butcher's Shop*. It portrays a passive lamb about to be slaughtered, surrounded by other butchered meat ready for sale. The lamb in the picture looks resigned; it knows what is coming next.

A paradox of Christian faith is proclaiming Jesus as both the Great Shepherd of the Sheep and the Lamb of God. As any Sunday school child will testify, images of Jesus carrying a young lamb aloft on his shoulder are powerful and resonant. Jesus rescues the lost; he raises up and restores the lost sheep that would otherwise have perished.

But Holy Week also does something unusual to this Great Shepherd of the Sheep. It turns Jesus into just another one of the flock, and leads him to be butchered at the cross in the same way as countless thousands of others would die that year, at the hands of fickle Roman justice. Led like a lamb to the slaughter.

Yet a faith that takes its shepherd and turns him into a sheep tells a deeper story. Christian tradition portrays Jesus as the Saviour, and in so doing reaches back to the Jewish perception of the Passover, of scapegoating and of the Pascal lamb. Here, in this death, and by the shedding of this blood, God will redeem his people. To be the victor, you must first be the victim.

COLLECT

Almighty and everlasting God,
who in your tender love towards the human race
    sent your Son our Saviour Jesus Christ
to take upon him our flesh
and to suffer death upon the cross:
grant that we may follow the example of his patience and humility,
and also be made partakers of his resurrection;
through Jesus Christ your Son our Lord,
who is alive and reigns with you,
in the unity of the Holy Spirit,
one God, now and for ever.

Psalms 42, 43
Leviticus 16.2-24
Luke 23.1-25

Thursday 29 March
Maundy Thursday

Leviticus 16.2-24
'Thus he shall make atonement ...' (v.16)

At the centre of Good Friday and Maundy Thursday is the image of the slaughtered lamb who atones for our lives. This animal offering to procure our righteousness before God – scripted by the Old Testament, and then reframed in the New Testament – is what links the faith of Christianity to its parental Judaism. And today, the image offers three ways of looking at the coming sacrifice.

First, this slaughtered lamb reflects a kind of tame compliance. In silence, Jesus absorbs the pain and the hatred that is visited upon him. The centre of Good Friday comes in the realization that this hurt and violence will not be passed on – they are to be absorbed by God.

Second, the blood and the wounds are salvific. Jesus' blood is somehow nourishing, and to feed off it is to participate in the abundant life of God. To be covered by the blood of the lamb symbolizes not only purity, but a new kind of intensity, in which the life of God washes away the pain, sickness and violence of the world.

Third, we know that Jesus' last words from the cross will be concerned not with protestations of his innocence, but with the spreading of forgiveness. Jesus seems to be powerfully aware that his executioners really *don't* know what they are doing. They too are simple instruments in a system where this engineering of cruel death is part of everyday life. With Jesus' words, our sins of ignorance are absolved.

And so the Lamb of God who was slain for the world invites us to his supper.

True and humble king,
hailed by the crowd as Messiah:
grant us the faith to know you and love you,
that we may be found beside you
on the way of the cross,
which is the path of glory.

COLLECT

Reflection by **Martyn Percy** | 109

Friday 30 March

Good Friday

Psalm 69
Genesis 22.1-18
John 19.38-end
or Hebrews 10.1-10

Genesis 22.1-18

'God himself will provide the lamb' (v.8)

It is easy to forget how precious Isaac was to his father and mother. Earlier in Genesis, 'the Lord appeared to Abraham' in the form of three mysterious men (Genesis 18.1). Abraham receives the strangers and gives them hospitality. These men then announce that Abraham's wife, the barren Sarah, now in her nineties (Genesis 17.17), will soon give birth to a son. Sarah laughs at this, but the three visitors reply gnomically: 'Is anything too hard for the Lord?' Nine months later, Sarah gives birth to Isaac.

So, what is too hard for the Lord? The answer is nothing, of course. But today of all days takes us to a place that is very hard, one that no human would ever want to arrive at. For who can ever sacrifice their own child?

No parent can imagine what Abraham is doing. But this story is not about appeasing the gods of old with a precious blood sacrifice, let alone killing the innocent to satisfy the God of Abraham, Isaac, Jacob and Moses. This story is about something else; it is a story that ends self-sacrifice.

There is nothing precious that we own or love that we can sacrifice in order to close the gap between ourselves and God. God, in Christ, has already reached us. The cross of Christ is God's signature and a pledge: we are fully loved. Nothing we can do, say or offer can change that. Even if we disown him, he will not disown us. That's why the sacrifice is God's, not ours. Truly, today is Good Friday.

COLLECT

Almighty Father,
look with mercy on this your family
for which our Lord Jesus Christ was content to be betrayed
    and given up into the hands of sinners
    and to suffer death upon the cross;
who is alive and glorified with you and the Holy Spirit,
one God, now and for ever.

Reflection by **Martyn Percy**

Psalm 142
Hosea 6.1-6
John 2.18-22

Saturday 31 March
Easter Eve

Hosea 6.1-6

'... the knowledge of God rather than burnt-offerings' (v.6)

Lent is over – yet on Easter Eve comes the call: time to repent! Talk of repentance makes modern-day Christians nervous, even squeamish. We are embarrassed by the stereotype of old-fashioned preachers hammering on about sin and guilt. We rush to assert that Jesus isn't really like that. He came out of love; he wants to help us. He knows us deep inside and feels our every pain, and his healing love sets us free.

That's true, of course, but nevertheless, repentance is the doorway to the spiritual life, the only way to begin. It is also the path itself, the only way to continue. Anything else is foolishness and self-delusion.

The ancient Christian literature on repentance can be quite beautiful – full of simplicity, humility, and peace. Those who know themselves to be so greatly forgiven are far from gloomy, but are flooded with joy and deep tranquillity. Those who are forgiven much, love much. They find it hard to hold grudges against others; they find it hard to hold anything in this life too tightly. For Christians, two things are ever-linked: sorrow over sin, and gratitude for forgiveness.

The resurrection will burst this all asunder. We are now asked to greet our saviour. Our sacrifices of old are to be replaced with a new knowledge of God. As we wait in darkness, the light is about the dawn: repentance will be met with forgiveness; mourning with joy; death with life. And so we turn to the One who is life, light and joy – who in his death and sacrifice, has freed us from death.

Grant, Lord,
that we who are baptized into the death
of your Son our Saviour Jesus Christ
may continually put to death our evil desires
and be buried with him;
and that through the grave and gate of death
we may pass to our joyful resurrection;
through his merits,
who died and was buried and rose again for us,
your Son Jesus Christ our Lord.

COLLECT

Reflection by **Martyn Percy**   111

Monday 2 April

Monday of Easter Week

Psalms 111, 117, 146
Exodus 12.1-14
1 Corinthians 15.1-11

Exodus 12.1-14

'Your lamb shall be without blemish' (v.5)

Images of shepherds, sheep and sacrifice pepper the Old and New Testament. These images are about reclaiming the purity of sacrifice, redeeming defilement. A Lamb shall be slain.

Yet although references to shepherds and lambs wind their way through many scriptural texts, they are difficult images for the Church to embrace. Most of us are far removed from the practices of shepherding. Furthermore, the notion has taken on a rather negative meaning – to describe someone as a sheep is an insult, implying they follow the crowd without question and expect someone else to be responsible for them.

The first Passover was a prelude to a journey. Now, we are all to be followers of the way, and we need to prepare and make ready. In the imagery of Passover, we encounter a journey of faith that is meant to carry us through our darkest hours. This trust, like the ways of a sheep with its shepherd, is not blind obedience. It is, rather, a radical trust that empowers us to believe that life has Christian meaning, even though our immediate experience may be telling us otherwise.

So, 'My sheep hear my voice. I know them, and they follow me' (John 10.27) is a message for Passover, and for Christian faith. But how easy can this be? Just ask any of the disciples whom Jesus called and who now stand on the other side of Easter. For the way of the Shepherd and Sheep leads to both life and death; safety and sacrifice; love and loss. It is to this we are called.

COLLECT
| Lord of all life and power,
who through the mighty resurrection of your Son
overcame the old order of sin and death
to make all things new in him:
grant that we, being dead to sin
and alive to you in Jesus Christ,
may reign with him in glory;
to whom with you and the Holy Spirit
be praise and honour, glory and might,
now and in all eternity.

| *Reflection by* **Martyn Percy**

Psalms 112, 147.1-12
Exodus 12.14-36
1 Corinthians 15.12-19

Tuesday 3 April

Tuesday of Easter Week

Exodus 12.14–36

'Take your flocks and your herds, as you said, and be gone' (v.32)

An exodus is a journey, and a costly one at that – a whole people on the move, fleeing war, oppression, famine or disaster. In one sense, Holy Week and Easter are all about making costly journeys, including those that ultimately embrace death, in the hope that this may lead to life.

An old Christian legend tells of St Peter fleeing Rome for fear of his life. As he hurries away from the city, he meets Jesus travelling in the opposite direction. Peter calls him: 'Master, where are you going?' In the tale, Jesus says: 'I am going to Rome to take your place.' At this point Peter turns round, returns to the city, and goes on to meet his death and his maker.

If we are resolved to move daily further into union with Christ, we must be ready for a journey – to face the things that hold us back. Repentance is the way back to the Father. Easter is the door and the path to a new life. To have the heart set on God is to choose wisdom, and to follow him who calls us, not to a life where desires are fulfilled, but to one where the restless heart is finally set at ease.

Remember what Jesus says: 'For where your treasure is, there your heart will be also' (Matthew 6.21). So the question we are asked, and which is ever before you and me, is simple: will you follow?

God of glory,
by the raising of your Son
you have broken the chains of death and hell:
fill your Church with faith and hope;
for a new day has dawned
and the way to life stands open
in our Saviour Jesus Christ.

COLLECT

Reflection by **Martyn Percy**

113

Wednesday 4 April

Wednesday of Easter Week

Psalms 113, 147.13-end
Exodus 12.37-end
1 Corinthians 15.20-28

Exodus 12.37-end

'This is the ordinance for the passover: no foreigner shall eat of it'
(v.43)

According to the Gospel of John (10.22), Jesus' visit on the Feast of Lights (or Dedication) was last trip that he made to Jerusalem before his final visit – and his own sacrifice. The next visit would be Christ's last, when he would return there for his final Passover and sacrifice.

The Feast of the Passover is a bitter–sweet affair – and literally so: bitter herbs, sweet meat. At the feast, it is traditional to spill some of the wine as a reminder that the cup of joy is not filled to the brim, let alone overflowing.

The joy of Easter, for Christians, must be tempered by the knowledge that the extraordinary life that bursts from the tomb does not just result in personal salvation for all who receive it. The resurrection, like the Passover, places responsibility on the community of the redeemed – to reach out to the alien and the stranger who also want to feast with us.

Whilst the feasting of the first Passovers was only for those initiated into the faith of the Old Testament, Easter reminds us that the salvation that comes through Jesus in the New Testament is to be universal. In Jesus, the boundaries between us – native and alien, family and stranger, kith and kin – are dissolved. Jesus asks us to make our meals inclusive, as it shall be in the Kingdom that is to come. This is a feast to which the whole world is invited.

COLLECT

Lord of all life and power,
who through the mighty resurrection of your Son
overcame the old order of sin and death
to make all things new in him:
grant that we, being dead to sin
and alive to you in Jesus Christ,
may reign with him in glory;
to whom with you and the Holy Spirit
be praise and honour, glory and might,
now and in all eternity.

| *Reflection by* **Martyn Percy**

Psalms 114, 148
Exodus 13.1-16
1 Corinthians 15.29-34

Thursday 5 April

Thursday of Easter Week

Exodus 13.1-16

'Consecrate to me all the firstborn' (v.2)

According to Luke's Gospel, Jesus as a firstborn male is brought to the temple to be consecrated, as custom demands. But as with all consecrations, the blessings are shared out. Simeon and Anna are blessed as much as those they came to bless.

I often think of that occasion in the temple, when Mary and Joseph, after their epic journeys, must have wanted to keep Jesus to themselves – to protect him, to keep him safe. But they are made to go to the temple, and offer him up.

It may seem extraordinary to us that after the trials and tumult of exodus, the Israelites are now to offer the very first fruits of everything to God. Yet it is the same for Christians. The only real possession we have – ourselves – is asked to be surrendered. And we cannot truly live a life of faith until we give up ourselves.

Giving and offering are part of God's provision of blessing. It is people and things being raised to their true and proper status before God. It is creation being returned to the creator. 'God rules creation by blessing' claimed the rabbis of Jesus' day. Quite so. Blessing is that comprehensive praise and thanks that returns all reality to God. Truly, it is more blessed to give than to receive. And that is how, in turn, we are blessed.

COLLECT

God of glory,
by the raising of your Son
you have broken the chains of death and hell:
fill your Church with faith and hope;
for a new day has dawned
and the way to life stands open
in our Saviour Jesus Christ.

Friday 6 April

Friday of Easter Week

Psalms 115, 149
Exodus 13.17 – 14.14
1 Corinthians 15.35-50

Exodus 13.17 – 14.14

*'The Lord went in front of them in a pillar of cloud by day ...
and in a pillar of fire by night' (13.21)*

The Old Testament is not only full of people demanding signs; it is also full of the strange signs by which God speaks to us. A burning bush; a rock that flows with water; a pillar of flame; a cloud; or even Balaam's ass – God speaks through all these things.

But the Easter faith confounds the need for signs and symbols. As Paul remarks in the New Testament, Jews demand signs; Greeks wisdom (1 Corinthians 1.22). But no sign shall be given, except the sign of the cross – foolishness to the Greeks, and a stumbling-block to us all.

The love of God, according to hymn writer Frederick William Faber, is broader than the measure of our mind. So it is with wisdom, which is why God uses simple things to shame the intelligent, and the foolish to confound the wise. Here we have a straggling rabble of people, led across the desert, guided by little more than a cloud by day and a sliver of light by night. But it is enough. It is through this journey that the story of salvation continues. And it will find its fulfilment in the bursting of light at Easter, and the deep cloudy haze of the transfiguration and ascension.

God's signs, symbols and messages often come through unexpected sources. We need to learn to read the utterly extraordinary in the perfectly ordinary. God's wisdom is not like ours; it surprises, undermines and disturbs. It does not confirm; it often confounds.

COLLECT

Lord of all life and power,
who through the mighty resurrection of your Son
overcame the old order of sin and death
to make all things new in him:
grant that we, being dead to sin
and alive to you in Jesus Christ,
may reign with him in glory;
to whom with you and the Holy Spirit
be praise and honour, glory and might,
now and in all eternity.

Psalms **116**, 150
Exodus 14.15-end
1 Corinthians 15.51-end

Saturday 7 April

Saturday of Easter Week

Exodus 14.15-end

'Israel saw the great work that the Lord did ...' (v.31)

The discipleship that God requires of us is one that is centred on journey and risk. There is no enchanted path. The road we travel in our faith is one in which God abides with us – but it is fraught with hazards, and dangers remain. We are asked to trust. And sometimes to take extraordinary risks.

Moses has taken his people as far as he can go. Now he finds himself caught between his pursuers and a seemingly insurmountable obstacle. There is nothing Moses can do. He is trapped. It is as this point that God speaks to Moses. God sees our plight. And at the point when we are beginning to feel utterly defeated, God somehow redeems us.

Many readers today will struggle with the huge loss of life contained in this story. But in some respects, this is not a story about victors and vanquished; it is, rather, a story about how God meets us in moments of dire despair and desolation. The game appears to be up for the Israelites. They are about to be recaptured. Yet this story says that God will not give up on us. When we cry out to God, we are heard.

Sometimes it is easy to feel defeated by the overwhelming odds we face or the sheer scale of needs we are attempting to address on behalf of others. So this story shows that God can snatch a victory from the jaws of defeat. What God needs us to be is not fearful, but rather watchful and faithful. Rather than face drowning or annihilation, we may yet find ourselves on some dry land, and with an unlikely path ahead.

God of glory,
by the raising of your Son
you have broken the chains of death and hell:
fill your Church with faith and hope;
for a new day has dawned
and the way to life stands open
in our Saviour Jesus Christ.

COLLECT

Reflection by **Martyn Percy**   117

Monday 9 April

Annunciation of Our Lord
to the Blessed Virgin Mary

Psalms 111, 113
1 Samuel 2.1-10
Romans 5.12-end

1 Samuel 2.1-10

'He raises up the poor from the dust;
he lifts the needy from the ash heap' (v.8)

The Feast of the Annunciation – celebrated late this year because Palm Sunday fell on March 25th – finds its connection to Hannah's song because the Magnificat, Mary's response to her meeting with the Angel Gabriel, is a kind of remix of this earlier song.

The word 'remix' is mostly associated with dance or hip hop music, where short samples are the basis for a completely new song. But the practice is not new; artists as various as Johnny Cash, Led Zeppelin, George Harrison, Radiohead, Beethoven and Handel are among those who have – consciously or subconsciously – borrowed and remixed from earlier music in their own or other people's repertoire.

Elizabeth's story, even more than Mary's, has close personal resonances with Hannah's. Both women had longed in quiet desperation for a child; each of them understood their unexpected sons to be God's gift not just to them, but for the service of the world. So strong are the links between their stories, and the similarities of the two songs, that scholars have speculated whether the Magnificat was originally attributed to Elizabeth. Whatever its provenance, the Magnificat clearly and deliberately recalls Hannah's story, with the exuberant joy and defiant faith of both songs standing not only as a declaration that God's promises are never broken, but also putting the spotlight on God's faithfulness to women, who are so often sidelined and ignored in the story of salvation.

COLLECT

We beseech you, O Lord,
pour your grace into our hearts,
that as we have known the incarnation of your Son Jesus Christ
    by the message of an angel,
so by his cross and passion
we may be brought to the glory of his resurrection;
through Jesus Christ your Son our Lord,
who is alive and reigns with you,
in the unity of the Holy Spirit,
one God, now and for ever.

| *Reflection by* **Maggi Dawn**

Psalms **8**, 20, 21 *or* **5**, 6 (8)
Exodus 15.22 – 16.10
Colossians 1.15-end

Tuesday 10 April

Exodus 15.22 – 16.10

'… the Lord showed him a piece of wood; he threw it into the water, and the water became sweet' (15.25)

Bitter water: not just bad to the taste, but the kind that gives you stomach cramps. The best solution to bitter water is to find an alternative source. For Moses, however, the choice was not between clean or contaminated water, it was between dirty water or none at all. God provided the answer in the shape of a piece of wood that, on contact with the water, miraculously made it fit to drink.

The Biblical texts are full of allusion, with old stories being re-interpreted through the lens of what happened later. But the best examples offer new layers of interpretation without overloading the text with equivalence. To say 'this equals that' flattens a text, but to float an allusion opens up the possibility of new meanings without crushing the original.

The story of Marah hangs around a miracle in which a piece of wood makes bitter water sweet. Without claiming precise equivalence, there are echoes of this ancient miracle in the central moment of redemption, where a death on a wooden cross opens up the possibility of new life; absorbing and cancelling the bitter power of sin, and opening the way to renewed and transformed life.

Almighty Father,
you have given your only Son to die for our sins
and to rise again for our justification:
grant us so to put away the leaven of malice and wickedness
that we may always serve you
in pureness of living and truth;
through the merits of your Son Jesus Christ our Lord,
who is alive and reigns with you,
in the unity of the Holy Spirit,
one God, now and for ever.

COLLECT

Reflection by **Maggi Dawn** | 119

Wednesday 11 April

Psalms 16, **30** *or* **119.1-32**
Exodus 16.11-end
Colossians 2.1-15

Exodus 16.11-end

'When the Israelites saw it, they said to one another, "What is it?"
For they did not know what it was' (v.15)

The story of the wilderness wanderings can read like a repeating cycle of complaints, miraculous signs – and more complaints. Why did they not learn? But a more compassionate reading emerges with the recognition that people lose heart when they live through prolonged uncertainty. The extensive migration of the previous few years had made clear the desperation of those who wandered the earth knowing they could not go back, but with no clear destination in view.

When the manna fell, the people did not recognize it as food; it had to be named before they could receive it. Generations later, in the days after the resurrection, the disciples repeatedly failed to recognize the risen Christ. Mary thought he was a gardener; on the road to Emmaus he was mistaken for a foreign tourist; and at the lake a whole round of fishing took place before they realized it was Jesus on the shore.

At times of stress, grief, dislocation or extreme tiredness, it's good to remember that the answer to our prayers could be right under our noses, even if we can't see it. Just as the ancient Israelites needed Moses to name the manna as food, we need friends, and spiritual guides, to read our situation back to us. All that stands between us and Easter joy may be the moment of recognition.

COLLECT

Almighty Father,
you have given your only Son to die for our sins
and to rise again for our justification:
grant us so to put away the leaven of malice and wickedness
that we may always serve you
in pureness of living and truth;
through the merits of your Son Jesus Christ our Lord,
who is alive and reigns with you,
in the unity of the Holy Spirit,
one God, now and for ever.

| *Reflection by* **Maggi Dawn**

Psalms **28**, 29 *or* 14, **15**, 16
Exodus 17
Colossians 2.16 – 3.11

Thursday 12 April

Exodus 17

*'From the wilderness of Sin the whole congregation of the
Israelites journeyed by stages, as the Lord commanded' (v.1)*

It's easy to forget that the season of Easter is longer than Lent: 50 days
in all. The time lag between Easter and Pentecost reminds us that, for
the disciples, there were weeks – or perhaps even months – between
Christ's resurrection and their empowerment in the Spirit. Easter was
not one cataclysmic moment, but a gradual revelation. This has a clear
resonance with the legendary stories of the wanderings in the
wilderness, when, step by painful step, they progressed from the land
of oppression to the land of promise.

Although wilderness stories are usually associated with Lent rather
than Easter, they are more appropriate to the season than we might
first suppose. We read the story of salvation retrospectively, knowing
the end from the beginning, but every chapter was once the lived
reality of a group of people who could not see the future and did not
know where they would end up.

After the resurrection the disciples journeyed one step at a time, just
as the ancient congregation had done. And, even though we know the
outcome of the story of Easter and Pentecost, we too live in uncertain
times. We share the common human experience of living one day at a
time, trusting God for the outcome.

COLLECT

Risen Christ,
for whom no door is locked, no entrance barred:
open the doors of our hearts,
that we may seek the good of others
and walk the joyful road of sacrifice and peace,
to the praise of God the Father.

Reflection by **Maggi Dawn** | 121

Friday 13 April

Psalms 57, **61** *or* 17, **19**
Exodus 18.1-12
Colossians 3.12 – 4.1

Exodus 18.1-12

'Jethro, Moses' father-in-law, brought a burnt offering and sacrifices to God' (v. 12)

Jethro was a priest of the Midianites, with worship practices quite different from those of Moses. Nevertheless, he was a strong support for Moses, taking care of the family while Moses was away, and then returning them safely to him.

Behind those who are busy doing what is acknowledged as God's work, there are always supportive people who pick up the stuff of everyday existence – tasks that are just as important, but may not get the same spiritual recognition. Joseph did it for Mary, Jonathan for David, Isaiah for Ahaz. But in order for Jethro to do this for Moses, he had to reach across religious boundaries.

Moses could certainly not have achieved what he did without help from his wife and her family. But perhaps the sweetest part of the story is to see a priest of the Midianites welcomed into the community and the worship of Moses' God.

It would be extravagant, I think, to read this as a conversion narrative. The beauty of the story, rather, is to recognize that genuine strength and support can be offered between people of different religions and cultures. Now as then, those who generously reach across such religious and cultural barriers still find that God's blessings are returned to them.

COLLECT

Almighty Father,
you have given your only Son to die for our sins
and to rise again for our justification:
grant us so to put away the leaven of malice and wickedness
that we may always serve you
in pureness of living and truth;
through the merits of your Son Jesus Christ our Lord,
who is alive and reigns with you,
in the unity of the Holy Spirit,
one God, now and for ever.

| *Reflection by* **Maggi Dawn**

Exodus 18.13-end

'Moses listened to his father-in-law and did all that he had said'
(v.24)

They always say that you shouldn't make decisions when you are tired or under serious pressure. The problem is, though, that jobs that demand important decisions also make you tired and put you under pressure. Moses was so tired he had somehow slipped from resolving problems by calling directly on God, to endlessly explaining the nitpicking detail of the law. Thank goodness for his father-in-law, who saw that Moses was so overburdened by multiplying administrative tasks, he was no longer doing what he was good at.

Unsolicited advice is not always welcome. But Jethro had three things in his favour. First, he had a track record; he had advised Moses before and proved himself trustworthy. Second, he had nothing to gain from the advice he was giving; he was speaking without prejudice. Third, he spoke out of genuine care for Moses.

The right person, at the right time, with the right words of wisdom, can reach out to those who are working themselves into an early grave. If leaders are criticized harshly, it reinforces their lonely path. But critique brought with kindness and care is more likely to be received as a route to the better health of the whole community.

With all this in place, there was still one final piece of the jigsaw: Moses listened. 'Let the reader understand.'

COLLECT

Risen Christ,
for whom no door is locked, no entrance barred:
open the doors of our hearts,
that we may seek the good of others
and walk the joyful road of sacrifice and peace,
to the praise of God the Father.

Reflection by **Maggi Dawn** | 123

Monday 16 April

Psalms **96**, 97 *or* 27, **30**
Exodus 19
Luke 1.1-25

Luke 1.1-25

'When he did come out, he could not speak to them' (v.22)

It has often been suggested that Zechariah's muteness was a punishment for not believing the angel's message. But this seems incongruous – there are so many other biblical figures who needed multiple reassurances. Only a few verses later Mary asked an identical question and received an answer that satisfied her.

It is not uncommon for people to lose their voice following a traumatic event, so it is not surprising that, coming face to face with God's presence in the Holy of Holies, Zechariah was rendered speechless. But his muteness may carry a more symbolic message. The people were waiting for him outside the sanctuary in order to receive the priestly blessing, which he was expected to announce after successfully completing the ritual. At the opening of Luke's Gospel, Zechariah was unable to pronounce the blessing, but at the very end (Luke 24.50), Luke describes Jesus blessing the disciples, after which they return to the temple to worship. The blessing is taken from Zechariah's lips, and put in the mouth of Jesus, the new 'High Priest'. The old patterns were giving way to a new order.

Zechariah's loss of voice was perhaps more gift than punishment, then: both an answer to his question and a prophetic sign that his priestly task was now to be reassigned to the Great High Priest. With the blessing thus deferred to Christ, Zechariah recovered his voice to name his son.

COLLECT

Almighty Father,
who in your great mercy gladdened the disciples
    with the sight of the risen Lord:
give us such knowledge of his presence with us,
that we may be strengthened and sustained by his risen life
and serve you continually in righteousness and truth;
through Jesus Christ your Son our Lord,
who is alive and reigns with you,
in the unity of the Holy Spirit,
one God, now and for ever.

Reflection by **Maggi Dawn**

Psalms **98**, 99, 100 *or* 32, **36**
Exodus 20.1-21
Luke 1.26-38

Tuesday 17 April

Luke 1.26-38

'The Holy Spirit will come upon you, and the power of the Most High will overshadow you' (v.35)

One of the vexed questions in recent discussions of the Annunciation is whether Mary had a choice. This is not merely a philosophical conundrum over the will of God. With the growing awareness of how little agency women have had over their own bodies, it is no surprise that questions are raised by Luke's brief account of the Annunciation. Even naming the feast as announcement rather than invitation can seem to suggest at least an imposition upon Mary, if not – as some have claimed – an abusive act.

If a careful reading of the Annunciation story fails to put paid to that worry, the Magnificat that follows leaves us in no doubt: Mary receives the gift of a son with joy, not fear; as invitation, not imposition. Edwin Muir, in 'The Annunciation', goes a step further, imagining that the Angel is more awestruck than Mary. The angel comes to her 'from far beyond the farthest star, feathered through time' – yet in her presence, his feathers 'tremble on his wings'.

Traditionally Mary's response ('Let it be to me …') has been regarded as a consent, and the intercessions for the Annunciation begin, 'By the consent of your handmaid …'. Abusive treatment has no place in God's story. The divine promises are fulfilled through invitation, not coercion.

Risen Christ,
you filled your disciples with boldness and fresh hope:
strengthen us to proclaim your risen life
and fill us with your peace,
to the glory of God the Father.

COLLECT

Reflection by **Maggi Dawn**

Wednesday 18 April

Psalm **105** *or* **34**
Exodus 24
Luke 1.39-56

Luke 1.39-56

'Surely, from now on all generations will call me blessed' (v.48)

Today we hear Mary's song, so reminiscent of Hannah's song that we read a few days ago on April 9th. There we observed that while Elizabeth's situation was closer to Hannah's than that of Mary, it was Mary who got to sing the great song of praise. Indeed, one of the things that is so striking about the Magnificat is its departure from much of the traditional imagery that surrounds Mary.

It is often noted that Mary lived in a world that gave women little control over their own lives; she lacked age, status or privilege, and in many ways had no power or independence. Her consent to God's invitation – 'Let it be to me according to thy word' – is often read in a way that is not only submissive, but subservient.

Yet the Magnificat is exuberant, triumphant even. It demonstrates a strong, even a defiant faith, and a refusal to accept the status quo. Mary does more here than meekly accept an honour bestowed; she grabs it with both hands and claims the political and spiritual triumph of the hour.

If ever we needed persuading that obedience to God's will is an act of strength, not of weakness, Mary's song is the mandate. Accepting the invitation to travel God's path is an act of tremendous and joyful strength.

COLLECT

Almighty Father,
who in your great mercy gladdened the disciples
   with the sight of the risen Lord:
give us such knowledge of his presence with us,
that we may be strengthened and sustained by his risen life
and serve you continually in righteousness and truth;
through Jesus Christ your Son our Lord,
who is alive and reigns with you,
in the unity of the Holy Spirit,
one God, now and for ever.

| *Reflection by* **Maggi Dawn**

Psalm **136** *or* **37***
Exodus 25.1-22
Luke 1.57-end

Thursday 19 April

Luke 1.57-end

'Then his father Zechariah was filled with the Holy Spirit and spoke this prophecy' (v. 67)

The Biblical canticles are passages that, apart from the Book of Psalms, stand out as songs rather than poetry or prose. But what makes a song successful? Luke claims that Zechariah was inspired by the Holy Spirit, yet the song draws heavily on the language of the prophets, and – in Luke's creative scheme – also shows a certain similarity to the Magnificat.

Luke's songwriting fits the formulae named by various experts on the brain, on memory, and on song structure, so closely that you could almost believe he had the benefit of their advice. Paul McCartney famously noted that nothing is original; writers take what they have heard and rearrange it. James Kellaris, from the University of Cincinnati, names a combination of simplicity, repetition and mild incongruity as the key to lodging music in the brain, which is very close to Paul Simon's observation that a hit song sounds familiar enough that you think you've heard it before, but has an element of surprise and originality that makes you want to hear it again.

So was Zechariah inspired, or had Luke unwittingly landed on good songwriting techniques? I think it is possible that both are true at the same time. My songwriting students learn to measure the criteria of a hit, but they cannot then create a recipe for a classic song. Natural ability and learned skill certainly count, but a song that lasts down the centuries still depends on inspiration.

Risen Christ,
you filled your disciples with boldness and fresh hope:
strengthen us to proclaim your risen life
and fill us with your peace,
to the glory of God the Father.

COLLECT

Reflection by **Maggi Dawn** | 127

Friday 20 April

Psalm **107** *or* **31**
Exodus 28.1-4*a*, 29-38
Luke 2.1-20

Luke 2.1-20

'... there was no place for them in the inn' (v.7)

This moment in the nativity story is traditionally interpreted as one of outsiders finding no welcome in a foreign town. As such, it is a story that can reflect the feelings and needs of outsiders, foreigners, minority groups, refugees – all who are excluded by society.

But there is another way to read it. The word for 'inn' – *kataluma* – can be translated as 'guest room'. And in first-century houses that have been excavated in the Holy Land, the stable or animal room is not an outhouse, but located at the centre of the house, where the warmth of the animals would radiate through the home.

If Joseph and Mary returned to the town of their origin, and were put up by family, then the guest room would have been full to the brim with people. No place for a baby to be born. But at the centre of the family home was the animals' room. Warm, dry and the only quiet room in the house, it was the best possible place for this young woman to bring her baby into the world.

Were they excluded and representative of outcasts and refugees everywhere? Or was their welcome into the warmest room in the house a lesson in offering Christ the best we have, however humble that may be? Whichever way you read the story, it tells us something about receiving Christ into our lives.

COLLECT

Almighty Father,
who in your great mercy gladdened the disciples
    with the sight of the risen Lord:
give us such knowledge of his presence with us,
that we may be strengthened and sustained by his risen life
and serve you continually in righteousness and truth;
through Jesus Christ your Son our Lord,
who is alive and reigns with you,
in the unity of the Holy Spirit,
one God, now and for ever.

| *Reflection by* **Maggi Dawn**

Psalms 108, **110**, 111 *or* 41, **42**, 43
Exodus 29.1-9
Luke 2.21-40

Saturday 21 April

Luke 2.21-40

*'Lord, now lettest thou thy servant depart in peace,
according to thy word' (v.29, KJV)*

Jazz saxophonist and composer John Coltrane had a turbulent life, and a career of highs and lows. Eventually, though, through a new-found Christian faith, he found the stability to complete his best work. *A Love Supreme* became his finest album, but as he toured the work, one particular evening he gave the performance of his life. Everything – his playing, the band, the audience – came together in one sweet moment, the pinnacle of his life's work, the realization that he had done what he came for. As he left the stage, his drummer heard him say two words: *Nunc dimittis*.

Two prophets, Anna and Simeon, spent their life in the temple. Praying, speaking God's words, but most of all watching and waiting for the promised salvation of God. As Jesus was brought to the temple for dedication, they both recognized that this was what they had been waiting for. Their responses were different: Anna began proclaiming the truth to all who would listen. Like Mary Magdalene at the resurrection, the first one to proclaim the revelation of God was a woman. But then Simeon spoke. All that he had waited for, all that his life's work had been leading up to, he saw in the tiny face of this infant. We will never know *how* he knew; he just did.

'Now, Lord,' said Simeon, 'I can die a happy man. I've done what I came for. *Nunc dimittis*.'

Risen Christ,
you filled your disciples with boldness and fresh hope:
strengthen us to proclaim your risen life
and fill us with your peace,
to the glory of God the Father.

COLLECT

Monday 23 April

George, martyr,
patron of England

Psalms 5, 146
Joshua 1.1-9
Ephesians 6.10-20

Joshua 1.1-9

'Be strong and courageous' (vv.6, 7, 9)

Joshua meets George! The ambivalent and problematic book of Joshua has had many strange adventures, but none more so than to be set as background and commentary on the Feast of St George!

Reading Joshua must always give us pause. On the one hand, here is the source of the chorus we learned as children: 'Be bold, be strong, for the Lord your God is with you'. Here, too, is the source of all those stirring stories of battle against the odds, of trumpets blowing 'and the walls came tumbling down', a book that has inspired courage and determination down the centuries. On the other hand, here is the grim and self-justifying account of invasion and ethnic cleansing, of God apparently commanding genocide, the displacement and replacement of indigenous peoples, the planting in of the invader over the dead bodies and trampled culture of their victims. It would be manageable if the story of Joshua was applied only to its historic origins, but we know that in the conquest and 'planting' of North America and of South Africa, the Christian invaders took the book Joshua as their pattern and their justification.

What to do? Since we know, in Paul's vital words, that we have not come to fight flesh and blood but spiritual wickedness (Ephesians 6.12), that the real conflict is not with people but with evil itself, in our own hearts and elsewhere, perhaps it is the allegorical story of St George's dragon-slaying that will prove the best expression and application of Joshua's courage!

COLLECT

God of hosts,
who so kindled the flame of love
in the heart of your servant George
that he bore witness to the risen Lord
by his life and by his death:
give us the same faith and power of love
that we who rejoice in his triumphs
may come to share with him the fullness of the resurrection;
through Jesus Christ your Son our Lord,
who is alive and reigns with you,
in the unity of the Holy Spirit,
one God, now and for ever.

| *Reflection by* **Malcolm Guite**

Psalm **139** or **48**, 52
Exodus 32.15-34
Luke 3.1-14

Tuesday 24 April

Luke 3.1-14

'What then should we do?' (v.10)

John the Baptist was clearly not working with the benefits of a modern PR consultant or a skilled press officer. All our contemporary arts of flattery, every subtle and not so subtle attempt to butter up the listeners and tell them how deserving and excellent they are, seem to have passed him by. 'You brood of vipers!' is scarcely a promising opening, and the Baptist seems almost to resent the crowd for having taken such heed of his warnings as to listen to him in the first place! But after the initial harangue, which would have given most political campaign managers nightmares, comes the most direct, sound and practical advice. John does not wrap his listeners in comfy layers of cotton-wool spirituality, but opens the doors of their wardrobes, the lids of their larders, the clasps of their wallets, and gets straight down to business: 'Share your clothes and your food, be fair with money, don't rip people off'.

Every one of those actions is not just a piece of humane economics or neighbourliness; it is also a spiritual practice that prepares the way for Christ, and welcomes him both into the soul and into the world. In a world whose politics are dominated by greed and fear, John the Baptist's prescription here is more than just a moral challenge; it's a call to an occupied people, a call in the name of their true King, a call to hope and resistance!

Almighty God,
whose Son Jesus Christ is the resurrection and the life:
raise us, who trust in him,
from the death of sin to the life of righteousness,
that we may seek those things which are above,
where he reigns with you
in the unity of the Holy Spirit,
one God, now and for ever.

COLLECT

Reflection by **Malcolm Guite**   131

Wednesday 25 April

Mark the Evangelist

Psalms 37.23-end, 148
Isaiah 62.6-10
or Ecclesiasticus 51.13-end
Acts 12.25 – 13.13

Isaiah 62.6-10

'... prepare the way for the people' (v.10)

It is St Mark's Day, but instead of the Isaiah passage 'prepare the way *of the Lord'* (Isaiah 40.3), which Mark quotes at the opening of his Gospel, we have this passage from the same prophet saying 'prepare the way *for the people'*. Of course Mark's Gospel does both. His breathless narrative, posted in haste with his favourite adverb 'immediately' winging each episode on its way, certainly has all the urgency of Isaiah's passage with his insistent repetitions: 'Go through, go through the gates ... build up, build up the highway'. I tried to evoke a little of Mark's dramatic immediacy in these lines from my sonnet on his Gospel:

Mark is the gospel of the sudden shift
From first to last, from grand to intimate,
From strength to weakness, and from debt to gift,
From a wide desert's haunted emptiness
To a close city's fervid atmosphere,
From a voice crying in the wilderness
To angels in an empty sepulchre ... *

Mark's Gospel does indeed clear away stones for the people, for us as his readers, and it does 'lift up an ensign'. But when it comes to going through the gates, it is Christ himself, going ahead of us through the gate of death, who really prepares the way. The first, earlier ending of Mark's Gospel leaves those gates open wide and the disciples astonished and, frankly, afraid of the power unleashed in the resurrection.

*Malcolm Guite, *Sounding the Seasons*, Canterbury Press 2012

COLLECT

Almighty God,
who enlightened your holy Church
through the inspired witness of your evangelist Saint Mark:
grant that we, being firmly grounded in the truth of the gospel,
may be faithful to its teaching both in word and deed;
through Jesus Christ your Son our Lord,
who is alive and reigns with you,
in the unity of the Holy Spirit,
one God, now and for ever.

Psalm **118** *or* 56, **57** (63*)
Exodus 34.1-10, 27-end
Luke 4.1-13

Thursday 26 April

Luke 4.1-13

'... he was tempted by the devil' (v.2)

Life, it's just one temptation after another! But Luke's ordering of these three primal temptations makes spiritual and psychological sense. We start with the most straightforward (and often most insistent!) of temptations: those generated by our bodily appetites and needs – the temptation to serve first our own creature comforts, to tend to our obsessions and addictions, before we even consider the needs of others. But then we move on to the deeper temptation: to serve and feed not just the body, but also its driving ego, its lust for power – the temptation to dominate in the kingdoms of this world. We may overcome the first temptation only because we are captivated by the second. We diet, and discipline our flesh in gyms; we submit to the dictates of personal trainers and fitness plans, but only because we hope thereby to spruce up our image so as to shine and succeed in the world!

And then comes the last, the subtlest and worst temptation of all: the temptation to spiritual pride. We may rise above worldly ambition, only to congratulate ourselves on how 'spiritual' we have become, how superior to our fat-cat neighbours! The very discipline and virtue designed to bring us closer to our saviour, and make us available as ambassadors of his love, become instead the proud possessions that separate us from the one whose strength is made perfect in weakness. Thank God these temptations have been overcome on our behalf, and we can partake in and be sustained by his victory.

Risen Christ,
faithful shepherd of your Father's sheep:
teach us to hear your voice
and to follow your command,
that all your people may be gathered into one flock,
to the glory of God the Father.

COLLECT

Friday 27 April

Luke 4.14-30

'Today this scripture has been fulfilled ...' (v.21)

Jesus returns from his struggle in the wilderness filled with the Spirit and able to set out with clarity the very core of his vocation as Messiah and our vocation as his followers. The so-called 'Nazareth manifesto', was already an ancient prophecy when Jesus declared and fulfilled it on this day. When we hear it now, 2,000 years later, it seems just as pertinent, just as much in need of fulfilment.

Yet here is the paradox: 'Today this scripture has been fulfilled in your hearing'. Yes and no. It was fulfilled, in the sense that Christ, the one about whom the scripture was written, was there in their midst, just as Isaiah had prophesied – the prophecy had come true. But it was not entirely fulfilled then, nor has it been even now, in the sense that the tasks the Lord set his anointed – bringing good news to the poor, release to captives, freedom to the oppressed – are not yet complete. Christ began this work, but he calls his followers, his Church, to continue and complete it, in him and with him.

To be a Christian is to be in Christ, which means 'anointed', and therefore to be part of the fulfilling of this prophesy, and therein lies our hope. Every sharing of this good news, every liberation of a captive, every proclamation of God's grace, in the teeth of opposition, against all odds, is a step towards that fulfilment. Our actions in his name are also Christ's actions in us, and in him the fulfilment of all these things will come.

COLLECT

Almighty God,
whose Son Jesus Christ is the resurrection and the life:
raise us, who trust in him,
from the death of sin to the life of righteousness,
that we may seek those things which are above,
where he reigns with you
in the unity of the Holy Spirit,
one God, now and for ever.

| *Reflection by* **Malcolm Guite**

Saturday 28 April

Luke 4.31-37

'What kind of utterance is this?' (v.36)

Thank goodness for inclusive synagogues! One of the most remarkable things about this passage is that the man with the unclean spirit was there in the first place. A man 'tainted' in the eyes of his contemporaries, a man whom we would describe as mentally deranged, a man who in either case was disturbing and disruptive, shouting out randomly in the middle of a religious service, was still allowed to attend, still somehow included. No one had frozen him out, or told his family or carers that perhaps it would be better if they didn't bring him next Sabbath because 'it's distracting for the rest of us'. No, he was there, and so, for that matter, was Jesus! After what happened at Nazareth in yesterday's reading, the synagogue elders might have been tempted to exclude Jesus as not being 'theologically sound', but there he was, free to say things that would startle and astonish a sleepy congregation till they sat up and said 'What kind of utterance is this?'

Can we say as much? How would either the suffering man or the outspoken prophet have fared with us? Do people in our community with mental health issues have a welcome place in our congregations, even if they cry out with a loud voice? Do we ever give a platform or pulpit to a visitor who might challenge us, change our minds, startle us into repentance?

Risen Christ,
faithful shepherd of your Father's sheep:
teach us to hear your voice
and to follow your command,
that all your people may be gathered into one flock,
to the glory of God the Father.

COLLECT

Monday 30 April

Psalm **145** *or* **71**
Numbers 9.15-end;10.33-end
Luke 4.38-end

Luke 4.38–end

'They wanted to prevent him ...' (v.42)

They wanted to prevent him from leaving them. What could be wrong with that? They'd found their Messiah and they wanted to hang on to him, to keep him, his wisdom and his healing powers as an exclusive and ever-ready resource for themselves. Why waste him on neighbouring towns that might not appreciate him so well? But Jesus will have none of it: 'I must proclaim the good news to other cities.'

We can understand their feelings, since sharing Jesus in the days before the Ascension meant actually losing his presence themselves, but it is not so with us. We know that the more we share him, the more present he is with us. Risen and ascended, enthroned at the hidden heart of things, he is, as the poet John Donne says, 'replenishingly everywhere'. Someone else's encounter with him, does nothing to diminish ours, and yet it's surprising how this attitude that says 'he's mine, not yours' persists. How easily an established church or congregation thinks that daughter churches or church plants haven't quite 'got it' yet, and should come back to the mother church for the true experience of proper Christianity. Even within one church there might be an 'inner group' who feel that their Sunday service is where Jesus essentially is, and rather resent the idea that he might be just as present in Messy Church or the Goth Eucharist!

But happily, we can't 'prevent him from leaving'. Happily, he himself 'continues proclaiming the message'.

COLLECT

Almighty God,
who through your only-begotten Son Jesus Christ
have overcome death and opened to us the gate of everlasting life:
grant that, as by your grace going before us
    you put into our minds good desires,
so by your continual help
we may bring them to good effect;
through Jesus Christ our risen Lord,
who is alive and reigns with you,
in the unity of the Holy Spirit,
one God, now and for ever.

Reflection by **Malcolm Guite**

Psalms 139, 146
Proverbs 4.10-18
James 1.1-12

Tuesday 1 May
Philip and James, Apostles

Proverbs 4.10-18
'... the way of wisdom' (v.11)

'I have taught you the way of wisdom.' This phrase opens out the path of an extended metaphor, a metaphor of path-finding and wayfaring that runs (or walks) through the rest of the reading. It is also picked up in today's Collect for St Philip and St James, with its petition 'that we may follow the steps of your holy apostles Philip and James, and walk steadfastly in the way that leads to your glory'. This metaphor of Wisdom as a 'way', and the whole Christian life itself as a 'way' in which we walk, is very attractive not least because it counters all the smug, static, 'finished' alternatives. Some evangelism can sound as though the speaker is arrogantly claiming to have 'arrived' already at perfect truth, to be already fully enlightened, and to assume that those who do not share their faith are in darkness and going nowhere.

This reading, and the example of the apostles, suggests instead we should be offering a more humble and collaborative invitation: 'I am still on a journey, would you like to join me on the way? Something is dawning on me, join me on a walk towards that sunrise', or, as Philip so succinctly put it when his cynical friend said 'Can anything good come out of Nazareth?', 'Come and see' (John 1.46).

Almighty Father,
whom truly to know is eternal life:
teach us to know your Son Jesus Christ
as the way, the truth, and the life;
that we may follow the steps of your holy apostles
Philip and James,
and walk steadfastly in the way that leads to your glory;
through Jesus Christ your Son our Lord,
who is alive and reigns with you,
in the unity of the Holy Spirit,
one God, now and for ever.

COLLECT

Reflection by **Malcolm Guite**   137

Wednesday 2 May

Psalms **30**, 147.13-end *or* **77**
Numbers 12
Luke 5.12-26

Luke 5.12-26

'Amazement seized all of them' (v.26)

There is a poem by Seamus Heaney, *The Skylight* , which turns on this Gospel story and shines an unexpected, a surprising light on it, a light that restores what writer and philosopher G.K. Chesterton calls 'the buried sunrise of wonder'. In the poem Heaney describes how they lifted the tiles and cut a hole in the roof of the cottage in Glanmore where he wrote poetry, and how after the slates were taken off, 'extravagant Sky entered and held surprise wide open'. Skimming through the too-familiar words of this story we can miss the surprise and shock, both of the roof being opened and also of Christ's sudden, extravagant offer of complete and unconditional forgiveness: 'Friend, your sins are forgiven you'! Just like that, without his even having asked, with out preamble, penitence, excuses, conditions or caveats – just sheer, free, release!

Then comes the second surprise, which for some proves Jesus' authority to spring the first surprise, but is also an image of what such forgiveness looks and feels like: the healing itself – 'he stood up before them ... and went to his home'. These things are still happening, less visibly perhaps, but just as powerfully: people paralysed with fear, with guilt, with self-loathing hear afresh from Christ's body, his Church, those words: 'Friend, your sins are forgiven you'. Extravagant mercy enters and holds surprise wide open. Heaney's poem ends with a link back to this story in which he says he felt like 'an inhabitant of that house' where this story had happened. An imaginative reading of this passage can make us feel that too.

COLLECT

Almighty God,
who through your only-begotten Son Jesus Christ
have overcome death and opened to us the gate of everlasting life:
grant that, as by your grace going before us
 you put into our minds good desires,
so by your continual help
we may bring them to good effect;
through Jesus Christ our risen Lord,
who is alive and reigns with you,
in the unity of the Holy Spirit,
one God, now and for ever.

Thursday 3 May

Luke 5.27-end

'Then Levi gave a great banquet for him' (v.29)

'An Unexpected Party', the first chapter title in *The Hobbit*, might well serve as a heading for this passage. Levi's 'great banquet for Jesus' is unexpected in every way. Like Bilbo when Gandalf called on him, Levi was living his complacent and unexamined life sitting at his tax booth, and like Bilbo, after hearing an unexpected 'Follow me', from the least likely of all callers, 'he got up, left everything, and followed him'.

There the parallels end, however. Bilbo's former life was dull but respectable; Levi, as a tax collector for the Romans, was a collaborator with the occupying force, widely seen as a betrayer and oppressor of his own kith and kin. It is not for nothing that 'tax collectors and sinners' are so often coupled in the same Biblical phrase. So it was unexpected, for many, certainly for Levi himself, that Jesus called him, rather than ignoring or cold-shouldering him as the Pharisees always did. When Levi's response to this unlooked-for grace is extravagant hospitality, 'a great banquet', it's even more unexpected that Jesus shows up at the party.

The Pharisees can be as shocked as they like, but Jesus' transforming and holy presence in the midst of our parties and pleasures is a consistent motif of the Gospels: from the first sign of his glory at Cana, through the mystery of the Last Supper, to this beautiful teaching that the kingdom is like new wine – too expansive, overflowing and abundant to be contained in the old skins.

Risen Christ,
your wounds declare your love for the world
and the wonder of your risen life:
give us compassion and courage
to risk ourselves for those we serve,
to the glory of God the Father.

COLLECT

Friday 4 May

Psalms **138**, 149 *or* **55**
Numbers 14.1-25
Luke 6.1-11

Luke 6.1-11

'... the withered hand' (v.8)

The miracles of Jesus often offer us an outward and visible picture of the inward and spiritual truths of his teaching. They are all, in that sense, sacramental. No more so than in this discussion of Sabbatarian legalism, which is suddenly accompanied by the healing of a man's withered right hand. Judaism, the faith that had led Isaiah to say, 'The Lord has bared his holy arm before the eyes of all the nations' (Isaiah 52.10), the faith that was meant to be the right hand of God's blessing, had withered and shrivelled into a judgemental religiosity so myopic and rule-bound that when the Lord himself appeared in their midst, instead of welcoming him, all that the Pharisees could do was nit-pick about the legality of gleaning grain. So self-concerned were they, so perverse in their judgements that they refused to recognize a good deed if it was done by 'the wrong person' on 'the wrong day'. Instead they were filled with fury. What fine internet trolls they would have made!

That man's withered hand was healed, but what of ours? Sabbatarian legalism is not the issue it once was, but our 'inner Pharisee' has plenty to work on. Do we refuse to recognize the good done by people with whom we disagree? Do we carp at rule-breakers so constantly that we forget what the rules were for in the first place?

Perhaps we do, but this passage gives us hope that we too can stretch out our withered hand and be restored.

COLLECT

Almighty God,
who through your only-begotten Son Jesus Christ
have overcome death and opened to us the gate of everlasting life:
grant that, as by your grace going before us
    you put into our minds good desires,
so by your continual help
we may bring them to good effect;
through Jesus Christ our risen Lord,
who is alive and reigns with you,
in the unity of the Holy Spirit,
one God, now and for ever.

| *Reflection by* **Malcolm Guite**

Psalms **146**, 150 *or* **76**, 79
Numbers 14.26-end
Luke 6.12-26

Saturday 5 May

Luke 6.12-26

'... for yours is the kingdom' (v.20)

Here is the world turned upside down! A blessing on those who suffer what we quite reasonably try to avoid – poverty, hunger, sorrow, defamation – and then a corresponding 'woe' to those who have actually achieved the goals for which we are all supposed to be striving – wealth, satisfaction, happiness, reputation. What are we to make of it?

It is not in itself blessed to be poor or hungry; if it were, then Jesus would not be asking us, as he clearly does, to relieve the poor and to feed the hungry. Nor is it necessarily a blessing to weep. And yet, paradoxically, Jesus asks us to look deeper, to look beneath the veil of these present sorrows and privations, and glimpse a change, a reversal, a hidden glory waiting to be made manifest. Everything turns on the movement in these verses from 'now' to 'will', turns on the hinge of hope: you weep *now*, but you *will* laugh; you are deprived *now*, but yours is the kingdom. We must dare to see through the veil of the present, and dare also to tear aside the veil of the false fulfilment, the temporary satisfaction, the purchase of the world that lost us our souls. I recently reflected, in a sonnet on the beatitudes, that Jesus speaks these words not to condemn, but to challenge and change, to lift the veil of time just enough to help us see that:

> *'... longing is the veil of satisfaction,*
> *And grief the veil of future happiness.*
> *We glimpse beneath the veil of persecution*
> *The coming kingdom's overflowing bliss.'**

*Malcolm Guite, 'Beatitudes', *Parable and Paradox*, Canterbury Press 2016

Risen Christ,
your wounds declare your love for the world
and the wonder of your risen life:
give us compassion and courage
to risk ourselves for those we serve,
to the glory of God the Father.

COLLECT

Monday 7 May

Psalms **65**, 67 *or* **80**, 82
Numbers 16.1-35
Luke 6.27-38

Luke 6.27-38

'Love your enemies, do good to those who hate you' (v.27)

These verses from Scripture are not easy. Jesus gets to the very nub of what it means to follow him. It is very beautiful – who doesn't want to live in a world where we love and help each other? But it also hard. Loving those who love us is something most of us can manage. But loving your enemy? Offering your aggressor the other cheek? Relinquishing your goods to the thief who robbed you? This seems impossible.

Many of us rationalize it away, saying Jesus presents an impossible ideal; it is therefore all right to carry on hating our enemies, and avenging and imprisoning our aggressors. But now and again we see this other beautiful way lived out. Like Mahatma Gandhi's non-violent resistance. Or Nelson Mandela's vision of a rainbow nation. Or a victim of violence forgiving the person who attacked them. And in Jesus himself we see it lived out perfectly. He forgives the soldiers who nail him to the cross. He doesn't fight back.

I don't find this teaching easy. But neither do I think we should explain it away. For I know that when I am able to forgive, and when I refrain from judgement and resist the temptation to condemn, I receive a blessing: the full measure of the gospel poured into my lap. And when I am judged, says Jesus, this will be the measure: my own capacity to love and forgive others.

COLLECT

God our redeemer,
you have delivered us from the power of darkness
and brought us into the kingdom of your Son:
grant, that as by his death he has recalled us to life,
so by his continual presence in us he may raise us
    to eternal joy;
through Jesus Christ your Son our Lord,
who is alive and reigns with you,
in the unity of the Holy Spirit,
one God, now and for ever.

| *Reflection by* **Stephen Cottrell**

Psalms 124, 125, **126**, 127
or 87, **89.1-18**
Numbers 16.36-end
Luke 6.39-end

Tuesday 8 May

Luke 6.39-end

'... it is out of the abundance of the heart that the mouth speaks'
(v.45)

I think it was the great English writer George Orwell who playfully observed that by the time you are 50, you have the face you deserve! You may be born with what the world currently deems beautiful and attractive, but in the end no amount of exercise or surgical intervention will prevent the real person shining through. What we do and say on the outside – and even what we look like to others – will be shaped by what is happening on the inside.

Jesus is making the same point here: each tree is recognized by its fruit – you can't pick figs from thorn bushes. A good person brings good things out of the good stored up in their heart.

Therefore, as his famous parable about the two houses makes clear, discipleship means paying attention to your foundations. What are the values, the attitudes, the predispositions that undergird our lives, and how can we make sure they are those of the gospel? If we do, it won't be that we need to try harder to be good; it will happen naturally because we are planted in good soil and bearing good fruit. We will also be able to see clearly the planks of hypocrisy and deceit in our own eyes and be less eager to point out the specks of dust in others.

Risen Christ,
by the lakeside you renewed your call to your disciples:
help your Church to obey your command
and draw the nations to the fire of your love,
to the glory of God the Father.

COLLECT

Reflection by **Stephen Cottrell** 143

Wednesday 9 May

Psalms **132**, 133 *or* **119.105-128**
Numbers 17.1-11
Luke 7.1-10

Luke 7.1-10

'... not even in Israel have I found such faith' (v.9)

A theme of Luke's Gospel is the way those on the edge – the excluded and neglected, the foreigner or the child – get things right. This is one such story. The centurion may be a person of power and standing within his own world, but to the Jews he is an outsider. He is not someone to mix with, and certainly not someone who can teach them about faith, though, as we learn here, this particular centurion was a good man who had showed kindness to the Jews and even helped them rebuild their synagogue. So he is obviously an enlightened and God-fearing man. Like many others, he has heard about Jesus and he likes what he hears.

So Jesus goes to him. He crosses boundaries of religious and political affiliation. He reaches out to the stranger, even one of the rich and powerful strangers who occupy his land.

But now it is the centurion who shows great faith. Hearing Jesus is on his way, he send friends with a message saying that as he too is a man under authority who gives orders to others then he is happy for Jesus to just 'speak the word' and he knows his servant will be healed.

And Jesus is amazed at his faith. For he trusts that Jesus' word is enough.

COLLECT

God our redeemer,
you have delivered us from the power of darkness
and brought us into the kingdom of your Son:
grant, that as by his death he has recalled us to life,
so by his continual presence in us he may raise us
    to eternal joy;
through Jesus Christ your Son our Lord,
who is alive and reigns with you,
in the unity of the Holy Spirit,
one God, now and for ever.

| *Reflection by* **Stephen Cottrell**

Psalms 110, 150
Isaiah 52.7-end
Hebrews 7.[11-25] 26-end

Thursday 10 May

Ascension Day

Isaiah 52.7-end

'... the Lord will go before you' (v.12)

The Ascension of our Lord Jesus Christ is not an ending, but a beginning; not a departure, but an arrival.

Jesus' resurrection appearances come to an end. He ascends to the Father and will not be seen on earth again in this way. But it is a beginning too. Because Jesus carries our humanity to heaven, his sacrifice is complete, and he brings us into union with God (see Hebrew 9.11-15). It is the beginning of the new age of reconciliation because of what God has done in Jesus Christ.

It is also an arrival: the arrival of the Spirit in a new, fresh and dynamic way. Jesus is now no longer confined by space and time. The Spirit is sent into the world in such a way that Jesus can be equally and completely present to every person who turns to him. This is why Jesus said on the night before he died, 'it is to your advantage that I go away, for if I do not go away, the Advocate [the Holy Spirit] will not come to you' (John 16.7).

This is all very good news indeed. As Isaiah foretells, God's servant will be lifted up, the Lord will comfort his people ('comforter' is one of the names the Bible gives for the Holy Spirit), and he has redeemed Israel. How beautiful are those who proclaim this good news!

Grant, we pray, almighty God,
that as we believe your only-begotten Son our Lord Jesus Christ
to have ascended into the heavens,
so we in heart and mind may also ascend
and with him continually dwell;
who is alive and reigns with you,
in the unity of the Holy Spirit,
one God, now and for ever.

COLLECT

Reflection by **Stephen Cottrell** | 145

Friday 11 May

Psalms 20, **81** *or* **88** (95)
Exodus 35.30 – 36.1
Galatians 5.13-end

Exodus 35.30 – 36.1

'... he has filled him with the Spirit of God' (35.31, ESV)

The readings for the next nine days as we prepare for the great feast of Pentecost are all about the Holy Spirit; they help us get ready to celebrate again the place and activity of God the Holy Spirit in the life of the Church. It is a broad and compelling vision.

What I love about today's reading is the way it celebrates the artistic skills and ingenuity of artists and craftsmen, the knowledge and appreciation of different materials and trades, and what human creativity can achieve, telling us that it is all a work of the Spirit. It is the Spirit of God who, with wisdom, understanding and knowledge, and with all kinds of skill, has equipped the stonemasons, engravers, designers and embroiderers who are at work here. Even the names of these artists are recorded.

Too often we narrow the work of the Spirit down to particular gifts and ministries, usually those most obviously associated with the work of the Church. But the whole world is alive with the glory of God. And human creativity is one of the best and most potent signs of the Spirit's presence in the world and of the Creator God who by the Spirit gives us gifts of imagination and vision.

Let us make sure these gifts are also treasured in our churches.

COLLECT

Grant, we pray, almighty God,
that as we believe your only-begotten Son our Lord Jesus Christ
to have ascended into the heavens,
so we in heart and mind may also ascend
and with him continually dwell;
who is alive and reigns with you,
in the unity of the Holy Spirit,
one God, now and for ever.

| *Reflection by* **Stephen Cottrell**

Psalms 21, **47** *or* 96, **97**, 100
Numbers 11.16-17, 24-29
1 Corinthians 2

Saturday 12 May

Numbers 11.16-17, 24-29

'Would that all the Lord's people were prophets ...!' (v.29)

Today's reading is about how the Spirit inspires and equips us for leadership, but also about the godly desire that all people would receive the Spirit of the Lord.

First of all, Moses is instructed by God to share his own leadership, though in this case it seems that the inspiration and equipping of the Spirit is limited in some way. A portion of the Spirit that Moses has received will be taken and shared out among Israel's elders.

Later on we discover that two of the elders, Eldad and Medad, who were not present when the Spirit was given to the others, are also prophesying. Some want to stop them. Their ministry hasn't been properly authorized! But Moses is not so precious, nor does he hold ministry to himself, or imagine it is up to him whom the Spirt of God chooses to empower. 'Would that all the Lord's people were prophets, and that the Lord would put his spirit on them!' is his reply.

This, of course, is the impact of Pentecost. The Spirit is given to everyone; and everyone has a part to play in God's ministry of peace and reconciliation for the world. We are all given different gifts, and we are called to use these gifts in the service of the gospel. We particularly pray for and cherish those whom God has called and equipped for leadership in the Church.

Risen Christ,
you have raised our human nature to the throne of heaven:
help us to seek and serve you,
that we may join you at the Father's side,
where you reign with the Spirit in glory,
now and for ever.

COLLECT

Reflection by **Stephen Cottrell** | 147

Monday 14 May

Matthias the Apostle

Psalms 16, 147.1-12
1 Samuel 2.27-35
Acts 2.37-end

Acts 2.37-end

*'Repent and be baptized … and you will receive the gift of the
Holy Spirit' (v.38)*

In this reading we learn how the transforming power of the Spirit, now
poured into the hearts of those who turn to Christ, enables those who
follow Christ to do the things he did and to live a new life with God.
Seeing themselves as the new Israel, having twelve of them was
important. Thus Matthias is added to the number of those whose
apostolic witness is the foundation of the Church.

This life is compelling, but also challenging. Peter exhorts those who
witness this new life to repent and be baptized and receive the Spirit
for themselves. On this first Pentecost 3,000 people are added to the
number of believers.

Verses 42 to 47 then give us a lovely picture of the life of the very first
Church. The disciples hold everything in common. They give to those
in need. They praise God. Devoting themselves to teaching and
fellowship, to the Eucharist and to prayer, those who see them are
filled with awe. More people join them.

This is what the Church becomes when we live the life of the Spirit and
when, as faithful disciples, we too pay attention to the foundations of
our faith, the things that really matter: the content of the faith itself;
community with one another; generosity to those in need and self-
sacrifice; prayer and the sacramental life. The Holy Spirit will be our
teacher.

COLLECT

Almighty God,
who in the place of the traitor Judas
chose your faithful servant Matthias
to be of the number of the Twelve:
preserve your Church from false apostles
and, by the ministry of faithful pastors and teachers,
keep us steadfast in your truth;
through Jesus Christ your Son our Lord,
who is alive and reigns with you,
in the unity of the Holy Spirit,
one God, now and for ever.

| *Reflection by* **Stephen Cottrell**

Psalms 98, **99**, 100 *or* **106*** (*or* 103)
1 Samuel 10.1-10
1 Corinthians 12.1-13

Tuesday 15 May

1 Samuel 10.1-10

'Then the spirit of the Lord will possess you' (v.6)

We rather jump in at the climax of this lovely story where Saul has been looking for his father's lost donkeys and ends up being crowned King of Israel! His obedience and faithfulness in one task has led him to be entrusted with another. It is good to reflect on this, and worth reading the previous couple of chapters to get the context of the story.

What it says to me is, don't fritter your life away dreaming about what you might be doing, but be faithful in the task that is before you. Indeed, when people ask me how it feels to be a bishop, or even what made me want to become a bishop, I often reply that all I have been doing is looking for the donkeys. Everything else has been a bonus and a surprise. In other words, I have sought to be faithful in the primary vocation I have been given. It has led to other things, but they were not things I was seeking.

But of course the reason we have this story here is because Saul, having been faithful in one task, and having been called to another greater and more responsible task, is now given the gift of the Spirit, which comes upon him powerfully ('possesses him') and equips him for the work ahead. Faithfulness is still required. But the Spirit is equipping and empowering.

O God the King of glory,
you have exalted your only Son Jesus Christ
with great triumph to your kingdom in heaven:
we beseech you, leave us not comfortless,
but send your Holy Spirit to strengthen us
and exalt us to the place where our Saviour Christ is gone before,
who is alive and reigns with you,
in the unity of the Holy Spirit,
one God, now and for ever.

COLLECT

Reflection by **Stephen Cottrell**

Wednesday 16 May

Psalms 2, **29** or 110, **111**, 112
1 Kings 19.1-18
Matthew 3.13-end

1 Kings 19.1-18

'... after the fire a sound of sheer silence' (v.12)

When we speak about the power of the Spirit, we are talking about the power of love. God is love, says St John (1 John 4.8), and one of the ways we test whether things are of God is by seeing if they carry the hallmark of love. The Scriptures often talk about the 'power' of the Spirit, and the 'signs and wonders' that accompany the Spirit's activity and presence, but, because it is God's Holy Spirit proceeding from the Father and the Son, then it is always the power of love; love that is patient and kind (1 Corinthians 13.4), love that is just as likely to be manifest in quiet and temperate ways as it is by dazzling displays of supernatural clout. St Paul famously reminds us in 1 Corinthians 13 that love is the Spirit's greatest gift, and without love we are a clanging cymbal, not a still small voice.

Therefore, when the Lord promises to Elijah that he will pass by, it is not in the wind or the earthquake or the fire that God is encountered, not in anything flashy, but a gentle whisper, a sound of silence. It is the gift of the enduring presence of love. When we patiently love, and when love endures in our own lives, these are the times when our lives manifest the presence of the Spirit.

COLLECT

O God the King of glory,
you have exalted your only Son Jesus Christ
with great triumph to your kingdom in heaven:
we beseech you, leave us not comfortless,
but send your Holy Spirit to strengthen us
and exalt us to the place where our Saviour Christ is gone before,
who is alive and reigns with you,
in the unity of the Holy Spirit,
one God, now and for ever.

Reflection by **Stephen Cottrell**

Psalms **24**, 72 *or* 113, **115**
Ezekiel 11.14-20
Matthew 9.35 – 10.20

Thursday 17 May

Ezekiel 11.14-20

'I will give them one heart' (v.19)

The readings today and tomorrow from the prophet Ezekiel point us towards the great climax of God's involvement with the world when all things will be gathered together into a new creation. The Spirit lifts Ezekiel up and shows him what will be. It is a beautiful vision of restoration. The scattered and exiled people of God are gathered together and God gives them a new spirit and a new heart: 'they shall be my people, and I will be their God.'

But with this comes the directive that they must keep God's ways and follow God's commandments. It will be easier for them, because they now have one, undivided heart. But obedience is still required. The freedom of the Spirit is not a freedom *from* the laws of God, but a freedom to *enjoy life as it is meant to be* under the rule of God and in the loving embrace of God's new creation. As Christians we know that this new humanity and new heart are made possible for us in Christ. But we too must live God's way and still look forward to that day when God will gather everything together in Christ. The gift of the Spirit is the sign and foretaste of this new creation. It carries with it certain responsibilities for the way we live.

Risen, ascended Lord,
as we rejoice at your triumph,
fill your Church on earth with power and compassion,
that all who are estranged by sin
may find forgiveness and know your peace,
to the glory of God the Father.

COLLECT

Friday 18 May

Psalms **28**, 30 *or* **139**
Ezekiel 36.22-28
Matthew 12.22-32

Ezekiel 36.22-28

'... a new spirit I will put within you' (v.26)

Even though the name of the Lord has been profaned, God is still going to gather his people together, and this will be a sign of God's goodness and faithfulness. Sprinkled with clean water, God's people will be cleansed from all their wrongdoing. They will be given a new spirit and a new heart.

This wonderful promise is also made to us. God wants to remove our hard hearts, though it is wise to remember that the promise of God is not a super bionic, never-to-be-broken heart, but a heart of flesh. We will not be immune from the sufferings of life. God removes what is inflexible and unyielding, but gives us instead a heart that is better able to feel pain.

The promise of a heart of flesh is nothing less than the promise of receiving a heart like Jesus, for he is the one who weeps and laments for the sin and brokenness of the world and whose own heart was broken on the cross. When we ask the Holy Spirit to make us more like Jesus, this is what we are asking for. We are asking for a heart that shares the delights and sorrows of the world and feels its pain keenly and participates in its joy. Then we will be God's people.

COLLECT

O God the King of glory,
you have exalted your only Son Jesus Christ
with great triumph to your kingdom in heaven:
we beseech you, leave us not comfortless,
but send your Holy Spirit to strengthen us
and exalt us to the place where our Saviour Christ is gone before,
who is alive and reigns with you,
in the unity of the Holy Spirit,
one God, now and for ever.

| *Reflection by* **Stephen Cottrell**

Micah 3.1-8

'I am filled ... with the spirit of the Lord' (v.8)

On the eve of the great feast of Pentecost, we are given a warning by the prophet Micah about what happens when we ignore God's justice and care only for our self-interest. Not only are people led astray, but to embrace injustice, to hate what is good and to love what is evil, is like eating people's flesh, stripping their skin from their bones, and chopping them up like meat for the pot.

Micah declares that he is filled with 'the spirit of the Lord', and this means he must declare the sins and transgressions of the people and witness to the justice of God. He cannot ignore either. Jesus also says that we are blessed when we hunger and thirst for what is right (Matthew 5.6). It is no good asking God to send us his Spirit, if we are not penitent about our sins, realistic about where we fall short, and hungry to see God's justice prevail. The Christian faith is about working with Jesus' agenda for the whole of life and for all the world. To receive the Spirit is to be enlisted in this work of the kingdom, and to challenge the unjust structures of our society as well as lament our individual failings. To do anything less is to invite the darkness that Micah sees coming as those who have gone astray cover their faces and turn from God.

Risen, ascended Lord,
as we rejoice at your triumph,
fill your Church on earth with power and compassion,
that all who are estranged by sin
may find forgiveness and know your peace,
to the glory of God the Father.

COLLECT

Reflection by **Stephen Cottrell** | 153

Monday 21 May

Luke 9.18-27

'... let them deny themselves and take up their cross daily' (v.23)

Jesus does not declare his identity in words to his disciples. Instead he waits for the penny to drop, letting them witness his miracles and be drawn into the intimacy of his prayer. It is only then that he challenges them with the ultimate question of who he is. The various answers reflect their hesitation and unease.

Even for those who were closest to him, there was something problematic about Jesus. He fulfilled certain expectations, but not others. Even when his actions recalled a figure of the past returned, he did not behave as might have been predicted. Typically, the impulsive Peter cuts through the fog, naming Jesus as the Messiah. In Luke's version this is not followed by Jesus' singling out of Peter as the 'Rock', but his warning to all the disciples that the Messiah's role, and by implication, theirs, is to suffer. The vocation of suffering is unavoidable for those who would follow Jesus. And that vocation is extended to those of us who follow Jesus today.

The call is sharpened in Luke's account – it is only Luke who has Jesus adding the word 'daily' to the call to take up the cross. That little word is worth reflecting on. To identify the daily 'cross' that goes with our following of Jesus is to come closer to his will.

COLLECT

O Lord, from whom all good things come:
grant to us your humble servants,
that by your holy inspiration
we may think those things that are good,
and by your merciful guiding may perform the same;
through our Lord Jesus Christ,
who is alive and reigns with you,
in the unity of the Holy Spirit,
one God, now and for ever.

| *Reflection by* **Angela Tilby**

Psalms **132**, 133
Joshua 2
Luke 9.28-36

Tuesday 22 May

Luke 9.28-36

'... they saw his glory' (v.32)

The transfiguration of Jesus is the pivot of the gospel story, the central event in the Lord's earthly life, both completing his ministry in Galilee and pointing ahead to his passion. This is emphasized in Luke's version where Moses and Elijah speak with Jesus of his *exodos* – his departure (v.31). This word can mean death – departure from life – but it also echoes the Exodus from Egypt, suggesting that the death of Christ will bring freedom to many.

After the transfiguration, Jerusalem becomes the only direction of travel. The disciples were drowsy, possibly asleep during the actual moment of the transfiguration, but they saw its after-effects and experienced the cloud that overshadowed the event. After the questioning of the previous verses, the transfiguration finally reveals Jesus' heavenly origin. For us, such a realization may come as a fleeting experience in worship or prayer. The icons that are so much a part of Orthodox spirituality remind us that God's glory is located in the face of Jesus Christ, but, earthbound as we are, we are only occasionally able to glimpse it.

O Lord, from whom all good things come:
grant to us your humble servants,
that by your holy inspiration
we may think those things that are good,
and by your merciful guiding may perform the same;
through our Lord Jesus Christ,
who is alive and reigns with you,
in the unity of the Holy Spirit,
one God, now and for ever.

COLLECT

Reflection by **Angela Tilby**

Wednesday 23 May

Psalm 119.153-end
Joshua 3
Luke 9.37-50

Luke 9.37-50

'... all were astounded at the greatness of God' (v.43)

The wonder of the transfiguration is rudely shattered as Jesus and the disciples come down the mountain to find a huge crowd waiting for them. The rest of the disciples have attempted unsuccessfully to heal a boy with violent convulsions, and now his father cries out for help.

What is striking here is Jesus' expression of frustration with the unbelief of the crowd and the failure of the disciples. To us his response seems harsh. But Jesus inhabits the glory of God. The transfiguration has revealed things as they really are. He is the Messiah. The present moment has already given way to the coming of his kingdom. And yet at the foot of the mountain he returns to the long age of waiting, the frustration before fulfilment comes.

As we reflect today on the sicknesses of the world, and on our own physical and emotional fragilities, we can take strength from Christ's impatience. He wants us well. He yearns for our peace, even though it will cost him everything. He strives for the least and last of us; the child is his envoy and messenger not the great ones of the world. A certain impatience in prayer is not a sign of unbelief, but of a true and urgent faith that is in tune with heaven itself.

COLLECT

O Lord, from whom all good things come:
grant to us your humble servants,
that by your holy inspiration
we may think those things that are good,
and by your merciful guiding may perform the same;
through our Lord Jesus Christ,
who is alive and reigns with you,
in the unity of the Holy Spirit,
one God, now and for ever.

| *Reflection by* **Angela Tilby**

Thursday 24 May

Luke 9.51-end

'... he set his face to go to Jerusalem' (v.51)

Today's passage begins in great solemnity. Jesus setting his face to go to Jerusalem marks a moment of intense commitment. He knows his destiny. But he still has to get there. Those who reject him at this stage of his ministry are signs and anticipations of the great rejection that lies ahead.

As Jesus takes the road to Jerusalem, so the destiny of many others is being played out. It is noticeable that Jesus is harder on the 'would-be' disciples who make the right noises but lack urgency, than he is on the Samaritans who refuse to give him hospitality. Rejection can be forgiven, but lukewarm or insincere acceptance grates because it misunderstands the ultimate nature of Jesus' call.

On the way to Jerusalem Jesus promises no easy road, and the road we are called to follow as Christians is always the *via crucis*, the way of the cross. This is extremely challenging, especially for those of us who have been Christians for many years, or all our lives. We may have integrated our faith so well into our personalities and lifestyles that we are no longer shocked by its extreme demands. We look for our spiritual life to bring us peace but this should not be the false peace of self-satisfaction. The kingdom of God demands more.

O Lord, from whom all good things come:
grant to us your humble servants,
that by your holy inspiration
we may think those things that are good,
and by your merciful guiding may perform the same;
through our Lord Jesus Christ,
who is alive and reigns with you,
in the unity of the Holy Spirit,
one God, now and for ever.

COLLECT

Friday 25 May

Luke 10.1-16

'... the Lord appointed seventy others' (v.1)

Luke has a very particular take on mission as we see from his account of the mission of the 70, who are sent out in pairs to herald the kingdom. They are to provoke a sense of urgency and to show that God's kingdom comes with healing and peace to all who are willing to receive it. Jesus links the reception of the 70 with the reception of himself. To reject the messenger is to reject the Lord.

The placing of the mission of the 70 after the transfiguration shows that Luke links the emergence of the Church to the coming passion. Christian discipleship will always involve a measure of sacrifice. This is hard for us to wrestle with in a society where security is prized and easy access to material plenty is so often taken for granted. But we should also take heart from this passage. Jesus trusts us with his message. We represent him in our ordinary lives and our day-to-day encounters.

There is also a call here to speak truth to all, including the complacent and indifferent. The kingdom is not only for Christians, and not all who call themselves Christians really get it. When nothing good seems to come out of our efforts and we are met with negativity, we are still called to demonstrate that the kingdom of God has come near.

COLLECT

O Lord, from whom all good things come:
grant to us your humble servants,
that by your holy inspiration
we may think those things that are good,
and by your merciful guiding may perform the same;
through our Lord Jesus Christ,
who is alive and reigns with you,
in the unity of the Holy Spirit,
one God, now and for ever.

| *Reflection by* **Angela Tilby**

Luke 10.17-24

'... rejoice that your names are written in heaven' (v.20)

There is nothing like this passage in the other Gospels – its content is unique to Luke. The 70 return having experienced success in their mission. While they have been away, Jesus has had a visionary experience of Satan falling from heaven. This signifies the defeat of evil; the overthrow of the forces opposed to God, who are the ultimate cause of the sickness, conflict and pain of the world.

The fall of Satan at this point in the gospel story brings the victory of Easter forward into the time leading up to the passion. Since Jesus 'set his face' to go to Jerusalem, the outcome has been inevitable; the age of the Messiah has already dawned. As one of the Easter Eucharistic prefaces puts it: 'The long reign of sin is ended, a broken world is being renewed, and humanity is once again made whole'. This vision of wholeness is not brought about by ideology or power or persuasion. The agents of God's will are 'infants', those who are simple, trusting, humble, poor. They are the ones who hold the secret of God's will; they are the ones who are truly intimate with the Father.

On the eve of Trinity Sunday this passage reveals to us that God is not a lone monarch but a community of love, a feast to which we are invited.

O Lord, from whom all good things come:
grant to us your humble servants,
that by your holy inspiration
we may think those things that are good,
and by your merciful guiding may perform the same;
through our Lord Jesus Christ,
who is alive and reigns with you,
in the unity of the Holy Spirit,
one God, now and for ever.

COLLECT

Reflection by **Angela Tilby** | 159

Monday 28 May

Psalms 1, 2, 3
Joshua 7.1-15
Luke 10.25-37

Luke 10.25-37

'Go and do likewise' (v.37)

It can be difficult to receive very well-known passages from scripture freshly because we have heard them too often. The parable of the Good Samaritan is surely one of those passages. It has become a hallmark for the response to suffering that everyone recognizes as truly and distinctively Christian. The Samaritan acts without guile; he has no need, as the lawyer does, to justify himself. He is moved by pure compassion. He does not weigh up the disadvantage to himself in acting compassionately, as the priest and the Levite do when they pass by. His response is direct and human. He 'feels with' the suffering of the robbed and wounded man. Such compassion cannot be faked; it springs from the heart.

But there is more in the story Jesus tells than a paradigm of Christian love. The mercy shown by the Samaritan mirrors the boundless mercy of God. The Samaritan's spontaneous response to human need reveals God's own heart. The fact that he is not an orthodox Jew drives the point home. God's love is not limited to those of the 'right' creed or practice. God's love is manifest whenever compassion for suffering results in the relief of suffering. The story invites us to examine our own hearts. We can all feel sorry for those in obvious need. But do we do anything about it?

COLLECT

Almighty and everlasting God,
you have given us your servants grace,
by the confession of a true faith,
to acknowledge the glory of the eternal Trinity
and in the power of the divine majesty to worship the Unity:
keep us steadfast in this faith,
that we may evermore be defended from all adversities;
through Jesus Christ your Son our Lord,
who is alive and reigns with you,
in the unity of the Holy Spirit,
one God, now and for ever.

| *Reflection by* **Angela Tilby**

Psalms **5**, 6 (8)
Joshua 7.16-end
Luke 10.38-end

Tuesday 29 May

Luke 10.38-end

'Mary has chosen the better part' (v.42)

It is important to remember that this little story of Mary and Martha is set in the context of Jesus having set his face to go to Jerusalem. There is an urgency behind the text which is not always noticed when the story is isolated from its setting. The point is that the passion lies ahead. This helps make sense of Jesus' response to the two sisters, which otherwise could seem unfair. After all, it is Martha who welcomes him into their home, Martha who gets on with the housework while Mary listens to the Lord. Jesus' judgement of Martha is not a condemnation of her work, but more a comment on her distractedness. She prefers to let herself be taken up with necessary, but perhaps not absolutely vital, tasks rather than spend precious moments listening to what the Lord is saying. Mary, on the other hand, grasps the moment, perhaps recognizing that it will not come again.

One wonders whether he is talking to Mary about his impending suffering and death and the need for sacrifice on the part of his disciples. Perhaps this is the part that Martha cannot bear, and she is not alone. All of us baulk at the challenge of Jesus to take up our cross 'daily' (Luke 9.23) and follow him. How much of our schedule today is calculated to avoid the things that really matter?

Holy God,
faithful and unchanging:
enlarge our minds with the knowledge of your truth,
and draw us more deeply into the mystery of your love,
that we may truly worship you,
Father, Son and Holy Spirit,
one God, now and for ever.

COLLECT

Reflection by **Angela Tilby** | 161

Wednesday 30 May

Luke 11.1-13

'... everyone who asks receives' (v.10)

Today's passage reflects Luke's take on Jesus' teaching about prayer. What emerges clearly is that Jesus expects his disciples to pray with boldness, trusting God to take care of their daily needs. The disciples clearly sense that there is something about the way Jesus prays to the Father that they need to inhabit for themselves. The 'model' prayer he gives them is fairly unremarkable, full of phrases familiar to any pious Jew. The teaching that follows stresses the need for persistence. The friend at midnight who at first refuses to provide food for an unexpected visitor stands here for our constant experiences of setback in prayer; our projections onto God of our own impatience and lack of compassion. We are not born trusting God; trust has to be discovered and learnt, and we are to persist in spite of any damage to our image of God that arises from past experience or wounded memories.

God is not like the friend at midnight; yet we may sometimes feel abandoned and that our requests are not heard. Praying with persistence requires discipline and courage. Our spiritual muscles need developing and exercising before we can rely on them to carry us through barren times. Once again, Jesus prepares the disciples for his passion. To interpret his suffering, and the suffering they themselves will endure, requires the consoling gift of the Holy Spirit.

COLLECT

Almighty and everlasting God,
you have given us your servants grace,
by the confession of a true faith,
to acknowledge the glory of the eternal Trinity
and in the power of the divine majesty to worship the Unity:
keep us steadfast in this faith,
that we may evermore be defended from all adversities;
through Jesus Christ your Son our Lord,
who is alive and reigns with you,
in the unity of the Holy Spirit,
one God, now and for ever.

Reflection by **Angela Tilby**

Psalm 147
Deuteronomy 8.2-16
1 Corinthians 10.1-17

Thursday 31 May

Day of Thanksgiving for the
Institution of the Holy Communion
(Corpus Christi)

Deuteronomy 8.2-16

'You shall eat your fill and bless the Lord your God' (v.10)

Today the Church gives thanks for Holy Communion, and we reflect on the way in which God makes provision for both our bodily and spiritual needs. There is a sacred continuity between the life of the body and that of the soul, and this means that the manna in the wilderness has two dimensions. It satisfies real hunger, but as it does so it provokes another hunger, which, as we are told here, can only be satisfied by the word of God. We do not live by bread alone, as Jesus demonstrated in his temptation in the wilderness. We are meant to live on what God communicates to us, feeding on the word, absorbing it into our very being. As the word comes to life in us, we should become more grateful and more generous. Even in the Old Testament account the manna has a sacramental dimension. In the psalms the manna is described as the bread of angels (Psalm 78.25).

Holy Communion gathers up these meanings but also adds another. The bread broken at communion is identified by Jesus as his body, given for us. This extra layer of meaning is what makes us members of Christ's body. He lives in us and we in him. This is the mystical heart of the Christian faith, which is why reception of the sacrament should never be an optional extra.

Lord Jesus Christ,
we thank you that in this wonderful sacrament
you have given us the memorial of your passion:
grant us so to reverence the sacred mysteries
of your body and blood
that we may know within ourselves
and show forth in our lives
the fruits of your redemption;
for you are alive and reign with the Father
in the unity of the Holy Spirit,
one God, now and for ever.

COLLECT

Reflection by **Angela Tilby** | 163

Friday 1 June

Visit of the Blessed Virgin Mary
to Elizabeth

Psalms 85, 150
1 Samuel 2.1-10
Mark 3.31-end

1 Samuel 2.1-10

'My heart exults in the Lord' (v.1)

Hannah's outpouring of praise to God for the birth of her son Samuel is the model for the song Mary sang when, pregnant with Jesus, she visited her cousin Elizabeth, herself pregnant with John the Baptist (Luke 1.46-55). Hannah worships God as the one who overturns the order of the world; the strong are put to shame and the weak raised to dignity. She rejoices because her humble but heartfelt prayer for a child has been heard, and now, in the generosity of her gratitude, she brings her son to the temple 'lending' him to the Lord (1 Samuel 1.28).

God is a generous giver and we are promised that he hears the prayers of our hearts. Our deepest needs and longings are already known to him; indeed, he inspires in us what will bring out the best in us. But the gifts he so freely gives are not for us to hoard or control. Hannah could have clung on to Samuel; Mary could have tried to determine the fate of Jesus; Elizabeth could have resisted the call of John the Baptist. The Christian pattern though is gift for gift; we give back what we are given, because only by doing so does God's gift reach its full potential. In the words of H. Montagu Butler's rousing hymn: 'Lift every gift that thou thyself has given; low lies the best till lifted up to heaven.'

Mighty God,
by whose grace Elizabeth rejoiced with Mary
and greeted her as the mother of the Lord:
look with favour on your lowly servants
that, with Mary, we may magnify your holy name
and rejoice to acclaim her Son our Saviour,
who is alive and reigns with you,
in the unity of the Holy Spirit,
one God, now and for ever.

| *Reflection by* **Angela Tilby**

Psalms 20, 21, **23**
Joshua 10.1-15
Luke 11.37-end

Saturday 2 June

Luke 11.37-end

'... you have taken away the key of knowledge' (v.52)

Jesus' contention with the Pharisees and lawyers is that they have become an elite, an exclusive club, failing to carry out their vocation as spiritual teachers and enablers of others. Jesus here acts as one of the prophets, whose witness against such distortions of faith is consistent through the generations. Jesus' concern here is for the 'little ones', the seekers and the needy whose desire for God's healing touch is not being met.

The scope and scale of the condemnation here is terrifying, and it speaks as much to our contemporary Church and to society as to the Jewish establishment of Jesus' time. There is a revolt against elitism in the world at the moment – a fear that global wealth is being hoarded by a smaller and smaller group of the super-rich while many struggle to cope. All professions have the tendency to become exclusive, to raise the bar to membership to keep others out. The Church itself has often shared this tendency, recruiting its ministry from a relatively narrow band within society. But the gospel is for everyone, and the art of Christian proclamation is to comfort the afflicted and afflict the comfortable – a vocation that stirs up inevitable hostility.

Almighty and everlasting God,
you have given us your servants grace,
by the confession of a true faith,
to acknowledge the glory of the eternal Trinity
and in the power of the divine majesty to worship the Unity:
keep us steadfast in this faith,
that we may evermore be defended from all adversities;
through Jesus Christ your Son our Lord,
who is alive and reigns with you,
in the unity of the Holy Spirit,
one God, now and for ever.

COLLECT

Reflection by **Angela Tilby** | 165

Monday 4 June

Luke 12.1-12

'Beware of the yeast of the Pharisees, that is, their hypocrisy' (v.1)

In the medieval City of London it was forbidden to wear masks in the streets during the twelve days of Christmas. Party-goers making their way home were too vulnerable to robbers hiding behind the festive masks of the season. The word used in Luke's Gospel for 'hypocrite' is derived from the Greek stage. It refers to one who wore a mask and who spoke from under it in a performance. It is an appropriate image for those of us who know what it is like to present to the world in one way whilst being very different at heart.

We all put on masks to get us through life. The trouble is that sometimes the masks fit too comfortably and eventually begin to eat into our faces so that we don't know the difference between the two. Masks can protect us, distract people from encountering the real 'me', as they vainly try and build relationships with a form of ourselves that is less than honest. Masks may work professionally, enabling boundaries between role and person, but they can never work spiritually, and Jesus had strong words for those who thought otherwise.

Disciples of Jesus learn from him that to live a life in the light is always healthier – for yourself and others. We might as well try it now, he suggests, because eventually 'Nothing is covered up that will not be uncovered'. As medieval City folk knew, at Christmas God had removed his mask of invisibility. From that moment, God invites us to do the same so that the kingdom, where we shall all see each other and our creator face to face, might come a little closer.

COLLECT

O God,
the strength of all those who put their trust in you,
mercifully accept our prayers
and, because through the weakness of our mortal nature
we can do no good thing without you,
grant us the help of your grace,
that in the keeping of your commandments
we may please you both in will and deed;
through Jesus Christ your Son our Lord,
who is alive and reigns with you,
in the unity of the Holy Spirit,
one God, now and for ever.

| *Reflection by* **Mark Oakley**

Psalms 32, **36**
Joshua 21.43 – 22.8
Luke 12.13-21

Tuesday 5 June

Luke 12.13-21

'... one's life does not consist in the abundance of possessions' (v.15)

It's been said that in the West we are spending money we don't have on things we don't want in order to impress people we don't like. Although we laugh at the accuracy, it should make us cry, because this circle of dissatisfaction ends up leaving us with lots to live *with* but little to live *for*. Jesus knew the spiritual shipwrecks that occur when greed takes over a life. He tells his followers to be on their guard and tells them a parable to bring home the point.

Jesus often taught with parables. They can infuriate because they don't always make easy sense. But this is the point. They were not intended to make easy sense but to make us, or rather re-make us, by way of an often puzzling but resonant story that reconfigures the heart by way of the mind. His parable of the man building more storage for yet more stuff is eerily relevant. It ends by asking us what it means to be 'rich towards God'.

All the things that matter most in this life – love, relationship, trust, wisdom, justice – these increase as you share them. If others win, so do I. Unlike wealth and power, where if you win I lose, the qualities of the kingdom that allow us to relate more deeply to God, ourselves and other people are all so rich that both the giver and receiver benefit in an exchange of sacred significance. To live within this economy, teaches Jesus, is to live as a citizen of God's kingdom and not just as a consumer of the world.

God of truth,
help us to keep your law of love
and to walk in ways of wisdom,
that we may find true life
in Jesus Christ your Son.

COLLECT

Wednesday 6 June

Luke 12.22-31

'... do not keep worrying' (v.29)

It can be a telling exercise during a day to stop occasionally and see what position your hands are in. It's an alarming revelation for many of us to discover how many times our hands are clenched tight. The anxieties and stresses of contemporary life are somehow symbolized in this gripped fist. The ancient Assyrians used a word for prayer that also meant to unclench the hand. Like a flower opening in the sun's warmth, so time spent with God was understood to release the tensions of worry, competition and endless self-justification.

Jesus similarly tells his followers not to allow anxiety to shape their lives. Nothing can be more irritating, though, than when someone tells you not to worry when you have genuine concerns about something. The question we face after hearing Jesus' teaching is 'when does a proper concern become an improper anxiety?' We are being asked not to be unduly concerned about life's needs or the future over which we have little control. Our desires need ordering and disciplining so that they don't take hold of us. The primary longing for God places all other hungers into their proper context for an integrated life. Good things lie on the other side of fear and Jesus dares us to test this out for ourselves.

Although many speak of 'faith' as if it means believing that something is the case and signing on the dotted dogmatic line, Jesus shows us that it actually means a relationship of believing in, trusting, and committing yourself to the God whom we do not fully understand and who yet is the source and focus of our deepest hope.

COLLECT

O God,
the strength of all those who put their trust in you,
mercifully accept our prayers
and, because through the weakness of our mortal nature
we can do no good thing without you,
grant us the help of your grace,
that in the keeping of your commandments
we may please you both in will and deed;
through Jesus Christ your Son our Lord,
who is alive and reigns with you,
in the unity of the Holy Spirit,
one God, now and for ever.

Reflection by **Mark Oakley**

Psalm **37***
Joshua 23
Luke 12.32-40

Thursday 7 June

Luke 12.32-40

'Be dressed for action and have your lamps lit' (v.35)

After the serenity of Jesus telling his followers not to be anxious about their lives, the intense urgency of his subsequent teaching here about being ready for his arrival at the end of time comes as a shock. The phrase 'dressed for action' used to be translated as having 'your loins girded', that is ensuring that your robes are pulled up and fastened high enough to allow your legs to run. Like a family at an airport arrivals lounge, they need to be ready to run with arms open – ready for a reassuring hug.

The first readers of Luke's Gospel may have been wondering why Jesus hadn't yet returned. Some may have been suffering as they waited. Contemporary readers may have similar questions as to why evil and pain are not brought to an end by the final reign of God on earth. Why is patience more virtuous than justice?

Jesus' teaching here reminds all of us that, for the Christian, all things are as yet unfinished. Our discipleship is a way, a journey, and it requires of us an alertness and readiness for discerning right decisions, movement and courage. The challenge is for us to be a continually expectant people, eager to have enough light in our lives to be able to see Christ when he comes to us in the frightened, hurting, oppressed and ignored. Unless we are ready to move towards such men, women and children living alongside us now, dressed for action with light shining, we may well miss him when he arrives at the 'unexpected hour', even though we were given many images of him before our eyes as we were looked to for help.

God of truth,
help us to keep your law of love
and to walk in ways of wisdom,
that we may find true life
in Jesus Christ your Son.

COLLECT

Friday 8 June

Luke 12.41-48

*'From everyone to whom much has been given,
much will be required' (v.48)*

Peter asks whether Jesus' teaching to be expectant is meant for the original disciples or for everyone – that is, us. The answer he gets, in more parabolic forms, is clear. Any follower of Christ who has grown indifferent has flabbiness of soul and needs to start exercising quickly. It is not enough to claim the name of Christ for yourself but then not translate the name into your life in such a way that makes a difference to your behaviour, words, priorities and generosity. Just because you are in a garage doesn't make you a car. Even if you stand in a church, singing and praying happily, it does not follow that you have yet learned what 'Christian' really means for your life.

Jesus teaches that 'everyone to whom much has been given' are those whom he expects to 'find at work'. If you have faith, if you have received the grace of God, then gratitude should find itself very busy in you, seeking ways in which you too, like Christ, can be graceful towards the failing and fragile. Sometimes a religious faith can solidify us in our prejudices and even our coldest hatreds. Jesus warns us here that unawareness is the root of all evil and that any who bear his name must be constantly self-scrutinizing as to whether they are genuinely about his work of love or merely enjoying a self-congratulating, but dangerously fraudulent, game.

COLLECT

O God,
the strength of all those who put their trust in you,
mercifully accept our prayers
and, because through the weakness of our mortal nature
we can do no good thing without you,
grant us the help of your grace,
that in the keeping of your commandments
we may please you both in will and deed;
through Jesus Christ your Son our Lord,
who is alive and reigns with you,
in the unity of the Holy Spirit,
one God, now and for ever.

Reflection by **Mark Oakley**

Psalms 41, **42**, 43
Joshua 24.29-end
Luke 12.49-end

Saturday 9 June

Luke 12.49-end

'... why do you not know how to interpret the present time?' (v.56)

It's been said that the heart of the human problem is the problem of the human heart. If to follow Christ means any change in that heart, and we claim readily that it does, it will entail significant consequences. These will lead us from time to time into conflict with the currents of society, the 'norms' that can be taken for granted by a generation, and even with those who are nearest and dearest to us. Jesus says that he has comes to bring fire to the earth, he has come to burn away human dross in a fire similar to that encountered by Moses, one that roars with the loving and eternal presence of God, defrosting the world of self-regard.

Jesus asks why we cannot interpret our own times. We might reply that there are too many people today interpreting and opinionating from every direction. Shouldn't the person of faith withdraw from them all and find a deeper stillness within? Yes, certainly, but only so that we can then discern with a fresh perspective the thoughts and actions that are controlling human motivations in our day and the ways in which people are being damaged or forgotten by them. Then comes the hard part. If we don't stand for something, we will fall for anything. Christians need to voice their challenge to the world, as well as to the Church itself of course. Christians will often be afraid to do this, but must do it anyway. Christian spirituality is a slow learning of speaking up for others, burning up with love whatever diminishes them.

God of truth,
help us to keep your law of love
and to walk in ways of wisdom,
that we may find true life
in Jesus Christ your Son.

COLLECT

Monday 11 June

Barnabas the Apostle

Psalms 100, 101, 117
Jeremiah 9.23-24
Acts 4.32-end

Acts 4.32-end

'He sold a field that belonged to him' (v.37)

Remembering Barnabas today, we celebrate an early Christian, named Joseph, who was given the name Barnabas by his friends and became prominent in the Jerusalem church. He accompanied Paul on missionary journeys and defended non-Jewish converts to Christian faith from those who were sceptical about their authenticity as disciples.

In this reading we learn that in the Church's earliest days it was considered faithful, for those who could afford it, to sell disposable property in order to create a surplus for charitable distribution amongst their community. Words from the First Book of Chronicles (29.14) were certainly in their minds: 'For all things come from you, and of your own have we given you.' We are told that Barnabas sold a field he owned and gave the proceeds to the apostles for them to discern its best use. There is a valid question for all of us: 'For whom is our money good news?'

The name Barnabas means, the author tell us, 'son of encouragement'. What a happy corrective it would be if Christians thought of ourselves as children of encouragement, people inspired to live life by the cherishing encouragement of God, but also men and women who bring hope and purpose to our locality and among those we share life with. As the early Christians knew, this often begins with learning to want what we have, instead of endlessly having what we want. This enables the generosity that Winston Churchill spoke of when he said: 'We make a living by what we earn, but we make a life by what we give.'

COLLECT

Bountiful God, giver of all gifts,
who poured your Spirit upon your servant Barnabas
and gave him grace to encourage others:
help us, by his example,
to be generous in our judgements
and unselfish in our service;
through Jesus Christ your Son our Lord,
who is alive and reigns with you,
in the unity of the Holy Spirit,
one God, now and for ever.

| *Reflection by* **Mark Oakley**

Psalms **48**, 52
Judges 4.1–23
Luke 13.10-21

Tuesday 12 June

Luke 13.10-21

'... there appeared a woman with a spirit that had crippled her'
(v.11)

Names are a vital part of our identity and self-worth. In this story, however, we meet someone who is simply known as 'the bent woman'. Her distorted back forced her to look at the ground. She was unable to look people in the eye, and presumably damage had been done to various organs of her body. The woman doesn't have an identity other than that of a victim. Her shoulders most probably carried a much heavier and isolating burden than anyone knew. She is there in the Gospel for everyone whose soul and beauty are not seen because of a label pinned on them – the 'gay', the 'Muslim', the 'immigrant', the 'pensioner'. We could extend the list ...

The healing from Jesus, this 'setting free', might be understood to be a physical one. Her back is put right and she can stand tall. But there is another healing given her. Jesus calls her a 'daughter of Abraham'. In all the Gospels, only here is this expression used. Jesus celebrates her as an heir to the one to whom, one starry night, a promise was given that a great and blessed people would come through him (Genesis 15.5-6). She is an heir to this blessing and is freed now to become a blessing herself to others. Once again, Jesus turns a person's full-stop into a comma so she can begin a new life with herself, her neighbours and her God.

When the world tries to bury us, God makes us seeds. I wonder how her life took shape after this day, as she began to live and grow into God's dreams for her?

Lord, you have taught us
that all our doings without love are nothing worth:
send your Holy Spirit
and pour into our hearts that most excellent gift of love,
the true bond of peace and of all virtues,
without which whoever lives is counted dead before you.
Grant this for your only Son Jesus Christ's sake,
who is alive and reigns with you,
in the unity of the Holy Spirit,
one God, now and for ever.

COLLECT

Reflection by **Mark Oakley** | 173

Wednesday 13 June

Luke 13.22-end

'... some are last who will be first' (v.30)

How will Christ recognize his followers? This question is at the heart of today's reading. We Christians often talk about being able to see Christ in another person, the stranger or the one in need. Here, though, the focus shifts onto us instead, and we are made to wonder whether there is enough love, faith and hope in us to be discernibly one of Christ's own. It will not be enough, it appears, to say that we attended the eucharist and listened to sermons for 'you will begin to say, "We ate and drank with you, and you taught in our streets." But he will say, "I do not know where you come from ..."'. Pleas of familiarity will not be adequate. Those who consider themselves first in line will have made themselves last.

We also hear how Herod wants to kill Jesus. Jesus then reflects on Jerusalem being a city where prophets are killed. Prophets are not people who foretell but rather forth-tell, they do not predict the future but they place a scalpel to the present and reveal all that has gone wrong. Prophets uncomfortably tell us who we have become as human beings and recall us to the divine vision for life and creation. We have a great capacity to resist change though. Sin can be a very conservative thing. We prefer to reach for a stone, or a cross, when a prophet comes to town.

COLLECT

Lord, you have taught us
that all our doings without love are nothing worth:
send your Holy Spirit
and pour into our hearts that most excellent gift of love,
the true bond of peace and of all virtues,
without which whoever lives is counted dead before you.
Grant this for your only Son Jesus Christ's sake,
who is alive and reigns with you,
in the unity of the Holy Spirit,
one God, now and for ever.

| *Reflection by* **Mark Oakley**

Psalms 56, **57** (63*)
Judges 6.1-24
Luke 14.1-11

Thursday 14 June

Luke 14.1-11

'... they were silent' (v 4)

It has been said that rather than answer all of people's questions, Jesus tends to question all their answers. Here is a good example, as Jesus at a sabbath meal asks whether it is lawful to heal a man. The lawyers and Pharisees are silent. It appears they know he is right to confront what they teach. Their religious script, when pushed, is clearly inhumane. Nobody and nothing is served well by it in this instance, except perhaps their pride in keeping to reassuring regulations.

Throughout his ministry Jesus used meals as signs of God's kingdom, where each has a place at the table and each enjoys the company with shared gifts and common purpose. As he looks around, though, he sees that the company has made this meal exclusive and not inclusive. It is a meal that reflects their pride rather than humility, as they jostle for the best places. He shows them a meal works best when your gratitude at being present outweighs any desire to push others aside. A meal becomes a feast when all feel welcome, all share the same foods and each looks to the other to make the occasion rich in friendship and hope. As in the meal, so in life. Those who exalt themselves miss out on the true shared beauty of the kingdom.

In Isak Dinesen's story called *Babette's Feast*, where extraordinary transformations happen to ordinary people eating together, the two sisters who hosted the meal watch the guests make their way home at the end and comment that 'the stars have come closer tonight'. Heaven draws nearer when humility makes place for everyone.

Faithful Creator,
whose mercy never fails:
deepen our faithfulness to you
and to your living Word,
Jesus Christ our Lord.

COLLECT

Friday 15 June

Luke 14.12-24

'... you will be blessed, because they cannot repay you' (v.14)

We all make excuses from time to time. Sometimes we have legitimate reasons for turning an invitation down; other times we make things up because we're not keen to accept. Which was the case with the three people in the parable? Were these good and understandable reasons to give to the host or were they inventing things to get out of going to the dinner? Either way, they fail to comprehend the urgency of the invite as well as the level of demand placed on them by their relationship with the host. Neither reasonable justifications for absence nor indifference meet the requirements faith in God lays on us.

The angry giver of the banquet decides now to issue his invitation to the outsiders of the city and then to those living in the country, resting in the quiet lanes. The attitude of the original invitees is self-excluding and all those who would never normally get an invitation to sit at table with others are now called, and even compelled, to join the party.

To Luke's first hearers, this parable would point to the inability of the Jewish people of God to take the call and ministry of Jesus seriously so that God has to reach out to the gentiles to bring his kingdom in. For us today, we can see how we often avoid the challenges faith asks of us only to see that others, whose lives are often much harder than our own in many ways, live up to expectancy with a more courageous and loving fidelity. God is not fussy when it comes to helpers. Accept an invitation today and see what might happen! It may be part of God's surprise for you.

COLLECT

Lord, you have taught us
that all our doings without love are nothing worth:
send your Holy Spirit
and pour into our hearts that most excellent gift of love,
the true bond of peace and of all virtues,
without which whoever lives is counted dead before you.
Grant this for your only Son Jesus Christ's sake,
who is alive and reigns with you,
in the unity of the Holy Spirit,
one God, now and for ever.

| *Reflection by **Mark Oakley***

Psalm **68**
Judges 7
Luke 14.25-end

Saturday 16 June

Luke 14.25-end

'Whoever does not carry the cross and follow me cannot be my disciple' (v 27)

The Christian community is called to be a school for relating, a place where we can learn how to relate more deeply to God, to each other and to ourselves. It focuses on the life and ministry of Jesus in order to learn the lessons of true human relationship. As we follow Christ, we begin to understand that a human self is more itself when not being selfish. To live this truth entails a distillation within us and an un-learning of much that the world encourages us to believe. In other words, there is a cost to Christian discipleship. For some, the cost is the ultimate one of life itself, and, says Jesus here, we therefore need to be serious in our decision as to whether really following him is something we are prepared to commit to.

To help us in this decision Jesus shocks us by implying that we will need to commit to him more than to our family. We will need to give up our possessions, that is, all those things that give us an inauthentic identity and which sadly in our own day can begin to possess us rather than we them. It means being willing to carry an instrument of public execution to remind us of the one we follow and the demands salvation makes. It entails a sometimes blind faith, a keeping-going, even when all seems lost. Christian faith is a pilgrimage of devotion and dereliction, and only when we have made the commitment named by Jesus do we realize the true nature of God and the beauty of the Christian vocation. As art critic and social thinker John Ruskin said: 'The highest reward for a person's toil is not what they get for it, but what they become by it.'

Faithful Creator,
whose mercy never fails:
deepen our faithfulness to you
and to your living Word,
Jesus Christ our Lord.

COLLECT

Reflection by **Mark Oakley** | 177

Monday 18 June

Psalm **71**
Judges 8.22-end
Luke 15.1-10

Luke 15.1-10

'This fellow welcomes sinners and eats with them' (v.2)

Here's a question: 'What does religion do?' Or to put it more personally: 'What's the effect in your life of your religious practice and belief?' It may not be a question you often ask, but today's reading invites such a reflection.

The Gospels tell a consistent story that many of those most committed to their faith were provoked by Jesus' behaviour and, in particular, his persistent, personal, generous engagement with those on the edge of society. For the Pharisees and others, faithful religious practice meant *separation* from those who failed to live up to the standards of holiness they set themselves, or believed that God set them. The sad thing is that the way their religion played out in their lives led them further away from the heart of God, not closer to it.

Jesus shows us the true heart of God: a love that, like the shepherd with his sheep and the woman with her coin, searches relentlessly and effectively for lives that seem to others – or perhaps to themselves – to be lost. That is the God we see in Jesus' words and actions.

It is that God who invites us to join with his Son in welcoming sinners and eating with them and who says to us, with the shepherd and the woman, 'Rejoice with me'!

So here's a question, and take a bit of time answering it honestly. Does your faith, in practice, lead you nearer to the searching, rejoicing, Jesus-shaped heart of God?

COLLECT

Almighty God,
you have broken the tyranny of sin
and have sent the Spirit of your Son into our hearts
    whereby we call you Father:
give us grace to dedicate our freedom to your service,
that we and all creation may be brought
    to the glorious liberty of the children of God;
through Jesus Christ your Son our Lord,
who is alive and reigns with you,
in the unity of the Holy Spirit,
one God, now and for ever.

| *Reflection by* **John Kiddle**

Psalm **73**
Judges 9.1-21
Luke 15.11-end

Tuesday 19 June

Luke 15.11-end

'His father ... ran and put his arms around him and kissed him' (v.20)

The three parables in Luke 15 address the attitude of those who grumbled about the behaviour of Jesus in welcoming sinners and eating with them. It is an attitude based on a deep misunderstanding of holiness. For Jesus, holiness is powerful and active. It does not, in fear, need to keep itself separate from all that would make it unclean. Rather, in love, it will embrace that which is lost and bring it to life.

The story of the father and two lost sons draws us into the life of a wounded family, and, in that mess, a father's broken heart shows us the heart of God. The father's deep humanity and vulnerability reveal the true holiness of God. The father waits and looks, sees and runs. He embraces his son, kisses him, and celebrates with a party. This, Jesus is saying, is what God does because this is who God is.

That holy and loving father knows his heart broken a second time as his elder son stands and stares, unable to share his father's love and joy. This son too is lost, not in the loose living and humiliation of his brother, but in pride, anger and self-righteousness.

He is near, but he is far; he is close at hand, but he is lost. He sees what is unfolding, but cannot recognize the wonder of welcome and restoration. His lostness is heart-breaking.

Where today might you have the opportunity to see and to recognize the transforming, loving holiness of God?

God our saviour,
look on this wounded world
in pity and in power;
hold us fast to your promises of peace
won for us by your Son,
our Saviour Jesus Christ.

COLLECT

Reflection by **John Kiddle** | 179

Wednesday 20 June

Luke 16.1-18

'Make friends for yourselves by means of dishonest wealth ...' (v.9)

This is a rather strange parable. A servant, seeing the end of his employment on the horizon, uses the wealth that is, for a few more days, in his hand. He has a cunning plan. With a bit of creative accounting, he 'invests' his master's resources to make friends for himself for the tricky future that is to come.

Jesus, or at least the master in the parable, appears to commend this dishonesty. What are we to make of this? There is a line of thought that in fact the master in the story was himself acting well beyond the spirit of the law by charging interest on the loans of oil and wheat. Perhaps the servant's dishonesty can be seen as righting a wrong.

However, this is a parable, and parables are not usually overcomplicated. Maybe Jesus is simply asking a question. What can you do with the wealth that is, for a season, in your hands? How might you, with creativity and imagination, use it for something lasting and good?

What is a shrewd investment? Finding the last 0.5% of interest? Or making a lasting difference in another person's life? How can I build a better future for others, not just for me and mine?

And in the spirit of the servant in the story, what would happen if you simply decided to invest some of all that God has given you in having a party for your neighbours? Making friends through generosity and celebration – which, of course, offers an intriguing link back to the previous chapter.

COLLECT

Almighty God,
you have broken the tyranny of sin
and have sent the Spirit of your Son into our hearts
    whereby we call you Father:
give us grace to dedicate our freedom to your service,
that we and all creation may be brought
    to the glorious liberty of the children of God;
through Jesus Christ your Son our Lord,
who is alive and reigns with you,
in the unity of the Holy Spirit,
one God, now and for ever.

| *Reflection by* **John Kiddle**

Psalm **78.1-39***
Judges 11.1-11
Luke 16.19-end

Thursday 21 June

Luke 16.19-end

'... between you and us a great chasm has been fixed' (v.26)

There is a terrible finality about this parable. It offers little hope for the rich man who failed to recognize his responsibilities towards Lazarus, the poor man who, covered in sores and hungry, lay at the door of his fine house. Neither is much hope offered for the rich man's brothers; nothing will change their mind set and lifestyle – not even if 'someone rises from the dead'.

The chasm between the rich man and Lazarus after their deaths only reflects the distance that separated them in life. They were neighbours, and it is clear that the rich man knew who Lazarus was and knew his name. However, the gap between them was as real in life as in death.

The rich man's wealth gave him both the responsibility and the opportunity to do something about Lazarus' poverty and suffering, but he failed to take action. His humanity should have moved him to pity and action, but he remained detached and uninterested. His faith would have told him of God's requirements, in both the law and the prophets, to live mercifully and to act justly, but he did the opposite.

There's a strong connection between this threefold disconnection and the parables we have looked at in the last three days. Our faith, our humanity and our wealth give us responsibilities towards others and opportunities to really make a difference. They are gifts to be used, not possessions to be guarded.

How might you make some connections and even bridge some chasms today?

God our saviour,
look on this wounded world
in pity and in power;
hold us fast to your promises of peace
won for us by your Son,
our Saviour Jesus Christ.

COLLECT

Reflection by **John Kiddle**   181

Friday 22 June

Luke 17.1-10

'... we have done only what we ought to have done!' (v.10)

Humility is a slippery thing. If we think we've got it, then we probably haven't. False humility, whether in fictional characters such as Uriah Heep in Dickens' *David Copperfield* or in ourselves, is a particularly unattractive quality. *True* humility is rooted in an honest and unanxious self-knowledge. It is liberating, freeing us to serve and also to lead.

In this passage, Luke has strung together sayings of Jesus like beads; the thread holding them together is the humility that shapes the lives of the disciples of Jesus. It means they will live with *care* (vv.1-2). They will tread cautiously as they touch the lives of others, not least the vulnerable. Clumsy and arrogant lives damage and trip up others.

The disciples will live with *grace* (vv.3-4). A humble heart bears with the faults of others and forgives freely; it is generous and is not preoccupied with its own recompense.

Humble disciples live with a *faith* that changes the world (vv.5-6). They know that the power of faith, like the smallest of seeds, does not stem from its greatness but from its ability to point us away from ourselves to God.

A life shaped by humility is a life that finds joy and freedom in *service* (vv.7-10). In a typically provocative way, Jesus describes his disciples as slaves; they freely choose to serve and so doing find liberation and life.

How might you live humbly today, living with care and grace, faith and service?

Almighty God,
you have broken the tyranny of sin
and have sent the Spirit of your Son into our hearts
    whereby we call you Father:
give us grace to dedicate our freedom to your service,
that we and all creation may be brought
    to the glorious liberty of the children of God;
through Jesus Christ your Son our Lord,
who is alive and reigns with you,
in the unity of the Holy Spirit,
one God, now and for ever.

| *Reflection by* **John Kiddle**

Psalms **76**, 79
Judges 12.1-7
Luke 17.11-19

Saturday 23 June

Luke 17.11-19

'Were not ten made clean? But the other nine, where are they?'
(v.17)

How do you receive a gift? Sometimes a gift is so eagerly anticipated or jealously guarded that we grab it and hold on with fingers clenched tight around it. Or a gift can be held lightly with an open hand, treasured but not grasped.

The nine, cured of their leprosy, excitedly and incredulously ran to the priest, as in fact they had been told, seizing their healing tightly in case it disappeared.

The one, cured of his leprosy, somewhat surprisingly stopped and thought about what had been given him and who had given him that gift. Quietly he returned to the giver and offered his thanks.

In returning he received a further gift, in Jesus' words of peace, 'Get up and go on your way; your faith has made you well'.

All that we have in this life comes to us as a gift; yet so often we hold on to it so tightly that we miss what life really offers.

All that is ours in Christ is grace, and yet often our uncertainty, anxiety and fear prevent us from fully experiencing the forgiveness and freedom he brings.

To live gratefully is to pause and to think. It is to return constantly to the source of the gift and say, 'Thank you'.

How might you live gratefully today? Holding all you have with an open hand, not fearing the moth and rust that destroys or the thief that steals, but able to receive with thanks and to share with generosity.

God our saviour,
look on this wounded world
in pity and in power;
hold us fast to your promises of peace
won for us by your Son,
our Saviour Jesus Christ.

COLLECT

Reflection by **John Kiddle** | 183

Monday 25 June

Psalms **80**, 82
Judges 13.1-24
Luke 17.20-end

Luke 17.20-end

'Those who try to make their life secure will lose it ...' (v.33)

Understandably and sensibly, we take precautions to make life more secure. We guard our health; we insure our possessions; we lock doors and look before we cross the road. Life is a gift and we want to treasure it, celebrate it and ensure we are able to care for and love those close to us.

However, in doing so, we can sometimes miss the point of life itself. We can become so anxious, so busy and perhaps even so guarded that the heart of life gets lost.

It is a common experience that unexpected events, even tragic ones, shake us out of the ruts we live in and give us new perspectives. These experiences can, paradoxically, sometimes feel like a gift; they allow us to see more clearly and more sharply the things that are truly important.

The words of Jesus that Luke has drawn together in today's passage speak about events that will come like lightning and disrupt the usual course and stuff of life – eating and drinking, planting and building.

Jesus is not inviting his followers to sit around fearfully waiting for the end of the world, or for some tragedy to strike, but to live each day with a different perspective. For as Jesus says, as we learn to embrace the insecurity of life and resist the constant pressure to accumulate more and more stuff, then we will find the freedom to live freely and fully.

COLLECT

O God, the protector of all who trust in you,
without whom nothing is strong, nothing is holy:
increase and multiply upon us your mercy;
that with you as our ruler and guide
we may so pass through things temporal
that we lose not our hold on things eternal;
grant this, heavenly Father,
for our Lord Jesus Christ's sake,
who is alive and reigns with you,
in the unity of the Holy Spirit,
one God, now and for ever.

| *Reflection by* **John Kiddle**

Psalms 87, **89.1-18**
Judges 14
Luke 18.1-14

Tuesday 26 June

Luke 18.1-14

'... to pray always and not to lose heart' (v.1)

It can be easy to lose heart in our prayers. Often it seems that prayers remain unanswered and God is, at best, powerless and, at worst, unmoved and uncaring. We lose heart when we fail to see what lies at the heart of prayer. Luke brings together two parables of Jesus that help show us that heart.

We lose heart in prayer when we forget *to whom* we pray. As he does in other parables, Jesus makes a point by contrasting the good character of God with that of 'sinful' human beings. If a grumpy, mean judge will eventually respond to a bothersome widow, how much more will God bring justice to the poor and oppressed. For justice and mercy are at the heart of God – God does not lose heart and nor should we.

We lose heart in prayer when we forget *who we are* in the presence of God. Jesus' second parable contrasts a man who seems to believe that the purpose of prayer is to vindicate himself before God with another who simply comes to God seeking mercy and grace.

The second man got it right. In his openness, humility and honesty, he discovered the heart of a welcoming and gracious God. We won't lose heart in prayer If we are constantly rediscovering that amazing love and acceptance.

So be persistent and be yourself. Pray and don't lose heart. God loves and God cares – not just for you, but for those you pray for.

Gracious Father,
by the obedience of Jesus
you brought salvation to our wayward world:
draw us into harmony with your will,
that we may find all things restored in him,
our Saviour Jesus Christ.

COLLECT

Reflection by **John Kiddle**

185

Wednesday 27 June

Luke 18.15-30

'... he became sad; for he was very rich' (v.23)

The sadness of the rich ruler is poignant and powerful. He knew that he was missing something; he saw it clearly and he truly wanted to take hold of the life that Jesus preached and lived.

Pope Francis wrote (in his encyclical on the environment): 'when people become self-centred and self-enclosed, their greed increases. The emptier a person's heart is, the more he or she needs things to buy, own and consume.'

The sadness of the rich man lies in the fact that his own buying and owning and consuming had become so powerful that he was unable to let go and reach out for what he could see was truly going to give his life purpose and joy. Jesus, I guess, shared his sadness.

Children show us a different way. Jesus insisted that infants were not prevented from coming to him. This insistence was not just for the children's sake but also for the disciples' sake.

If we take time to look and see the simplicity, trust and joy with which young children come to God, we might rediscover for ourselves the freedom to let go of the things that hold us back and open our hands to receive all that God wishes to give so freely and generously.

Today, what could you let go of in order to take hold of something that is liberating, life-giving and true? Whose example might help give you the power to do so?

COLLECT

O God, the protector of all who trust in you,
without whom nothing is strong, nothing is holy:
increase and multiply upon us your mercy;
that with you as our ruler and guide
we may so pass through things temporal
that we lose not our hold on things eternal;
grant this, heavenly Father,
for our Lord Jesus Christ's sake,
who is alive and reigns with you,
in the unity of the Holy Spirit,
one God, now and for ever.

| *Reflection by* **John Kiddle**

Thursday 28 June

Luke 18.31-end

'What do you want me to do for you?' (v.41)

It seems a silly question – a bit like asking a grieving person how they are feeling. Wasn't it obvious that the blind beggar wanted Jesus to heal him?

Jesus hears the man and sees more than a 'blind beggar'. People seek to bar his way, but Jesus will have none of it; he stands still and waits for the man to come to him and offers him a moment of quiet dignity.

Jesus creates a space of stillness and quietness in which to ask a question that is neither silly nor crass; it is kind and gently probing: 'What do you want me to do for you?'

We might often feel like the beggar sitting unseeing and unseen by the side of the road crying out for help as the crowds push past. Prayer often begins with that helpless cry from the side of the road, but it doesn't need to remain in that place.

Prayer is hearing Jesus' invitation to stand up and walk to him. Prayer is discovering the space in which we can encounter him. Prayer is knowing that he sees not only our needs but also the person often hidden by those needs.

Take time today to get up from the side of the road and make the space to stand in stillness with the Lord who, knowing you and loving you, asks: 'What do you want me to do for you?'

COLLECT

Gracious Father,
by the obedience of Jesus
you brought salvation to our wayward world:
draw us into harmony with your will,
that we may find all things restored in him,
our Saviour Jesus Christ.

Reflection by **John Kiddle**   187

Friday 29 June

Peter the Apostle

Psalms 71, 113
Isaiah 49.1-6
Acts 11.1-18

Isaiah 49.1-6

*'I will give you as a light to the nations,
that my salvation may reach to the end of the earth' (v.6)*

Today we celebrate St Peter. It is encouraging for us that Jesus chose
Peter to be the rock on which he built his Church. Peter often put his
foot in it or in some other way messed up. He also often got it right;
he stepped out in faith, he spoke up and he knew, in the end, that he
loved his Lord. He was willing to learn, ready to admit when he was
wrong, get up and start again. He was in fact just the sort of rock that
God loves to use.

Read the story of Peter's big eye opener in Acts 10. It began with a
daydream and finished with an interrupted sermon. It was a shock to
discover God's plans were far bigger than anything he had imagined,
and included people – the gentiles – whom he had considered beyond
the scope of God's love.

It's all there in Isaiah. Out of the painful experience of exile comes a
beautiful insight that God's plans are far bigger than the longed-for
return. God's purposes, through his servant, were not simply to bring
Israel home but also through that return to bring hope to *all* nations.

To limit God's love or goodness only to people like us is to miss who
God really is. Isaiah learned it. Peter learned it. We need to go on
learning it.

God's love is for all.

COLLECT

Almighty God,
who inspired your apostle Saint Peter
to confess Jesus as Christ and Son of the living God:
build up your Church upon this rock,
that in unity and peace it may proclaim one truth
and follow one Lord, your Son our Saviour Christ,
who is alive and reigns with you,
in the unity of the Holy Spirit,
one God, now and for ever.

| *Reflection by* **John Kiddle**

Psalms 96, **97**, 100
Judges 18.1-20, 27-end
Luke 19.11-27

Saturday 30 June

Luke 19.11-27

'Lord, your pound has made ten more pounds' (v.16)

There's a wonderful truth at the heart of creation that's called growth. Seeds fall in the ground, produce plants and trees that give life to flowers and fruit in plenty, containing the seeds of continuing growth. It's full of colour, abundance, sweetness and fragrance. It's the way God works in creation. It's beautiful, it's generous and it's life-giving. It's the way God wants to work in us, with the same generosity and beauty and the same joyful purpose to bring life in all its fullness.

The third servant missed the point. His master was, in his view, to be feared, someone who was quick to condemn, who took before he gave. So he wrapped the money up safely and hid it away.

The first servants saw their master differently. They saw his desire and joy at seeing what his wealth could achieve. They used what they had been given and produced more.

The servants acted according to what they understood their master to be, and on his return that was the master each encountered.

How we use all that we have been given in this life – our time, our skills, our love, our wealth – will entirely depend on what we fundamentally believe about the one who gives.

Take time today to reflect on the generous, life-giving, creative God we see at work around us and then do what you do today with that same imagination, beauty and abundance.

O God, the protector of all who trust in you,
without whom nothing is strong, nothing is holy:
increase and multiply upon us your mercy;
that with you as our ruler and guide
we may so pass through things temporal
that we lose not our hold on things eternal;
grant this, heavenly Father,
for our Lord Jesus Christ's sake,
who is alive and reigns with you,
in the unity of the Holy Spirit,
one God, now and for ever.

COLLECT

Reflection by **John Kiddle** 189

Monday 2 July

1 Samuel 1.1-20

'I have asked him of the Lord' (v.20)

Samuel stands at a transition point in the story of the people of Israel. Over the course of 1 and 2 Samuel, Israel changes from a loose federation of tribes to a nation. The tribes were led by judges whose authority came partly from personal strength and partly from a recognition of God's presence and action through them; the nation, on the other hand, is led by kings, some of whom have divine approval, some of whom do not. It is Samuel who anoints the first king, and who establishes the pattern of kings and prophets, whose different kinds of authority in the land are not always at ease with each other.

Samuel himself stands in the line of judges and prophets: his authority is a divine gift, not an inherited right or one won by the sword. We are not told that David is born as an answer to prayer, but Samuel is. His life is God's from before his conception, like Isaac, the child of the promise to Abraham and Sarah. God is tender towards these barren women, and somehow, because they are dependent on God's action rather than ordinary human processes, their children are transparent to God's call in a particular way.

As Eli disapprovingly watches Hannah weeping, he is already showing blindness to the action of God, a blindness that Samuel is to remedy on behalf of the nation.

COLLECT

Almighty and everlasting God,
by whose Spirit the whole body of the Church
    is governed and sanctified:
hear our prayer which we offer for all your faithful people,
that in their vocation and ministry
they may serve you in holiness and truth
to the glory of your name;
through our Lord and Saviour Jesus Christ,
who is alive and reigns with you,
in the unity of the Holy Spirit,
one God, now and for ever.

| *Reflection by* **Jane Williams**

Tuesday 3 July
Thomas the Apostle

John 11.1-16

'Thomas ... said to his fellow-disciples,
"Let us also go, that we may die with him."' (v.16)

The story of the raising of Lazarus is multi-layered, as John's narratives always are. It is set at a time of life-threatening conflict between Jesus and the local religious leaders, who have just tried to stone him for blasphemy, and are making repeated attempts to either kill him or get him in custody.

The story also highlights different sets of relationships that Jesus has with his friends and followers. John tells us, very simply, that Jesus loves Martha and her family, and there is a hint of rivalry perhaps, between these old friends and Jesus' disciples. Certainly, the disciples are exasperated at the thought that Jesus is planning to put himself in danger again, just because Martha and Mary snap their fingers.

But Jesus is fearless in his knowledge that God alone dictates the time when he will be vulnerable. Then, as now, death will be God's opportunity to manifest his glory (v.4). There is a strange elation in Jesus as he sets out to bring his dead friend back to life.

Gloomily, but doggedly, Thomas persuades the others to follow Jesus back into the trouble zone, expecting the worst. When, much later, Thomas has the opportunity to die with Jesus, his courage fails him and he, like all the others, runs. Thomas does not understand the glory of God until he puts his fingers into the marks of the nails in the risen Christ.

COLLECT

Almighty and eternal God,
who, for the firmer foundation of our faith,
allowed your holy apostle Thomas
to doubt the resurrection of your Son
till word and sight convinced him:
grant to us, who have not seen, that we also may believe
and so confess Christ as our Lord and our God;
who is alive and reigns with you,
in the unity of the Holy Spirit,
one God, now and for ever.

Reflection by **Jane Williams** | 191

Wednesday 4 July

1 Samuel 2.12-26

*'His mother used to make for him a little robe
and take it to him each year' (v.19)*

Trustingly, Hannah gives her son into Eli's care. Samuel is a gift from God, an answer to Hannah's desperate prayer, and her response makes it clear why God sees her and gives her her heart's desire. Although Hannah longs above all else for this gift of a child, she knows that gifts are to be shared, and she gives him back to God. The little robe (v.19) that she makes for him every year is a testimony that she does not do this easily: she carries Samuel's measurements in her heart, even though she sees him so rarely.

In stark contrast, Eli's sons have turned the service of God into a job, not a gift. They seem to have no idea that they are dealing with the Mighty One of Israel – for them, the regular rituals of praise and sacrifice are a convenient way for lazy and dishonest people to make a comfortable living. Eli does have some vague memory of his calling, as he remonstrates with his sons: they are meant to be interceding for sinners, not committing the sins themselves. But even for Eli, God is distant, not very likely to call in.

Yet he watched Hannah weep and saw God's answer. He should have felt some frisson of the presence of the living God.

COLLECT

Almighty and everlasting God,
by whose Spirit the whole body of the Church
  is governed and sanctified:
hear our prayer which we offer for all your faithful people,
that in their vocation and ministry
they may serve you in holiness and truth
to the glory of your name;
through our Lord and Saviour Jesus Christ,
who is alive and reigns with you,
in the unity of the Holy Spirit,
one God, now and for ever.

| *Reflection by* **Jane Williams**

Thursday 5 July

1 Samuel 2.27-end

'Why ... honour your sons more than me?' (v.29)

1 Samuel has set up two clear and contrasting pictures. On the one hand, we have Hannah and Samuel, a story of dependence upon God's generosity, which evokes in its turn a generosity in the receiver. In this story, God is at the heart of all that happens, living, responsive and utterly trustworthy. Hannah and Samuel live in the company of this God, and respond to him as flowers to sunshine: they grow towards him.

On the other hand, we have Eli and his sons. They have institutional-ized God and forgotten his reality; their work in the temple is a family business, not an entrusted gift. They deal with his power routinely, so that they have become inured to it. Day by day, they charge for God's forgiveness, in the sacred sacrifices that restore the sinner, but they don't believe a word of it. They trust themselves and their own exploitative plans, never dreaming that God has any say in the matter. Eli has indulged his sons and so failed them: they do not know God.

The man of God who comes to Eli tells the sombre truth: God cannot be dealt out like loose change, or inherited as a right. God is not bound by history, but utterly free to create a people for himself again, just as he did when he called the slaves out of Egypt.

Eli is caught between these two stories. He remembers enough to be anxious, but not enough to change.

Almighty God,
send down upon your Church
the riches of your Spirit,
and kindle in all who minister the gospel
your countless gifts of grace;
through Jesus Christ our Lord.

COLLECT

Friday 6 July

1 Samuel 3.1 – 4.1*a*

*'And all Israel from Dan to Beer-sheba knew that Samuel was
a trustworthy prophet of the Lord' (3.20)*

We catch a glimpse of Samuel's strange and lonely childhood with Eli,
an ageing man, with failing sight, which could almost be his chosen
defence mechanism: out of sight, out of mind. And then at night, the
little boy sleeps in the temple, amidst the smell and smoke of the burnt
offerings, the flickering light of the lamp, and with the terrifying
presence of the ark of God for company.

Yet, in the midst of all of these reminders, Samuel does not immediately
understand his call. It's hard not to see this as Eli's failing: just as he
failed to give his own sons any sense of the reality of God, so he has
apparently not given Samuel any expectation of the presence of God in
the sacred space where he lives, works and sleeps.

The first message God gives to Samuel is a brutal one, a hard test of
whether Samuel is willing to be a truthful speaker of the word of God.
Samuel is not to know that Eli has already heard this news, but we, the
readers, know and wait to see what Samuel will do. Samuel chooses,
and sets the pattern of faithful response that is to shape the rest of
his days.

With awe, God's people, who have come to despise Shiloh under the
ministry of Eli and his sons, come back, to hear and meet their God
again, at last.

COLLECT

Almighty and everlasting God,
by whose Spirit the whole body of the Church
    is governed and sanctified:
hear our prayer which we offer for all your faithful people,
that in their vocation and ministry
they may serve you in holiness and truth
to the glory of your name;
through our Lord and Saviour Jesus Christ,
who is alive and reigns with you,
in the unity of the Holy Spirit,
one God, now and for ever.

| *Reflection by* **Jane Williams**

Psalms 120, **121**, 122
1 Samuel 4.1*b*-end
Luke 20.27-40

Saturday 7 July

1 Samuel 4.1*b*-end
'The glory has departed from Israel' (v.21)

The ark of the covenant plays its own significant role in the trajectory of the story that 1 and 2 Samuel tells: it is a story of a great change in God's interaction with his people, culminating in the anointing of David, and looking ahead to Solomon's temple. In our passage today, the ark leaves Shiloh, and when it returns, David brings it to its new home in Jerusalem (2 Samuel 6). An order is passing in this narrative.

The ark is built to hold the 'covenant', the tablets of stone on which the law is miraculously carved (see Exodus 25). It accompanies the people of God on their journey through the desert and into the promised land, going ahead of them, guiding and guarding them. It becomes a symbol of God's promised presence and faithful speech with his people.

So no wonder the soldiers of Israel turn to it for help in battle. They, like their opponents, see it as a magical object, to be deployed like a weapon. They have forgotten, apparently, that it is a sign of the action of God, who cannot be coerced. So, ironically, as the Philistines in their terror throw all their force against the ark, they are facilitating what we already know must happen: the departure of God's 'glory' from Shiloh.

The death of Eli and his sons is the end of an era, and there is only Samuel to stand in the breach until the new day dawns.

Reflection by **Jane Williams** | 195

Monday 9 July

1 Samuel 5

*'Dagon had fallen on his face to the ground before the ark
of the Lord' (v.4)*

This is a wonderfully vivid chapter, describing the fate of the ark after the terrible battle of chapter 4 – except, of course, that it actually describes the fate of those who think that their victory in battle means a victory over the ark's god. The Philistines put the symbol of the defeated god in the temple of their own victorious god, Dagon, so that the lesser can pay homage to the greater, which is exactly what happens, though not in the way the Philistines expected. Dagon is forced to pay homage to Israel's God.

The force of that is clear: God was not defeated on the battlefield, so the defeat of the Israelites was sanctioned by God. The people of Gath, boastfully, assume that they can conquer where Ashdod failed, but they soon learn their lesson, and the people of Ekron have no such illusion: they know that the God of Israel has power over their lives. As the ark wreaks havoc in the Philistine cities, it manifests God's power to defend himself, if he so chooses.

It is ironic that back in 4.13, Eli sits fretting about the safety of the ark, while here in chapter 5, it is quite clear that the ark can take care of itself. God's own people have lost touch with the power and presence of God, so apparent now to the Philistines.

COLLECT

Merciful God,
you have prepared for those who love you
such good things as pass our understanding:
pour into our hearts such love toward you
that we, loving you in all things and above all things,
may obtain your promises,
which exceed all that we can desire;
through Jesus Christ your Son our Lord,
who is alive and reigns with you,
in the unity of the Holy Spirit,
one God, now and for ever.

Reflection by **Jane Williams**

Tuesday 10 July

1 Samuel 6.1-16

'After he had made fools of them, did they not let the people go?'
(v.6)

The holy people of the Philistines are an astute bunch, with a good eye for dealing with the sacred. They devise a clever way of getting rid of the ark without risking further damage to themselves and their countrymen. The story of what happened when Pharaoh opposed God over the freeing of his people is apparently well known to the Philistine priests and diviners, and they decide it is simpler to make a virtue of necessity: since God is going to have his way, it makes sense to co-operate.

First of all, they acknowledge the power of the ark by making golden images of the plagues that struck them; they demonstrate that they have understood where their tribulations came from. But, just in case, they set a little trap for the ark. After all, it might just have been a malign coincidence that all their troubles started when the ark arrived on their territory. The cart that is to carry the ark to the place of its own choice is pulled by two cows that have recently given birth and been separated from their calves, so that all their instincts would be to return home to find their young and suckle them. If the cows head off in another direction, then it will be clear that the ark is overruling their instincts. And that is, of course, what happens: lowing in pain, the cows take the ark to its home, not their own.

Creator God,
you made us all in your image:
may we discern you in all that we see,
and serve you in all that we do;
through Jesus Christ our Lord.

COLLECT

Wednesday 11 July

Psalm **119.153-end**
1 Samuel 7
Luke 21.20-28

1 Samuel 7

'Do not cease to cry out to the Lord our God for us' (v.8)

The homecoming of the ark is a strangely subdued affair. It wanders about a bit and finally comes to rest in a backwater, with one man to act as guardian and attendant. The mighty ark, which had shown such power in the land of the Philistines, is becalmed and the focus shifts to Samuel. There is a precariousness to the whole situation, now that the era of fierce conquest, marked by Joshua and the Judges, has passed, and the long tradition of priesthood, ending in Eli and his sons, has come to an end. The people lack purpose and direction: they are still surrounded by foes, but they seem to have lost their sense of the presence and protection of God.

It is Samuel who holds the vital but lonely position of straddling two worlds. In this time of insecurity, Samuel can still exercise the role of the Judge (v.15), like Deborah, although we have been told that his calling is more as a prophet, one who carries the words of God, and he can also pick up the priestly task that Eli and his sons abandoned. In these multiple roles, Samuel calls the people to repentance, and intercedes for them with sacrifices, and the Lord answers him and protects the people. Samuel alone holds all the roles that enable connection between God and the people. It is for this that Hannah gave him to the Lord.

COLLECT

Merciful God,
you have prepared for those who love you
such good things as pass our understanding:
pour into our hearts such love toward you
that we, loving you in all things and above all things,
may obtain your promises,
which exceed all that we can desire;
through Jesus Christ your Son our Lord,
who is alive and reigns with you,
in the unity of the Holy Spirit,
one God, now and for ever.

Thursday 12 July

1 Samuel 8

'... they have rejected me from being king over them' (v.7)

In view of how much the safety and well-being of the people depends on Samuel, it is not surprising that they start to worry as Samuel grows old. Samuel's sons, like Eli's, cannot share Samuel's calling, which is personal, not institutional. Samuel, the child born from God's gift, cannot then turn the gift into an hereditary office. The irony of this theological point is going to become clearer, as the people press Samuel to give them stable institutions of state, and not leave them at the whim of God. The people want a king, like other nations, despite the fact that they only exist at all because God has been their king. God brought them out of Egypt, made them a nation, gave them a home, and now they would like him to bow out.

The conversation between God and Samuel (vv.7-9) is telling. God has never pulled his punches with Samuel, from the time when he gave the small boy the terrible message of destruction for Eli, and now, again, God is frank. Samuel has heard this request for a king as a rejection of his own ministry and that of his sons, but God shows him the bigger picture. The people are rejecting God himself, and God is going to let them. God is going to work with their choices, hurtful as they are.

Creator God,
you made us all in your image:
may we discern you in all that we see,
and serve you in all that we do;
through Jesus Christ our Lord.

COLLECT

Friday 13 July

1 Samuel 9.1-14

'There was not a man ... more handsome than he' (v.2)

We, the readers, come fresh from overhearing the conversation between God and Samuel. We have heard Samuel laying it on thick: the people will be exchanging their God-won freedom for a virtual slavery to an earthly king. And we have heard the people insisting that they want a king, like the other nations. So now, tongue in cheek, the story moves to show us Saul, everyone's ideal of a king. He's rich, young, tall and good looking, and it is clear that God, almost jokingly, is going to give his people exactly what they thought they wanted. God is co-operating with his people's wishes, but that doesn't mean he can't laugh at them.

Insidiously, the story is showing us Saul on two levels at the same time. Blandly, the narrative describes Saul's outward appearance, while also describing his inability to find a few lost donkeys, and his total lack of initiative, which makes him dependent upon his more proactive boy. It is the boy, not Saul, who has a strategy and the wherewithal to make it happen.

So, as the young women of Zuph fall over themselves to help this tall, dark stranger, we await his meeting with Samuel, knowing that what is to come is not going to be an unmixed blessing. Poor Saul, unwittingly walking into a new world.

COLLECT

Merciful God,
you have prepared for those who love you
such good things as pass our understanding:
pour into our hearts such love toward you
that we, loving you in all things and above all things,
may obtain your promises,
which exceed all that we can desire;
through Jesus Christ your Son our Lord,
who is alive and reigns with you,
in the unity of the Holy Spirit,
one God, now and for ever.

| *Reflection by* **Jane Williams**

Psalm 147
1 Samuel 9.15 – 10.1
Luke 22.14-23

1 Samuel 9.15 – 10.1

'The Lord has anointed you ruler over his people Israel' (10.1)

Although Saul set off in all innocence to look for some missing donkeys, Samuel and God had other plans. Samuel and God are arranging a transfer of power, though neither of them mentions the fact openly.

Samuel has been the sole authority in Israel since his boyhood, but now he follows God's directions and greets the new king. But while he does this with impressive graciousness, the end result must be utterly bewildering to Saul, who has not been part of the consultations between God and Samuel. Samuel may have felt that this was an abnegation of power, but his every word and deed must make Saul feel like an ignorant child. Samuel knows who he is and what his fate is to be – he even knows where the missing donkeys are – while Saul knows nothing. Samuel anoints him king, offers him fealty with a kiss, and declares God's purpose to him, all without giving Saul any explanation at all.

God, too, is allowing Saul to exercise borrowed power. Where once God defended his people from the Philistines with one roar of his voice (see 7.10), now Saul is going to be the people's saviour, since that is what the people have requested

And so Samuel anoints the first human king of Israel, and a new chapter begins. But if Saul has any sense, he will read the situation aright and know where true power still resides.

Creator God,
you made us all in your image:
may we discern you in all that we see,
and serve you in all that we do;
through Jesus Christ our Lord.

COLLECT

Monday 16 July

1 Samuel 10.1-16

'Is Saul also among the prophets?' (vv.11, 12)

'No', is the answer. Saul is not among the prophets. A different destiny awaits him.

So begins the story of Israel's first king. Having read the preceding chapters, we know that the writer is deeply ambivalent about the whole idea of kingship. On the one hand, if the nation is to establish itself amongst its neighbours, it needs a ruler who can represent them effectively. On the other hand, they who are ruled by the God of Israel need no human ruler. Samuel, who is among the prophets, reluctantly agrees to give the people what they want, even though he suspects it will not turn out well.

So Saul's kingship is born. Saul is anointed on a visit to consult Samuel about missing donkeys, hardly an auspicious beginning. Nor is being overtaken by a prophetic frenzy likely to do him much good when strategic state decisions need to be made. Saul gives the impression of being a passive, rather puzzled player in events. What he has going for him, we are told in the previous chapter, is height and looks, which while a bonus in a king, are not necessarily a qualification.

Israel has, perhaps, sold out. It has opted to become a nation like any other. We are invited to ask ourselves what kind of leadership is appropriate for the people of God, as we follow this leader's story.

COLLECT

Lord of all power and might,
the author and giver of all good things:
graft in our hearts the love of your name,
increase in us true religion,
nourish us with all goodness,
and of your great mercy keep us in the same;
through Jesus Christ your Son our Lord,
who is alive and reigns with you,
in the unity of the Holy Spirit,
one God, now and for ever.

Reflection by **Gillian Cooper**

Psalms **5**, 6 (8)
1 Samuel 10.17-end
Luke 22.31-38

Tuesday 17 July

1 Samuel 10.17-end

'... today you have rejected your God' (v.19)

Israel has turned from allegiance to the God who saved them from slavery, made them a people and gave them a land. In God's place they want to put a king, a human ruler they will be able to see and hear, who will speak for them and protect them in a way they can understand. We sympathise, perhaps, more than the biblical authors appear to do.

The contrast is stark. Israel can be ruled by the God who created them, or by a young man who hides from the task among the baggage. How foolish they seem when they respond with such enthusiasm to his height. Yet how we understand, we whose national leaders have to look and sound good on the television.

Trouble is already brewing for Saul, however. Not everyone is happy with his kingship, and there are ruthless enemies to deal with. This king is not going to sit peacefully in a palace. The people are going to need him to turn into a proper king.

We are reading the start of perhaps the most tragic story in the Bible. We want things to work out for poor Saul, chosen against his will, but already we suspect that he will not easily grow into the task. Perhaps we even wonder whether it is a cruel God who uses him to show the inadequacy of human rule. We will make our judgments as the story unfolds.

Generous God,
you give us gifts and make them grow:
though our faith is small as mustard seed,
make it grow to your glory
and the flourishing of your kingdom;
through Jesus Christ our Lord.

COLLECT

Wednesday 18 July

1 Samuel 11

'... the spirit of God came upon Saul in power' (v.6)

Despite everything, it is a good start for King Saul. He finds the strength of will and courage to lead his people to a victory that is both decisive and merciful.

This sudden instance of strong leadership does not, however, arise out of Saul's own character and ability. 'The spirit of God came upon Saul' we are told. At the beginning of his journey to the kingship, Saul was caught up in the frenzied worship of a band of prophets; so now, he is taken over again by the divine spirit. The resulting violence of his actions shows a man who is under external influence. This is not the young man who hid away from his calling

So it should be, we may think. If he is God's choice, naturally he will be able to draw on God's inspiration at these moments when he needs to lead decisively. God ignites him, and he gains both confidence in himself and the respect of his people.

We remember, however, the uncertainty about whether there should be a king at all. For the moment, the experiment seems to be a success, but it all hinges on God's active favour. What will happen if that favour is ever withdrawn? Even now, Saul's rule sits on a knife edge.

Do leaders, perhaps, need character of their own as well as the blessing of God?

COLLECT

Lord of all power and might,
the author and giver of all good things:
graft in our hearts the love of your name,
increase in us true religion,
nourish us with all goodness,
and of your great mercy keep us in the same;
through Jesus Christ your Son our Lord,
who is alive and reigns with you,
in the unity of the Holy Spirit,
one God, now and for ever.

| *Reflection by* **Gillian Cooper**

Psalms 14, **15**, 16
1 Samuel 12
Luke 22.47-62

Thursday 19 July

1 Samuel 12

'... consider what great things he has done for you' (v.24)

We thought the matter of Saul's kingship was settled. Today we discover that is far from the case. Samuel is not happy, and neither, he insists, is God.

In a compelling piece of rhetoric, Samuel (or rather the writer of 1 Samuel) sets out the past and the future of the people who stand accused before Samuel and before God. They have forgotten their history. From slaves they became a nation, and they have forgotten that they did not do it themselves. They are guilty of profound ingratitude. They have demanded to be like other nations, but they are not like other nations. They are God's people, and God alone is their king.

In a moment of insight, the people realize what they have done. In response Samuel offers some good news: God will go along with the king plan. There is a condition, however. They and the king must be servants of God.

The writer knows where this story will end. History once forgotten can be forgotten again. Kings naturally get above themselves, and woe betide God's people now as then if they set human leaders above God. Israel will have to lose everything, including its king, before it learns this lesson. For now, however, Saul is king, with God's blessing, albeit conditional. He will have to demonstrate that a human king can rule effectively under God. We suspect that this king is not up to the task.

Generous God,
you give us gifts and make them grow:
though our faith is small as mustard seed,
make it grow to your glory
and the flourishing of your kingdom;
through Jesus Christ our Lord.

COLLECT

Friday 20 July

1 Samuel 13.5-18

'You have done foolishly' (v.13)

Saul seemed to be doing well, holding back the ever-present Philistines. But there needs to be prayer and sacrifice to convince the Israelites that they fight with God on their side. Only the prophet Samuel can properly offer the sacrifice, and Saul has been told to wait. But finally a desperate Saul, seeing his troops losing their nerve, performs the rite himself. He has decided that he knows best, and that decision represents a turning away from God and his calling that will never be reversed.

It may seem to us a sensible decision, by a commander who knows the fragility of his soldiers' morale. Samuel's view is very different, and his condemnation is devastating. This apparently small act of disobedience marks the beginning of the end for Saul. Indeed, his successor is already waiting in the wings. We have several chapters to wait before we discover the identity of this mysterious 'man after the Lord's own heart', already selected. Meanwhile, Saul is left to deal with the Philistines without the backing of God or his prophet.

This story is tragic enough to make one weep. The tall, handsome charismatic man is bowed down with the knowledge that he can never be the king God needs. And Israel is discovering the hard way a lesson for us all, that it is not always good for us to get from God exactly what we want.

COLLECT

Lord of all power and might,
the author and giver of all good things:
graft in our hearts the love of your name,
increase in us true religion,
nourish us with all goodness,
and of your great mercy keep us in the same;
through Jesus Christ your Son our Lord,
who is alive and reigns with you,
in the unity of the Holy Spirit,
one God, now and for ever.

| *Reflection by* **Gillian Cooper**

Psalms 20, 21, **23**
1 Samuel 13.19 – 14.15
Luke 23.1-12

1 Samuel 13.19 – 14.15

'... the Lord has given them into our hand' (14.10)

Today we meet a new character in this drama, Saul's son Jonathan. Jonathan is very different from his father: decisive rather than vacillating; brave rather than tentative; commanding support; and crucially, backed by God.

Background detail tells us of the weak position of the Israelites, without even the skill to make proper weapons. Taking on the Philistines will require something special, and Jonathan provides it with his daring raid into the enemy camp.

No military leader would commend Jonathan's actions. They are foolhardy in the extreme. Yet it is the careful Saul who is condemned by the biblical writers, and Jonathan who is the hero. This is not the story of a military campaign; rather it is about the ongoing formation of God's people. The big question is the extent to which they are a nation like any other, with a monarchy and sensible military strategy, or a people faithful to a God who has led them from slavery to a land of their own.

In other circumstances we might want to ask why God was, unfairly, not also interested in the wellbeing of the Philistines. But that would be the wrong question here. The Philistines are incidental to the main story. We are invited to ask instead about the nature of faithfulness between God and his people. Where do the true loyalties of the people of God lie? That is a question we might well ask of ourselves also.

> Generous God,
> you give us gifts and make them grow:
> though our faith is small as mustard seed,
> make it grow to your glory
> and the flourishing of your kingdom;
> through Jesus Christ our Lord.

COLLECT

Monday 23 July

Psalms 27, **30**
1 Samuel 14.24-46
Luke 23.13-25

1 Samuel 14.24-46
'Saul committed a very rash act' (v.24)

Oh dear, here we go again. Even Saul's best attempts at piety backfire. First there was a sacrifice that should not have been made. Now his sacrificial act, intended to please God, is described as 'rash'. We find ourselves relieved that Jonathan does not pay the penalty for his unwitting transgression. Clearly both God and the people recognize that Jonathan is the member of this family with the most leadership potential and deserves a measure of protection.

What are we to make of this extraordinary story? The storyteller is working with some basic principles. First, promises matter and are not to be made lightly. Second, an individual's transgression, even an accidental transgression of a ridiculous rule, has an effect on the whole community and has to be dealt with.

Although the story, with its drawing of lots and eating from honeycombs, has some features that strike us as primitive, we recognize the force of these principles. We know how much damage can be done by the unwise decisions of world leaders, for example. We know too about the effect on the wider community of individual wrongdoing, whether that is deliberate abuse or an accidental collision. The Church is in the business of repentance and healing on more than an individual level.

For Saul, though, healing is a long way off. For the moment, it is stalemate with the Philistines, and Saul appears to have learned nothing.

COLLECT

Almighty Lord and everlasting God,
we beseech you to direct, sanctify and govern
    both our hearts and bodies
in the ways of your laws
    and the works of your commandments;
that through your most mighty protection, both here and ever,
we may be preserved in body and soul;
through our Lord and Saviour Jesus Christ,
who is alive and reigns with you,
in the unity of the Holy Spirit,
one God, now and for ever.

208 | *Reflection by* **Gillian Cooper**

Tuesday 24 July

1 Samuel 15.1-23

'I have gone on the mission on which the Lord sent me' (v.20)

Saul gets it wrong yet again. He has apparently not learned that it is best to follow instructions to the letter. Nor has he learned not to have anything to do with sacrifices, his alleged reason for holding onto the pick of the Amalekite animals. He is defensive in the face of Samuel's accusation: 'I have obeyed the voice of the Lord,' he says. He cannot understand why he is being condemned and threatened yet again.

Saul's story poses many questions for the reader. We are rightly squeamish about God's demand for wholesale slaughter of defeated enemies, including their children, and we rightly question the ethics of the writer as a result. But that is not where we are supposed to focus our attention. Instead, we turn our gaze on the protagonists: Saul – defensive, weak, anxious, out of his depth; and Samuel – certain, determined, wanting only to secure the future of the nation after his death, with or without a king.

We do not read the saddest verse in this whole story, right at the end of the chapter. 'Samuel did not see Saul again until the day of his death, but Samuel grieved over Saul' (v.35). Saul is now truly on his own. The kingship experiment has gone disastrously wrong, and God and Samuel knew it would. There must be a new start. Saul's tragedy is heading for its inevitable end.

Lord God,
your Son left the riches of heaven
and became poor for our sake:
when we prosper save us from pride,
when we are needy save us from despair,
that we may trust in you alone;
through Jesus Christ our Lord.

COLLECT

Wednesday 25 July
James the Apostle

2 Kings 1.9-15
'O man of God, please' (v.13)

We leave Saul's story today to celebrate James the Apostle. James wanted to call down fire from heaven on Samaritans who did not welcome Jesus. In the gospel story the fire did not fall; here it does, and it is part of an ongoing power struggle.

The king needs help. And because he is a king, he can command it. He has not reckoned with the refusal of God's prophet to obey commands from anyone except God. Elijah has a track record of stubborn and destructive resistance in the face of kings and queens who throw their weight around, and he is not going to be ordered about by a nonentity like Ahaziah. It needs someone to say please nicely, which the third captain sent wisely does. Not that it benefits Ahaziah, who dies anyway.

Many years have passed, but we hear echoes of Saul and Samuel facing up to each other. Kings or prophets? Structured, hierarchical systems or freedom of inspiration? Human rule or God's rule? The books of Samuel and Kings describe the attempt of God's people to have both. Sometimes the balance is right; often it is not.

What of us? Hierarchical, stable structures of Church leadership? Or the voice of inspiration and resistance? The biblical stories tell us that both are needed. Getting the balance right, though, can be a matter of life or death.

COLLECT

Merciful God,
whose holy apostle Saint James,
leaving his father and all that he had,
was obedient to the calling of your Son Jesus Christ
and followed him even to death:
help us, forsaking the false attractions of the world,
to be ready at all times to answer your call without delay;
through Jesus Christ your Son our Lord,
who is alive and reigns with you,
in the unity of the Holy Spirit,
one God, now and for ever.

| *Reflection by* **Gillian Cooper**

Psalm 37*
1 Samuel 17.1-30
Luke 23.56*b* – 24.12

Thursday 26 July

1 Samuel 17.1-30

'David left the things in charge of the keeper of the baggage'
(v.22)

We have missed the vital moment, the introduction of our storyteller's hero, the golden boy of Israelite history, ruddy, with beautiful eyes, and handsome (1 Samuel 16.12). Despite God's assertion that this time he will look only on the heart, God's second choice for king is gorgeous. He is also musical, we have learned, and has found his niche as a favourite with Saul.

Today we meet him again, as if for the first time. Clearly one introduction to the story is not enough for David. In this version David is still in charge of the family sheep, and has not yet met Saul. Our clever storyteller subtly sets up the contrast between the two. Whereas Saul hid in the baggage, David drops his delivery there so that he can rush off to find out about the campaign. David's first recorded words are illuminating; he wants to fight for God, and he wants a reward. After the defiant talk, however, he turns back into a petulant boy: 'It was only a question'.

It is a perfect introduction to perhaps the most charismatic, fascinating and complex character in the Old Testament story. It sets the tone for a life full of heroism and devotion, damaged by serious weaknesses of character. But we would not, of course, expect God's choice to be perfect in every way. If he was, what hope would there be for any of us?

Almighty Lord and everlasting God,
we beseech you to direct, sanctify and govern
both our hearts and bodies
in the ways of your laws
and the works of your commandments;
that through your most mighty protection, both here and ever,
we may be preserved in body and soul;
through our Lord and Saviour Jesus Christ,
who is alive and reigns with you,
in the unity of the Holy Spirit,
one God, now and for ever.

COLLECT

Reflection by **Gillian Cooper**

Friday 27 July

1 Samuel 17.31-54

'... in the name of the Lord of hosts' (v.45)

So our hero fights his Philistine, and an idiom is born. In a scene reminiscent of a James Bond film, the bad guy fatally pauses for conversation before getting on with the killing. Meanwhile, David shows himself to be as psychologically skilled as he is brave. Again, the contrast with Saul is striking. David does not hesitate. He is not afraid of unequal odds. Above all, he is certain of the support of the Lord in whose name he acts.

David will eventually become the touchstone against whom all other kings are measured. He will turn out to be every bit as flawed as Saul, but Saul is a born loser, and David is a winner. There is much injustice in this story. We can, of course, argue that Saul is disobedient, whereas David has more faith. But it is difficult to avoid the inconvenient perception that Saul has been set up to fail, and David will succeed however badly he behaves. It may not be fair, but it is at least realistic. Contrast the charm of a John Kennedy or Bill Clinton with Richard Nixon for a more recent example.

David will, however, become much more than the greatest king of Israel. He will be the ancestor of a 'son of David' who also fought the powers of evil and won by unconventional means. David fires the theological imagination, and so his flaws can largely be forgiven.

COLLECT

Almighty Lord and everlasting God,
we beseech you to direct, sanctify and govern
    both our hearts and bodies
in the ways of your laws
    and the works of your commandments;
that through your most mighty protection, both here and ever,
we may be preserved in body and soul;
through our Lord and Saviour Jesus Christ,
who is alive and reigns with you,
in the unity of the Holy Spirit,
one God, now and for ever.

| *Reflection by* **Gillian Cooper**

Psalms 41, **42**, 43
1 Samuel 17.55 – 18.16
Luke 24.36-end

Saturday 28 July

1 Samuel 17.55 – 18.16
'... all Israel and Judah loved David' (18.16)

As well they might. Everyone falls in love with David, even poor tormented Saul, who knows when he is beaten.

Curiously, Saul seems here never to have met the young man who has been his court musician. Inconsistencies are not always ironed out in this story. Its writer seems to want to include all the stories about David, even when they contradict one another. David became an almost mythical figure, around whom stories gathered. So we let the inconsistency go, and focus on David in the court of King Saul. He has won the affection of Saul's son; soon he will marry Saul's daughter. Saul's people sing songs praising David above Saul. We might dislike David if any of this were his own doing. Saul, angry and afraid, makes the first of many half-hearted attempts to kill David. David, however, thrives because 'the Lord was with him'.

Public opinion tends to favour the fresh face over the establishment. David has courage, charm and looks, and he wins battles while Saul sits moodily at home. Israel is heading for a golden age, ruled by a king who has an ongoing close relationship with the Lord. It cannot of course last, while the king is human – all too human as it turns out. It will need a very different king from the line of David to fulfil all David's promise.

Lord God,
your Son left the riches of heaven
and became poor for our sake:
when we prosper save us from pride,
when we are needy save us from despair,
that we may trust in you alone;
through Jesus Christ our Lord.

COLLECT

Monday 30 July

Acts 1.1-14

'... as they were watching, he was lifted up' (v.9)

Luke–Acts is a two-volume work. Luke is the gospel of Jesus; Acts is the gospel of the Holy Spirit. Already we see an excited anticipation of the Holy Spirit in verses 5 and 8. The disciples will then cease to be confused by what's happening, as they have been all through Luke, and will be ready to stand tall and tell people the extraordinary, life-changing story of Jesus. And then the apostles will reverse the journey Jesus took from Galilee through Samaria to Judaea and Jerusalem, and start their journey from Jerusalem through Judaea to Samaria and then to the ends of the earth – that is, Athens and finally Rome.

But first comes one of the story's strangest episodes, at least to the modern, literal mind. Jesus 'was lifted up, and a cloud took him out of their sight'. This was not mere primitive thinking. It was a way of saying that Jesus was finally leaving 'our space' and going to 'God's space', God's dimension of reality – though 'earth' and 'heaven' were actually both God's reality and would one day be joined together in what we call the 'second coming'.

'I'll be back,' said Jesus (as well as Arnold Schwarzenegger's Terminator). In the meantime the disciples committed themselves to expectant prayer, awaiting this strange 'Holy Spirit' and the return of Jesus. I wonder what the return of Christ means for us today?

COLLECT

Almighty God,
who sent your Holy Spirit
to be the life and light of your Church:
open our hearts to the riches of your grace,
that we may bring forth the fruit of the Spirit
in love and joy and peace;
through Jesus Christ your Son our Lord,
who is alive and reigns with you,
in the unity of the Holy Spirit,
one God, now and for ever.

| *Reflection by* **John Pritchard**

Tuesday 31 July

Acts 1.15-end

*'So they proposed two, Joseph ... also known as Justus,
and Matthias' (v.23)*

Two things happen here. Judas meets his sticky end, described almost with relish, and the disciples have to be returned to their full complement of twelve, echoing the twelve tribes of ancient Israel as those who were central to God's plan and purpose. Indeed there is a sense – made even clearer in the Greek – that these are *necessary* events, not just matters of chance. For Judas, Scripture 'had to be fulfilled, which the Holy Spirit [no less] ... foretold'. And for the disciples, 'one of these *must* become a witness ...'. Clearly the Holy Spirit is already in charge.

In the Spirit-led ballot Matthias is the one chosen. The crucial qualification was to have been a witness to the resurrection, as this was the explosive event that gave birth to the missionary movement that became the Church. But I always have a soft spot for Justus. He wasn't chosen and had to return to the shadows. Such is the experience of many in our society and in church life. They aren't chosen; they aren't 'the special one'. But these are the people who make up the majority and quietly get on with the job, as Justus doubtless did, following Christ and living faithfully.

Perhaps today we could keep a look out for a Justus and somehow honour that person, as Christ would have done.

Gracious Father,
revive your Church in our day,
and make her holy, strong and faithful,
for your glory's sake
in Jesus Christ our Lord.

COLLECT

Wednesday 1 August

Psalm **119.57-80**
1 Samuel 20.18-end
Acts 2.1-21

Acts 2.1-21

'... there came a sound like the rush of a violent wind' (v.2)

Now we see the promised Spirit in action. We have the sights and sounds of fire and wind, reminding us of the Spirit coming on Jesus at his baptism, an event with its own sight (the dove) and sound (the voice from heaven). We're shown the power that will drive through the rest of Acts, the 'violent wind' that will take Peter, Paul and the others to the ends of the earth (Rome), changing people's lives as it sweeps through the known world. The tongues of fire symbolize the speeches that make up one third of Acts, here foreshadowed in Peter's speech that was preached to 'every nation under heaven'. A map of the places mentioned shows a complete circle around the ancient near east. The Spirit is up and running!

The question we can't avoid is why the Spirit seems only to be 'up and dawdling' in the lives of many of us. Certainly we can imagine the need for a turbocharge to start the process off at the beginning of Acts, so the effect of the Spirit may not always be so overwhelming, but still, aren't we missing something rather vital? Perhaps we could invite God's Spirit – even tentatively, and even today – to blow through the cold, dusty rooms of our lives, and bring us a touch of the sun-drenched life of the Spirit that we see in Acts.

COLLECT

Almighty God,
who sent your Holy Spirit
to be the life and light of your Church:
open our hearts to the riches of your grace,
that we may bring forth the fruit of the Spirit
in love and joy and peace;
through Jesus Christ your Son our Lord,
who is alive and reigns with you,
in the unity of the Holy Spirit,
one God, now and for ever.

| *Reflection by* **John Pritchard**

Psalms 56, **57** (63*)
1 Samuel 21.1 – 22.5
Acts 2.22-36

Thursday 2 August

Acts 2.22-36

'... it was impossible for him to be held in [death's] power' (v.24)

It doesn't actually sound like the sort of sermon the occasion needed. The rather complicated argument about David sounds somewhat convoluted, when a rousing call to action based on the life of Jesus might have seemed more appropriate. However, Luke is using the sermon to tell the reader what he thinks is going on, and the use of Psalm 16 and the reference to God's foreknowledge demonstrate that the Scriptures do indeed refer to Jesus and, again, that the Holy Spirit is running the show.

The touchstone and source of this confidence is always the resurrection, referred to at the beginning and the end of the speech. 'God raised him up [from death] because it was impossible for him to be held in its power' – 'This Jesus God raised up, and of that all of us are witnesses'. The resurrection ricochets around the early Church, making everything new and hopeful. The Good Friday fear of the disciples has been sent packing and now nothing seems impossible. Isn't this the confidence we need today, that Christianity isn't weary with age and misuse, but freshly minted for this generation, as for every other?

And isn't this a good way to face the day – quietly confident in God's lively presence in every challenge and opportunity that will come our way?

Gracious Father,
revive your Church in our day,
and make her holy, strong and faithful,
for your glory's sake
in Jesus Christ our Lord.

COLLECT

Friday 3 August

Acts 2.37-end

'... they spent much time together' (v.46)

Many a preacher has been envious of the effectiveness of Peter's first sermon – 3000 converts! And many a vicar has been challenged by the lovely picture of the close fellowship described by Luke in his summary of life in the early Church. There's a clear emphasis on the quality of their life together. They had all things in common, looked after anyone in need, broke bread in their homes, ate joyfully and shared food generously. It sounds idyllic – though we see in Paul's letters that rivalries, arguments and controversy would soon appear, men and women being as they are. But for now it's all good news and people were fascinated and impressed. 'And day by day the Lord added to their number.'

It's usually a mistake to try and read off directly from the New Testament what to do in a contemporary situation, as if historical, social, cultural and other contextual issues don't matter. But this familiar description of life in the early Church, particularly the fourfold 'apostles' teaching and fellowship ... breaking of bread and the prayers', does give a valuable template for a contemporary Church to re-contextualize. A vibrant church will be learning, loving, praying, and sharing the meal that says it all. I wonder how effectively your own church is doing those things? And what you could do to help your church to do them better?

COLLECT

Almighty God,
who sent your Holy Spirit
to be the life and light of your Church:
open our hearts to the riches of your grace,
that we may bring forth the fruit of the Spirit
in love and joy and peace;
through Jesus Christ your Son our Lord,
who is alive and reigns with you,
in the unity of the Holy Spirit,
one God, now and for ever.

| *Reflection by* **John Pritchard**

Saturday 4 August

Acts 3.1-10

'Peter looked intently at him ... and said, "Look at us."' (v.4)

In 2010 performance artist Marina Abramović sat at a table in the New York Museum of Modern Art with an empty chair opposite her where visitors could sit for as long as they wanted. She sat there whenever the museum was open for three months, and the faces of the visitors were all photographed. Their responses were hugely varied; some were disconcerted, unsure, some bold, belligerent – and some of them wept. There's great power in looking.

Peter looked 'intently' at the lame man begging at the gate and told him to look back. This is so different from the embarrassed averting of the eyes that goes on when we pass homeless people on the streets of our cities. But Peter needed the transparency of true encounter if he was to pass on the most precious thing he had – the healing power of Jesus. He didn't have money (that was shared in common), but he had much more. Peter gave all that love could give. He gave healing 'in the name of Jesus'. It was not his own, it was the continuing work of Jesus, and it continues right down to our own day.

But it starts with transparency, openness and genuine need. Then God can act. The challenge to us is to look honestly and without averting our gaze at the needs of the world and then to do what we can do 'in the name of Jesus'. Today will have its own opportunities – if we'll look.

Gracious Father,
revive your Church in our day,
and make her holy, strong and faithful,
for your glory's sake
in Jesus Christ our Lord.

COLLECT

Reflection by **John Pritchard** | 219

Monday 6 August
Transfiguration of our Lord

Psalms 27, 150
Ecclesiasticus 48.1-10
or 1 Kings 19.1-16
1 John 3.1-3

1 John 3.1-3

'... we will be like him, for we will see him as he is' (v.2)

'And our eyes at last shall see him, through his own redeeming love.' We sing these words from 'Once in Royal David's City' at carol services every year, but do we realize how amazing that claim really is? We are already seen by God as brothers and sisters of Jesus and so 'we are God's children now'. So far, so very good. But the promise in 1 John goes further than this. It says we will eventually see Jesus as he is, and because of this '*we will be like him.*' (Pause to recover.)

Of course it begs the question of what Jesus will be like, and basically we have no idea. The transfiguration gave three of the disciples the briefest of glimpses, and they saw in that moment that he belonged to both heaven and earth, a promise of the final new reality when both worlds, heaven and earth, will have fused together. So does this mean that we will be ourselves (earthly) but infinitely more so (heavenly)? Does it mean that we will enjoy everything of value here (earth) but transformed into what it was ultimately meant to be (heaven)? Does it mean we will love like him?

We can't know. But what we can do in the meantime is to *practise* seeing Christ as he is; we can practise the direction of our gaze.

COLLECT

Father in heaven,
whose Son Jesus Christ was wonderfully transfigured
before chosen witnesses upon the holy mountain,
and spoke of the exodus he would accomplish at Jerusalem:
give us strength so to hear his voice and bear our cross
that in the world to come we may see him as he is;
who is alive and reigns with you,
in the unity of the Holy Spirit,
one God, now and for ever.

| *Reflection by* **John Pritchard**

Tuesday 7 August

Acts 4.1-12

'... by what name did you do this?' (v.7)

Not often, but occasionally, I've been able to say to someone, 'Just use my name; that'll get you in.' The 'name' can operate as a key to open doors. So it was with the name of Jesus; his name is used throughout Acts as the key to new possibilities, often access to healing. But that name wasn't welcome in many parts of post-resurrection Palestine, just as it often isn't welcome today. In Jerusalem it was a threat to the established power structures. The aristocratic Sadducees didn't believe in the resurrection, so they didn't believe in the power of a dead 'messiah' to heal. Annas, Caiaphas and the others didn't want the delicate political, social and economic relationships in Jerusalem to be jeopardized, because they were top of the pile. So this claim of resurrection and the healing of the lame man had to be faced head on.

And here we see a Peter almost unrecognizable from the defeated deny-er of Jesus who avoided the crucifixion and then skulked through the streets of Jerusalem trying to avoid a similar fate. Here is a confident, carefree Peter challenging these pious authorities with the crime of crucifying Jesus, the stone they had rejected but who is in fact the cornerstone of a new world. What made the difference? The resurrection and the Holy Spirit.

Are we beginning to get the message?

COLLECT

Let your merciful ears, O Lord,
be open to the prayers of your humble servants;
and that they may obtain their petitions
make them to ask such things as shall please you;
through Jesus Christ your Son our Lord,
who is alive and reigns with you,
in the unity of the Holy Spirit,
one God, now and for ever.

Wednesday 8 August

Acts 4.13-31

'... recognized them as companions of Jesus' (v.13)

They were stuck. There before them was a man who had been sick and lame and was now clearly fit and well. And there before them were two men who had no rabbinic training, just ordinary fishermen from Galilee, who were spiritually fit and well because they had one undeniable trump card – they had been 'companions of Jesus'. What could these establishment figures do? Answer: what establishment figures have always been tempted to do – threaten and bully their opponents. They warned them 'not to speak or teach at all in the name of Jesus'. They might as well have tried to shut the door on a gale, and Peter and John told them so. Nothing was going to stop them talking about Jesus.

I wonder why Christians, who have been gifted with the good news about Jesus, are almost the opposite of Peter and John – it often seems that nothing can get us talking about Jesus. Peter and John returned to their lodgings and they prayed with their friends not that the authorities would be nicer to them or be struck down with a plague, but that they, the followers of Jesus, would be given all the boldness they needed to keep up the pressure of their witness. And in answer there was a minor earthquake and they were re-filled with the Holy Spirit.

It's a good lesson. We all leak. Pray daily for more of God's Spirit.

COLLECT

Let your merciful ears, O Lord,
be open to the prayers of your humble servants;
and that they may obtain their petitions
make them to ask such things as shall please you;
through Jesus Christ your Son our Lord,
who is alive and reigns with you,
in the unity of the Holy Spirit,
one God, now and for ever.

| *Reflection by* **John Pritchard**

Thursday 9 August

Acts 4.32 – 5.11

*'Look, the feet of those who have buried your husband are
at the door, and they will carry you out.' (5.9)*

This doesn't exactly feel like a moral tale. Indeed it sounds grimly unforgiving and fits badly with the joyous, Spirit-filled, property-sharing community growing steadily at the heart of Jerusalem. Presumably Luke is wanting Theophilus and other readers to realize that there are high stakes at play in this fast-growing movement. God's holiness is not something to treat lightly. In David's time Uzzah had also found this out when he simply went to steady the Ark as it trundled towards Jerusalem and was immediately and tragically struck down for his pains (2 Samuel 6). The holiness of God has the terrible power of both glory and destruction. Moral? Don't mess with it.

The other moral is to do with straight dealing. We have to assume that Ananias lied and that when he brought the proceeds of the land-sale to the apostles he'd said this was all the money he had raised. Otherwise he could simply have been open and said that he was giving such and such a proportion of the sale money. But lying cuts at the heart of community; it undermines trust and fractures the community's integrity. Nevertheless, the swift despatch of both husband and wife without opportunity of repentance inevitably grates with us as we read it now.

Did it happen exactly like this? Who knows. But at least we can see that actions have consequences. In belief and behaviour God always calls us to aim high.

Lord of heaven and earth,
as Jesus taught his disciples to be persistent in prayer,
give us patience and courage never to lose hope,
but always to bring our prayers before you;
through Jesus Christ our Lord.

COLLECT

Friday 10 August

Acts 5.12-26

'... tell the people the whole message about this life' (v.20)

Now the healing power of the risen Christ begins to take off. Even getting into Peter's shadow seems to be sufficient, because Peter had been with Jesus. People are pouring in to be healed (v.16) and joining the believers in 'great numbers'. It was time for the authorities to take a stand. Unfortunately those authorities didn't realize what they were up against. It's no good trying to put God's power into prison. Angels come and let it out. And the angel this time tells the apostles to get back to the temple and 'tell the people the whole message about this life'.

'This life.' It's a strange description of what was not yet 'the Way', and certainly not yet 'Christianity'. It was a way of life, a movement, a distinctive approach to life and faith, rooted in the life, death and new life of Jesus, and lived out in prayer, communal ownership, breaking of bread, mutual care, healing, and telling the story. It was no use trying to hold back such a driving force for good. 'This life' was unstoppable. So it can be today when we Christians get beyond living the Western dream with a religious add-on, and instead embrace the full-on, radical discipleship of 'this Life'.

Still, there's no time like today.

COLLECT

Let your merciful ears, O Lord,
be open to the prayers of your humble servants;
and that they may obtain their petitions
make them to ask such things as shall please you;
through Jesus Christ your Son our Lord,
who is alive and reigns with you,
in the unity of the Holy Spirit,
one God, now and for ever.

| *Reflection by* **John Pritchard**

Psalms **76**, 79
2 Samuel 2.1-11
Acts 5.27-end

Saturday 11 August

Acts 5.27-end

'... if it is of God, you will not be able to overthrow them' (v.39)

Gamaliel is one of the good guys. He was already a deeply respected rabbi and he knew something more important was at stake here than a gang of northerners getting people excited about an upstart 'messiah'. They needed to ask a deeper question. Peter, newly released by the angel and newly re-arrested by the temple police, had just had another go at the high priest. Every time Peter was called to account by the authorities, he told them off for killing Jesus and reminded them that God had put that right and exalted him as Leader and Saviour. It was not only monotonous, it was infuriating. The Council was all for the death penalty.

But Gamaliel was made of wiser stuff. His deeper question was about origins; where does this movement come from? If it's just a deluded group of fanatics, it'll shrivel away; if it's from God, watch out – you don't want to be in the position of fighting God. What good advice! There are many human problems that would benefit from the Gamaliel test: 'Time will tell'. All too often society rushes to 'fix' problems with instant solutions – and the sticking plaster comes away all too soon.

I wonder if we might be facing some issue today where applying the Gamaliel test would be the wiser course of *in*action?

Lord of heaven and earth,
as Jesus taught his disciples to be persistent in prayer,
give us patience and courage never to lose hope,
but always to bring our prayers before you;
through Jesus Christ our Lord.

COLLECT

Reflection by **John Pritchard**   225

Monday 13 August

Acts 6

'... the Hellenists complained against the Hebrews' (v.1)

It is gloriously ironic (isn't it?) that only a few months after Jesus' death and with his words about being as humble as servants ringing in their ears, the early Christian movement started squabbling. One group thought that they were being treated unfairly and that the 'others' were getting an advantage.

And how was the dispute solved? In time-honoured fashion (and via classic displacement activity) the Apostles recommended that new structures were needed. So they appointed a small group of administrators whose task it was to ensure fair play.

The early Church is often regarded by Christians as representing a golden age. Back then, goes the argument, all was sweetness and light and the Church grew apace. The implication is that if only today's Churches could emulate the pristine innocence and enthusiasm of those first Christians, the world would be transformed. Such an argument does not look carefully enough at the biblical evidence. The fact is that in the early Church there were arguments aplenty: Peter and Paul had strong differences of opinion (Luke even wrote Peter out of the story); Paul fell out with Barnabas and John Mark; the synagogue in Corinth split and with a complete lack of tact, Paul set up a meeting for the Christians right next door to the synagogue that he and some others had just left.

The question this raises is whether splits are part of normal human behaviour – or is there a dynamic instability in the faith that keeps it vibrant?

COLLECT

O God, you declare your almighty power
most chiefly in showing mercy and pity:
mercifully grant to us such a measure of your grace,
that we, running the way of your commandments,
may receive your gracious promises,
and be made partakers of your heavenly treasure;
through Jesus Christ your Son our Lord,
who is alive and reigns with you,
in the unity of the Holy Spirit,
one God, now and for ever.

Reflection by **Christopher Herbert**

Psalms 87, **89.1-18**
2 Samuel 5.1-12
Acts 7.1-16

Tuesday 14 August

Acts 7.1-16

'The God of glory appeared to our ancestor Abraham ...' (v.2)

Stephen's defence in front of the Jewish Council was to appeal to history, to the overarching story of God's dealings with Israel. In it Stephen traced the story from Abraham to Jesus. The final shape of Stephen's narrative was created by Luke when he composed Acts and therefore, though this was not his intention, we are given a glimpse of the early Church's foundational message. Designed for an audience who knew the Jewish story, it was the relationship between Jesus and the unfolding history of Israel that was central. In this mode the message was designed to convince a sceptical Jewish audience that Jesus really was the expected Messiah.

Two thousand years later, the audience for the Christian message is quite different. It is very mixed indeed. It cannot be assumed that the Jewish story is known or recognized, nor can it be assumed that the Jewish interpretation of history is one that is universally shared. Christianity now has to speak into a world that consists of a range of faiths and to communities that have a variety of ways of interpreting the meaning of history.

In such circumstances it is unlikely that people will be convinced of the truths of Christianity simply because we shout the loudest or use social media slickly. So what can we do?

Perhaps, paradoxically, we shall be more convincing if we learn to listen than if we are constantly on transmit, because that way reciprocal understanding can grow.

> God of glory,
> the end of our searching,
> help us to lay aside
> all that prevents us from seeking your kingdom,
> and to give all that we have
> to gain the pearl beyond all price,
> through our Saviour Jesus Christ.

COLLECT

Reflection by **Christopher Herbert**   227

Wednesday 15 August
The Blessed Virgin Mary

Psalms 98, 138, 147.1-12
Isaiah 7.10-15
Luke 11.27-28

Luke 11.27-28

*'Blessed is the womb that bore you and the breasts that
nursed you!' (v.27)*

On a hill 417 feet (127 metres) above sea level is a gem of an Italian
town. From its heights looking eastwards there is a glorious view of
the Croatian coastline. But the chief attraction of Loreto is its Holy
House. Sheltered by a great basilica, Mary's house is encased by
beautifully worked marble. Legend says that it was flown by angels
from Nazareth to Loreto in the 13th century just before the Crusaders
were expelled from the Holy Land; ever since it has been a pilgrimage
site.

If you look at the marble base on which the Holy House stands you can
see two shallow grooves running around the exterior of the building.
Those grooves have been worn into the marble by pilgrims circling the
house on their knees. It is a moving symbol of human yearning and of
the affection in which Mary is held.

Loreto is not the only Holy House. Walsingham in Norfolk also claims
a Holy House. It is said that an 11th-century Lady of the Manor was
taken to Nazareth 'in the spirit' and then commanded to build a replica
of Mary's house on English soil. Walsingham too has welcomed
thousands of pilgrims across the centuries.

There is something about Mary that attracts the human heart; perhaps
it is her humility, perhaps it is her gentleness. Whatever it may be, her
encounter with the angel at the Annunciation has intrigued the minds
of artists and storytellers and continues to tug gently at our souls.

COLLECT

Almighty God,
who looked upon the lowliness of the Blessed Virgin Mary
and chose her to be the mother of your only Son:
grant that we who are redeemed by his blood
may share with her in the glory of your eternal kingdom;
through Jesus Christ your Son our Lord,
who is alive and reigns with you,
in the unity of the Holy Spirit,
one God, now and for ever.

| *Reflection by* **Christopher Herbert**

Thursday 16 August

Acts 7.44-53

'... the Most High does not dwell in houses made by human hands' (v.48)

Stephen's speech is roaring to its climax – and now comes the final thrust. He compares the audience to their ancestors, describing these God-fearing Jews, the leaders of their community, as 'heathen'. It was no wonder that they 'ground their teeth' with fury (v.54).

But stop for a moment. Were the words those of Stephen himself, or of Luke? It seems unlikely that anyone in the crowded meeting would have recorded Stephen's speech verbatim. However, we do know that wax tablets were sometimes used to take notes, so it is not impossible that the gist of what Stephen said was summarized by someone and that those notes were later passed to Luke, though that does stretch credibility.

If the speech was largely Luke's construction, then presumably he wanted it to fit into the purpose of his bigger narrative, which was to show how and why the early Christians broke out from their Jewish matrix. In other words, not for the first or last time, 'historical' events were shaped by the author to fulfil an ulterior purpose.

Before we recoil in surprise, consider the way you construct your own stories. Do you not tell stories in such a way that your audience will want to listen? Might those stories be a way, not of deceiving people, but of helping to crystallize the direction of your own personal narrative?

Luke wanted to share his enthusiasm for his world view, one that had been transformed by his radically new understanding of Jesus. Isn't that a reasonable thing to do?

O God, you declare your almighty power
most chiefly in showing mercy and pity:
mercifully grant to us such a measure of your grace,
that we, running the way of your commandments,
may receive your gracious promises,
and be made partakers of your heavenly treasure;
through Jesus Christ your Son our Lord,
who is alive and reigns with you,
in the unity of the Holy Spirit,
one God, now and for ever.

COLLECT

Reflection by **Christopher Herbert** | 229

Friday 17 August

Psalms **88** (95)
2 Samuel 7.18-end
Acts 7.54 – 8.3

Acts 7.54 – 8.3

'I see the heavens opened and the Son of Man standing at the right hand of God!' (v.56)

There was a moment, recalled by Brian Keenan in his book 'An Evil Cradling' about his long captivity as a hostage, when, in the terrible and fear-filled solitary confinement of his Lebanese prison cell, he was given an orange. The vibrancy of the colour of that single piece of fruit was like a revelation to him. He rejoiced in its beauty and wrote about it with vivid and memorable freshness.

Extreme stress in some people, it would seem, can lead to a heightening of their perceptual awareness. What is ordinary becomes charged with meaning. Perhaps this was the case with Stephen, who had spoken out bravely in his own defence but under duress suddenly had a vision of God, a vision which revealed Christ at God's right hand, a vision which took away all his fear.

Luke treats the experience with understated simplicity and follows it with a stark statement about the man who was behind the killing, Saul. It's an astute and powerful piece of writing, which, as he intends, will lead to the story of Saul's dramatic conversion to the Christian movement.

Stephen, the first person to be killed because of his Christian faith, became an icon for succeeding generations. Like his Master, as he was dying in agony, he forgave his killers. It was an act of supreme spiritual courage. Inevitably, such an act raises questions about our own integrity and our own depths of courage: facing such an extreme situation, how would we react?

COLLECT

O God, you declare your almighty power
most chiefly in showing mercy and pity:
mercifully grant to us such a measure of your grace,
that we, running the way of your commandments,
may receive your gracious promises,
and be made partakers of your heavenly treasure;
through Jesus Christ your Son our Lord,
who is alive and reigns with you,
in the unity of the Holy Spirit,
one God, now and for ever.

| *Reflection by* **Christopher Herbert**

Psalms 96, **97**, 100
2 Samuel 9
Acts 8.4-25

Saturday 18 August

Acts 8.4-25

'Now those who were scattered went from place to place, proclaiming the word' (v.4)

We have now left the hubbub of the city of Jerusalem and Stephen's martyrdom and are taken by Luke out into the countryside and into a different culture where magicians ply their wares. He has inserted these stories between ones about Paul, and in doing so has acted like a film director hinting at what is to come but for the moment distracting us from the main theme with a subplot. With a few deft strokes he assures his readers that in spite of persecution the work of spreading the Good News has continued.

It is comforting to realize that the foot soldiers in this small hidden army of volunteers are given no names. They are the extras in the plot with humble walk-on parts. But their effect is greater than they can ever know. They stand in no limelight; they have no memoirs by which they are commemorated; they are unknown heroes, part of that great band of people of all races and nationalities that through the ages has quietly but bravely proclaimed the kingdom and lived the gospel in each generation.

And still that hidden work continues.

Think of those people who have influenced you by their faith. Few of them will be well known; most have simply got on with their lives and through their gentle and courageous service have emulated Christ. Most saints are unknown, except, of course, they are known to God. And we, shaped by their faithful example, should offer to God our quiet alleluias for them.

God of glory,
the end of our searching,
help us to lay aside
all that prevents us from seeking your kingdom,
and to give all that we have
to gain the pearl beyond all price,
through our Saviour Jesus Christ.

COLLECT

Monday 20 August

Psalms **98**, 99, 101
2 Samuel 11
Acts 8.26-end

Acts 8.26-end

'Then an angel of the Lord said to Philip, "Get up and go toward the south to the road that goes down from Jerusalem to Gaza."' (v.26)

Luke has a bit of a thing about angels. They are at the forefront of his Gospel (think of the Annunciation), they are there at the Resurrection, and here they are again, this time directing Philip where he should travel. The angels are Luke's way of indicating that eternity and time are being pushed in a new direction; the divine plan is unfolding as it should.

The gospel has been proclaimed in Jerusalem, then it was heard in Samaria and now it is beginning its journey further outwards. The high official whom Philip met on the desert road was an Ethiopian (or, perhaps, as some scholars suggest, a Sudanese). But the gospel is not just moving outwards geographically like the ripples in a pond, it is also breaking down barriers. The Old Testament (Deuteronomy 23.1) had made clear that eunuchs could not be full members of the community of Israel, yet here is the new Israel coming into being where all are welcome. Is it any wonder that the message was called 'Good News' and is it any wonder that the eunuch asks to be initiated into this new way of living?

Sometimes our familiarity with the New Testament stories blinds us to the radical changes that accepting Christ entails. We take it for granted, for instance, that Christian compassion embraces all people. But in societies where the disabled and the mentally ill are not accorded equal human value, the story of liberation that Christianity brings is life-changing.

COLLECT

Almighty and everlasting God,
you are always more ready to hear than we to pray
and to give more than either we desire or deserve:
pour down upon us the abundance of your mercy,
forgiving us those things of which our conscience is afraid
and giving us those good things which we are not worthy to ask
but through the merits and mediation
of Jesus Christ your Son our Lord,
who is alive and reigns with you,
in the unity of the Holy Spirit,
one God, now and for ever.

232 | *Reflection by* **Christopher Herbert**

Psalm **106*** (*or* 103)
2 Samuel 12.1-25
Acts 9.1-19*a*

Tuesday 21 August

Acts 9.1-19*a*

'Saul, Saul, why do you persecute me?' (v.4)

Paul's conversion experience has influenced the stories that people over the centuries have told about their own conversions. They too recall a moment of flashing insight. They too have felt in need of being 'led by the hand'. They too have wanted to proclaim their experience of having been overwhelmed by God.

But look at this story from another angle. Look at it not so much as a prototype of 'conversion' but as a way of understanding who Christ really is. The question that Saul heard was of immense significance. Technically speaking, Saul had *not* persecuted Jesus. To the best of our knowledge Saul had never even met Jesus, let alone set the attack dogs on him. All that Saul had done was to be the witness at the killing of Stephen, one of Jesus' followers. Yet Saul recognized (and this was the amazing insight – note the words) that in killing Stephen and in going after the Christians, he was in reality attacking Christ himself. The new followers embodied the very being of Christ. They and their Lord were one.

It was of course, a moment that changed history and one on which Saul/ Paul continued to reflect deeply. It led him to see that the new way was one which was about liberation. It was about humanity becoming one with the Creator ('For all who are led by the Spirit of God are children of God', Romans 8.14). It was about recognizing that all barriers between people were now abolished.

> God of constant mercy,
> who sent your Son to save us:
> remind us of your goodness,
> increase your grace within us,
> that our thankfulness may grow,
> through Jesus Christ our Lord.

COLLECT

Reflection by **Christopher Herbert** 233

Wednesday 22 August

Psalms 110, **111**, 112
2 Samuel 15.1-12
Acts 9.19*b*-31

Acts 9.19*b*-31

*'... and immediately he began to proclaim Jesus in the synagogues,
saying, "He is the Son of God"' (v.20)*

The shift in Paul's thought-world seems to have been instantaneous.
One minute he was plotting to destroy the followers of Jesus; the next
he had joined them and was speaking out boldly about his new
convictions. But here we face a problem. According to Paul's own
account (it can be found in his letter to the Galatians), after his
conversion he did not go up to Jerusalem; instead he went off to
Arabia for three years. In Luke's version of events, however, following
a brief stay in Damascus, Paul went to Jerusalem to see the Twelve.
A long sojourn in Arabia is not mentioned. The two accounts cannot
be squared.

In such circumstances what are we to do? Which version do we believe?
Presumably we trust Paul's own account and therefore we have to
assume that Luke's version is garbled. However, what is clear is Luke's
determination to show that Paul's powerful proclamation of Jesus as
Son of God began very early on.

It's worth noting where that proclamation was located. It was not on
street corners, nor inside houses, but it was in the heart of the Jewish
community's religious, social and educational hub: in the synagogues.
These were places where discussion and debate were part of the
tradition and, in that sense, Paul was continuing his rabbinic practice.

Now ask yourself a question: if you felt called to proclaim Jesus as the
Son of God, what would be your first-choice location for doing so?

COLLECT

Almighty and everlasting God,
you are always more ready to hear than we to pray
and to give more than either we desire or deserve:
pour down upon us the abundance of your mercy,
forgiving us those things of which our conscience is afraid
and giving us those good things which we are not worthy to ask
but through the merits and mediation
of Jesus Christ your Son our Lord,
who is alive and reigns with you,
in the unity of the Holy Spirit,
one God, now and for ever.

| *Reflection by* **Christopher Herbert**

Thursday 23 August

Acts 9.32-end

*'Now as Peter went here and there among all the believers,
he came down also to the saints living in Lydda' (v.32)*

Luke now switches his attention away from Paul to Peter. Paul had been sent away by the Apostles to Caesarea and then on to Tarsus, and so Peter enters the narrative. He goes on a tour of the Christians living in Lydda (now called Lod, north-west of Jerusalem), and then he is summoned by some of the Christians to Joppa (present-day Jaffa).

Here, the story that Luke tells has a number of echoes of the healings associated with the Prophets, Elijah and Elisha, as well as the healing of Jairus' daughter by Jesus. In other words, Peter is portrayed as continuing the powerful healing work of God.

There is just one subtlety however, and that concerns the woman in Lydda, named in Greek, Dorcas, and in Aramaic, Tabitha. It's a deft signal that the gospel is moving out of its Jerusalem-centred locale. And, if the echo of Elijah's healing is intentional, that too reinforces the sense of God being available to all; the woman in the Elijah story was not a Jew but a Phoenician who lived near Sidon.

The Spirit, implies Luke, is at work and is beginning to break down barriers; to liberate people from illness and even death. Could there be any greater sign of God's universal grace and purpose?

Now recall who the transmitter of God's love is – it is Peter, the very man who had denied Jesus just before the trial but to whom Jesus had appeared at the resurrection. A new world beckons ...

God of constant mercy,
who sent your Son to save us:
remind us of your goodness,
increase your grace within us,
that our thankfulness may grow,
through Jesus Christ our Lord.

COLLECT

Reflection by **Christopher Herbert** | 235

Friday 24 August
Bartholomew the Apostle

John 1.43-end

*'When Jesus saw Nathanael coming toward him, he said of him,
"Here is truly an Israelite in whom there is no deceit!"' (v.47)*

Here's an interesting chain of connections. Eusebius (c.260–340) is commonly regarded as 'The Father of Church History'. In his writings he tells of a man called Pantaenus, a skilful teacher in Alexandria in the 2nd century, who journeyed to India. There he found a copy of the Gospel of Matthew in Hebrew, which, it was claimed, had been left behind by Bartholomew when he too had visited India in the 1st century. Who knows? Is it just a delightful legend, or is there a tiny kernel of truth hidden within it?

The fact is, very little is known about Bartholomew except that he was one of the Twelve especially chosen and commissioned by Jesus. He is named by Luke as being in an upper room after the resurrection with the disciples, Mary the mother of Jesus, and some other women. But then he disappears from the written records. He is not seen or heard from again, which perhaps explains the growth of legends about him. He is, by the way, also thought by some scholars to be the person called 'Nathanael' in today's reading.

It's a bit frustrating. Did Bartholomew actually go to India? If not, where was his patch? What really happened to him? There are far more questions than answers. In some ways that is a comfort. Imagination and storytelling are an integral and necessary part of Christianity. Without them everything would be cut and dried, and that would be tedious and dull, wouldn't it?

COLLECT

Almighty and everlasting God,
who gave to your apostle Bartholomew grace
    truly to believe and to preach your word:
grant that your Church
may love that word which he believed
and may faithfully preach and receive the same;
through Jesus Christ your Son our Lord,
who is alive and reigns with you,
in the unity of the Holy Spirit,
one God, now and for ever.

| *Reflection by* **Christopher Herbert**

Saturday 25 August

Acts 10.17-33

'... Peter was greatly puzzled about what to make of the vision that he had seen' (v.17)

Here come the angels again. At the beginning of Luke's Gospel it is an angelic visitation that reduces Zechariah to awed silence. In this second part of Luke's narrative, an angel appears to a secular member of the occupying Roman forces. And Peter, within 24 hours of the angel's visit to Cornelius, has a vision that shakes him to the core. The vision was a foretelling of the barrier-breaking nature of the gospel: the old rules no longer applied; instead, a new age had dawned.

It is not at all surprising that Peter was perplexed; his whole thought-world was being turned upside down and inside out. It was his equivalent of Paul's vision on the Damascus road and led to a similarly radical response: gentiles were to be baptized and were to be welcomed into the growing Christian family.

The response from the Jerusalem-based headquarters was one of angry astonishment. How could such a profound break with the past be tolerated? Well. It's a cameo of what happens in all organizations, big or small, when radical changes are proposed. There is always resistance, though sometimes, let's be honest, the resistance might be necessary and correct. But it is also a picture of individuals when facing major new choices. We really do not like change.

But suppose that the proposed change is something that God wants for us. Could it be that out of that change, new life and new opportunities will arise? Might angels be nearby?

Almighty and everlasting God,
you are always more ready to hear than we to pray
and to give more than either we desire or deserve:
pour down upon us the abundance of your mercy,
forgiving us those things of which our conscience is afraid
and giving us those good things which we are not worthy to ask
but through the merits and mediation
of Jesus Christ your Son our Lord,
who is alive and reigns with you,
in the unity of the Holy Spirit,
one God, now and for ever.

COLLECT

Reflection by **Christopher Herbert** | 237

Monday 27 August

Psalms 123, 124, 125, **126**
2 Samuel 18.1-18
Acts 10.34-end

Acts 10.34-end

'Then Peter began to speak to them' (v.34)

The audience Peter is speaking to is a gathering of the family and friends of a Roman centurion, Cornelius, who is stationed in the town of Caesarea. The previous verses have been full of the detailed preparations for this visit, which has been spiritually inspired on both sides, given that it is unlawful for Peter to visit a gentile at home. We know that Peter is a powerful speaker; all that we see of him in the Gospels is that he is passionate, sometimes impetuous, but always totally committed. Earlier in Acts we heard that the crowd were 'cut to the heart' by how Peter spoke, and here his words seem just as influential.

Cornelius' household begin to accept the truth of his testimony and want to change their lives in response. Peter in turn declares that they should be baptized: included, admitted, welcomed right then and there. It's dramatic stuff, and begins a series of rather helter-skelter events in the streets, synagogues and houses of the towns visited by these first apostles. The way Peter tells the story of Jesus' life, death and resurrection and the effect it has had on him personally is something people can't resist; it becomes an irresistible invitation to live differently. Crowds of people from every layer of society want to hope again, want to start a new life. Now. At once.

The infectious energy of this meeting leaps off the page, and maybe convinces us that it's never too late to make new choices, take a different path. It reminds us that it's never too late to be surprised by God.

COLLECT

Almighty God,
who called your Church to bear witness
that you were in Christ reconciling the world to yourself:
help us to proclaim the good news of your love,
that all who hear it may be drawn to you;
through him who was lifted up on the cross,
and reigns with you in the unity of the Holy Spirit,
one God, now and for ever.

| *Reflection by* **Lucy Winkett**

Tuesday 28 August

Acts 11.1-18

'... in a trance I saw a vision' (v.5)

Now Peter has to go back and face the music. His vision of developing friendships and sharing the good news across the boundaries of ethnicity and belief is not shared by everyone. Perhaps recalling his former employment, he's remembering the words of Jesus to him and his friends: I will make you fish for people. In any case, he's facing criticism for eating with uncircumcised men, for breaking the laws by which he's lived up to now. He responds with his description of a vision that challenges this way of life profoundly.

It's striking that the picture he paints of his mystical experience is listened to respectfully by the others. When this vision is combined with evidence from his visit to Cornelius, of the presence of the Holy Spirit, tested against the apostles' own experience at Pentecost, his leadership on this issue is accepted, seemingly without question.

Peter's authority rests on both his own personal spiritual testimony together with his recounting of events among the new community he has started to create. As a piece of change management, it's genius. Both charismatic and personal communication are combined with real-life hard evidence. Taking all of this together, the centuries-old rules they have been living by are transformed. And such is the openness of these new Christians to receiving new truth that their reaction is not to begrudge or complain about the change but to rejoice that things will never be the same again.

Almighty God,
you search us and know us:
may we rely on you in strength
and rest on you in weakness,
now and in all our days;
through Jesus Christ our Lord.

COLLECT

Wednesday 29 August

Psalm **119.153-end**
2 Samuel 19.8*b*-23
Acts 11.19-end

Acts 11.19-end

'Then Barnabas went to Tarsus to look for Saul' (v.25)

Stephen's preaching earlier in Acts had had a tumultuous effect, and his execution triggered widespread persecution that scattered the men and women he would have known. Acts is peppered with stories of individual suffering and sacrifice, murder and imprisonment. So now we meet Barnabas, who goes to find Saul, now Paul, to take him to one of the most important cities of the Roman empire: Antioch.

Antioch was a political, commercial and military centre for communication and trade between Rome itself and Palestine and Asia Minor. A hugely important place, a large and thriving Jewish community was resident there. Paul and Barnabas spend a year here, Paul serving a sort of apprenticeship alongside Barnabas, with whom he would eventually argue irrevocably. But for now, they are fellow toilers in the vineyard, teaching, preaching, organizing.

The beginnings of an economic structure emerge here, too, across the ever-widening geographical reach of the new Christian communities. Believers in Judea are suffering through famine, and so the urban Antioch church sends cash with Saul and Barnabas to help them. We are seeing before our eyes the development of Christianity from the villages and hillsides of Galilee to the towns and cities of the Roman empire. The expansion will not be without bloodshed, argument and broken friendships along the way. It's a matter for both recognition and repentance, that from its very beginning, Christianity is contested in both culture and belief.

COLLECT

Almighty God,
who called your Church to bear witness
that you were in Christ reconciling the world to yourself:
help us to proclaim the good news of your love,
that all who hear it may be drawn to you;
through him who was lifted up on the cross,
and reigns with you in the unity of the Holy Spirit,
one God, now and for ever.

| *Reflection by* **Lucy Winkett**

Psalms **143**, 146
2 Samuel 19.24-end
Acts 12.1-17

Thursday 30 August

Acts 12.1-17

'Peter continued knocking' (v.16)

The events in the Acts of the Apostles read sometimes like a film script. At the rather breathless beginning of chapter 12 we are plunged into the violence and precariousness of first-century life with the summary execution of James (probably about eleven years after Stephen's execution) and an overwhelming four squads of soldiers (sixteen men), who are detailed to seize and then guard one man, Peter.

Peter is sprung from prison by a mysterious messenger, so unexpected that the lovely detail is given us by Luke that Peter didn't realize what was happening to him; he thought it was a vision or a dream. Then, presumably alone outside on the street, he makes his way to John Mark's mother's house to see if he can find safety there. The maid Rhoda is so shocked she doesn't immediately let him in but leaves him standing outside the gate while she goes to tell the family she has recognized Peter's voice. As usual, this low-status woman is not believed, a common theme of the New Testament, but Peter persists in knocking.

The minute-by-minute account of this unexpected arrival is enthralling. It gives us a strong sense of the day-by-day fragility of communications, meetings and organization of this religion-in-hiding. That Peter is left outside while they all argue inside is a beguiling image, adding to the twists and turns, confusions and perilous decisions made by the first bearers of this world-changing story.

Almighty God,
you search us and know us:
may we rely on you in strength
and rest on you in weakness,
now and in all our days;
through Jesus Christ our Lord.

COLLECT

Reflection by **Lucy Winkett** | 241

Friday 31 August

Acts 12.18-end

'... no small commotion' (v.18)

In contrast to the Middle Eastern hyperbole so common in the New Testament, this is a delightful understatement. All hell must have broken loose when the soldiers realized that they had lost their prisoner. It was their job to guard him, sixteen to one. And they've lost him. According to this account, they pay for this mistake with their lives. Violence begets violence, and as we saw yesterday, Herod was no stranger to summary judgement and execution.

Today we are back with the court of King Herod Agrippa. Favoured by the Roman Emperor Caligula, he is in the ascendancy. We learn that his chamberlain Blastus, seems to be open to bribes; Acts tells us that the embassy delegation from Tyre and Sidon, in dispute with Herod, have made him their 'friend'. And it's in response to this delegation that Herod seems to give in to hubris, accepting the adulation of the crowd that he is in fact a divine not a human leader. This is given as the reason for his sudden death, once again making the theological point that leaders, religious and political, are subject to the presence and authority of God.

The entwined relationship between politics and religion is on open display; the conversion of the Roman Emperor Constantine is still centuries away, but the messiness of Christianity's relationship with politics and power is beginning here, right at the start.

COLLECT

Almighty God,
who called your Church to bear witness
that you were in Christ reconciling the world to yourself:
help us to proclaim the good news of your love,
that all who hear it may be drawn to you;
through him who was lifted up on the cross,
and reigns with you in the unity of the Holy Spirit,
one God, now and for ever.

| *Reflection by* **Lucy Winkett**

Psalm 147
2 Samuel 24
Acts 13.1-12

Saturday 1 September

Acts 13.1-12

'When the proconsul saw what had happened, he believed' (v.12)

The multinational, multicultural nature of early Christianity is clear from today's passage. Apart from the increasingly mixed-ethnicity group of what we read are 'prophets and teachers', we come across the intelligent and thoughtful Sergius Paulus, the Roman proconsul of Cyprus at the time. After talking to Paul, John Mark and Barnabas, and seeing the miracle Paul performs, Sergius Paulus converts to Christianity.

The introduction of Roman and Greek culture, philosophy, assumptions, and especially structures, is beginning to shape the new Christian communities. At some point, Paul and Barnabas will have to return to Jerusalem and report that their message is having a turbulent effect, not only in the synagogues as they might have expected, but also in the government, the army, the civil service. They will have to report that the occupiers seem to be receiving this news as gladly as the occupied.

The original apostles may want to resist Paul (who never met Jesus) and his interpretation of the life, death and resurrection of a man that they knew personally and loved dearly. Guarding the legacy of someone or something that is precious to us personally can lead us to become resistant to new truths, new perspectives, different interpretations.

How does a new movement grow, and who claims the power to define what happens next? The locus of authority is becoming less clear as Paul travels further away from the original disciples who remember the 'locked door' behind which they hid after Jesus' death.

COLLECT

Almighty God,
you search us and know us:
may we rely on you in strength
and rest on you in weakness,
now and in all our days;
through Jesus Christ our Lord.

Monday 3 September

Psalms 1, 2, 3
1 Kings 1.5-31
Acts 13.13-43

Acts 13.13-43

'Paul stood up and with a gesture began to speak' (v.16)

We read elsewhere that Paul (unlike Peter) is not an impressive public speaker, and in imagining this scene, it is intriguing to picture him beginning to speak to the crowd in the synagogue, 'with a gesture'. He then, as the urbane, educated speaker he is, sets out what he hopes will be received as incontrovertible proof, tracing the action of God in the lives of the Israelites from their liberation from Egyptian slavery through the reigns of Saul and David right up to the message of John the Baptist pointing towards Jesus of Nazareth as the Messiah promised by God. Paul uses the very phrase made famous by John the Baptist which by now no doubt is a saying familiar and repeated by the faithful: '... one is coming after me. I am not worthy to untie the thong of his sandals' (John 1.27).

Paul's learning and ability to set out arguments are evident here. He is painstaking in building the case for Jesus. This is the man who is capable of the most extraordinary poetry about love (in his letter to the Corinthians) while at the same time providing cool-headed quasi-legal arguments to convince anyone who will listen that he was wrong and that Jesus is the Christ. Such a talented and able person is marshalling his considerable ability in the service of Christ, who, he tells us elsewhere, is simply everything to him. It's inspiring that he brings all that he is to this task – his emotion, his intellect, his energy – leaving nothing in reserve.

COLLECT

Almighty God,
whose only Son has opened for us
a new and living way into your presence:
give us pure hearts and steadfast wills
to worship you in spirit and in truth;
through Jesus Christ your Son our Lord,
who is alive and reigns with you,
in the unity of the Holy Spirit,
one God, now and for ever.

| *Reflection by* **Lucy Winkett**

Psalms **5**, 6 (8)
1 Kings 1.32 – 2.4; 2.10-12
Acts 13.44 – 14.7

Acts 13.44 – 14.7

'... speaking boldly for the Lord' (14.3)

In this unfolding story of increasing conflict and discontent caused by Paul and Barnabas' visits to synagogues, it is important, as twenty-first century readers, that we take care with the terms used. As in John's Gospel, the term 'the Jews' is sometimes used pejoratively to describe a group of people who become opposed to Jesus or the message about Jesus. The loose use of this term has had catastrophic historical consequences. A closer reading, however, shows us a more accurate and nuanced description of the deep split not only among the synagogue leaders; the point is powerfully made that both Jews and Greeks are both believers and unbelievers in this new message about Jesus. It's divisive for everyone.

Nevertheless, as the story goes on, it's becoming obvious that Paul doesn't believe that he is there simply to announce the coming of the Messiah to those who were waiting for him, but also to those who never acknowledged he was coming. This is a universal message of salvation that is radically unconcerned with ethnicity, background, social status or wealth. And it's a message freely preached, to anyone who is free to reject it too. Paul and Barnabas 'shook the dust off their feet' when it was clear they were not getting anywhere. A direct reference to the teaching of Jesus, it's an affirmation of freewill, freedom of speech and freedom to leave at any time.

It's a noticeable feature of the manner of Paul's ministry that he seems to remain agile, energetic and unconfined by what others want from him. He's an extraordinary presence in these pages, someone who feels himself accountable only to God.

Merciful God,
your Son came to save us
and bore our sins on the cross:
may we trust in your mercy
and know your love,
rejoicing in the righteousness
that is ours through Jesus Christ our Lord.

COLLECT

Reflection by **Lucy Winkett** | 245

Wednesday 5 September

Psalm 119.1-32
1 Kings 3
Acts 14.8-end

Acts 14.8-end

'Then they stoned Paul and dragged him out of the city' (v.19)

Archeological excavations have discovered that a temple to Zeus existed at the gates of Lystra, an important market town in what is now central Turkey. Derbe, about 60 miles away, was on the trading route from Iconium, from where Paul and Barnabas had fled, following threats of violence against them. The superstitious citizens of Lystra were simply interpreting Paul and Barnabas' spiritual impact as being due to their being Hermes and Zeus themselves – a natural assumption, given the existing religious culture of their town. The frame of reference by which any group, organization or community measure new truths is normally the one with which they are most familiar, so it's perfectly sensible that this community should interpret the teaching and healing they see Paul and Barnabas perform in the way they did. Sometimes, however, as here, the new truths are so ground-breaking and life-changing that they require new parameters, new definitions, new paradigms.

This is the nature of the resurrection message proclaimed by Paul and the others in this book. Even so, it's instructive to see how persistently some of each crowd they encounter struggle to understand that the world has changed fundamentally now that someone has been raised from the dead. For many, the struggle goes on.

COLLECT

Almighty God,
whose only Son has opened for us
a new and living way into your presence:
give us pure hearts and steadfast wills
to worship you in spirit and in truth;
through Jesus Christ your Son our Lord,
who is alive and reigns with you,
in the unity of the Holy Spirit,
one God, now and for ever.

| *Reflection by* **Lucy Winkett**

Psalms 14, **15**, 16
1 Kings 4.29 – 5.12
Acts 15.1-21

Thursday 6 September

Acts 15.1-21

'The apostles and the elders met together to consider this matter'
(v.6)

Back at base camp, Paul and Barnabas report the amazing spread of the message they are proclaiming among both Jews and gentiles. It's an obvious point of debate in this fledgling community of new believers in Jesus as to what the rules should be. Institutionalization is starting to happen before our eyes here in Acts, and the beginnings of a new set of structures, religious boundaries and expectations of behaviour are forming.

The two contentious issues are food laws and circumcision. Here the focus is on circumcision, a fundamental expectation in Judaism. A debate is had, and in the end, James, the respected leader in Jerusalem, makes a ruling in favour of the new, radically inclusive proposals of Paul. From this point, it is becoming ever clearer that this is not simply, as they might have at first expected, a reform movement within Judaism, but it is becoming a new distinctive fusion religion, combining Jewish inheritance with Greek insight, to produce something utterly new.

The words and stories about Jesus are still told and his lineage rehearsed for the crowds, but it is the astonishing news of the resurrection – that the power of death has been overcome, transformed – that is the shape-shifter for once-held, seemingly unbreakable adherence to religious rules or ancient philosophies.

Merciful God,
your Son came to save us
and bore our sins on the cross:
may we trust in your mercy
and know your love,
rejoicing in the righteousness
that is ours through Jesus Christ our Lord.

COLLECT

Reflection by **Lucy Winkett** | 247

Friday 7 September

Acts 15.22-35

'... certain persons ... have unsettled your minds' (v.24)

As this movement grows and codifies, it requires ever more wise counsel from the elders in Jerusalem. We saw yesterday that, led by James, they have made their decision about circumcision for gentiles (it's not required), and they have provided some guidance on eating laws (they remain, but in a more relaxed form), but this time, they ask Silas and Judas Barsabbas to accompany Paul and Barnabas to Antioch to deliver the letter containing these instructions. In the letter, they want to reassure Antioch's new Christians who have developed 'unsettled minds'. They want to make sure that the gentile church understands where the authority lies in this emergent organization: with them in Jerusalem, not with Paul on the road. Sending other leaders who will reiterate this will achieve what they want.

Ecclesiastical politics is evident right at the heart of the story of Acts. In among the policy-making of James and the Jerusalem leaders, the excitement generated by Paul's good news of Jesus leaps off the page. Perhaps, after the example of Acts, we learn that it's necessary that at the centre, policy is debated and documented and letters issued to the outposts. At the margins, though, the possibility of change is closer to the surface where good news of new truth remains volatile and free.

According to the stories of Acts, both the centre and the margins are necessary for the establishment of the much-heralded kingdom of God.

COLLECT

Almighty God,
whose only Son has opened for us
a new and living way into your presence:
give us pure hearts and steadfast wills
to worship you in spirit and in truth;
through Jesus Christ your Son our Lord,
who is alive and reigns with you,
in the unity of the Holy Spirit,
one God, now and for ever.

248 | *Reflection by* **Lucy Winkett**

Psalms 20, 21, **23**
1 Kings 8.1-30
Acts 15.36 – 16.5

Saturday 8 September

Acts 15.36 – 16.5

'The disagreement became so sharp that they parted company'
(15.39)

It's possible to get a little weary reading Acts, because there is so much conflict, not only between the new believers and their mother religion, but also between the new believers themselves. Here, Barnabas and Paul, who have been through so much together and have faced such great dangers together, argue so sharply that Barnabas sails away to Cyprus, leaving Paul to travel back to Lystra and then on to Syria.

They fall out over a person known as John Mark. It seems that Paul believes he has let them down, but Barnabas wants to re-admit him to the fold. Underneath the straightforward description of events, it's hard to sense the real atmosphere, but given the finality of this argument and the drama of Barnabas simply leaving Paul to it, we can assume that this was a serious and upsetting disagreement.

It's clear from Acts, that from its very beginnings, Christianity has been contested. It remains so. In some ways we can't be surprised, because as Peter, Barnabas, John Mark, Silas, Judas, Paul and all the others repeatedly teach, their faith is founded on the life, death and resurrection of Jesus. The life of Jesus is a life, not a set of instructions, and ever since the missionary journeys these pages describe, the meaning of that life lived by Jesus has been pondered, scrutinized, admired, rejected, loved by generations.

The book of Acts teaches us that straightforward agreement doesn't seem to be in the Christian DNA: but love of – and even at-a-distance solidarity with those with whom we disagree – certainly and enduringly is.

Merciful God,
your Son came to save us
and bore our sins on the cross:
may we trust in your mercy
and know your love,
rejoicing in the righteousness
that is ours through Jesus Christ our Lord.

COLLECT

Reflection by **Lucy Winkett** | 249

Monday 10 September

Acts 16.6-24

'... having been forbidden by the Holy Spirit to speak the word in Asia' (v.6)

Discerning the will of God as opposed to following a path merely of our own design is one of the toughest issues we face as Christians. Making the 'right' decisions can often feel like a shot in the dark. Reassuringly, there are various methods to help a process of discerning God's will, notably from the Ignatian tradition. In this tradition, you accept the ebb and flow of positive and negative periods in life, towards God ('consolation') and away from God ('desolation'). Focusing on previous experiences of consolation can lift us out of desolation, knowing that it will not last forever, and the voice of God will again become clearer.

The author of Acts seems quite clear about what God's will is when it comes to Paul's latest missionary journey. It is surprising to read that Paul and his companions had been 'forbidden by the Holy Spirit to speak the word in Asia' and that the 'Spirit of Jesus did not allow them' to go to a certain region. We rarely expect to hear that God does *not* want us to spread the gospel or enter a certain neighbourhood.

Maybe if we listen closely, God may be telling us to be more cautious, to wait for the right moment to begin our work. Perhaps the time is not right and so God is forbidding us to 'speak the word in a certain place'. Then, when the time *is* right, our mission will be nurtured by the Holy Spirit, because we will be 'convinced that God' is calling us to make this decision.

COLLECT

God, who in generous mercy sent the Holy Spirit
upon your Church in the burning fire of your love:
grant that your people may be fervent
in the fellowship of the gospel
that, always abiding in you,
they may be found steadfast in faith and active in service;
through Jesus Christ your Son our Lord,
who is alive and reigns with you,
in the unity of the Holy Spirit,
one God, now and for ever.

| *Reflection by* **Christopher Woods**

Psalms 32, **36**
1 Kings 8.63 – 9.9
Acts 16.25-end

Tuesday 11 September

Acts 16.25-end

'... he and his entire family were baptized without delay' (v.33)

We are witnesses in today's reading to a conversion that is both dramatic and comforting. While Paul and Silas are imprisoned, an earthquake causes the jail to become insecure. The prison guard tasked with holding them struggles to understand what has happened and blames himself for the jailbreak. Rather than run away, however, Paul and Silas save the prison guard. This act of kindness encourages the prison guard to receive the joy of faith, and he returns the kindness, very naturally and effortlessly, with acts of healing and hospitality at his home.

Reciprocal kindness is a gateway to receiving faith in God and experiencing the joy of salvation. But kindness is only the beginning. The prison guard is baptized along with his whole family, without delay. There is an urgency about this sacramental act, almost as if nothing at all must prevent the salvation of God penetrating the life of this man and his next of kin.

If we meet someone who has a change of heart in life, and who wants to know God more closely, do we show kindness or do we treat them with suspicion? Do we encourage the sacrament of Baptism 'without delay' – or do we want them to wait until *we* feel they are totally ready to make the promises?

Lord God,
defend your Church from all false teaching
and give to your people knowledge of your truth,
that we may enjoy eternal life
in Jesus Christ our Lord.

COLLECT

Reflection by **Christopher Woods** | 251

Wednesday 12 September

Acts 17.1-15

'Jason has entertained them as guests' (v.7)

Who is Jason? And why has he courageously been entertaining as guests people who have been 'turning the world upside down'?

Now conventionally known as 'Jason of Tarsus', he was an early convert from Judaism to Christianity and became well known in Thessalonica as one who took other Christians into his home. In particular, he gave refuge to Paul, Timothy and Silas when they visited the region.

Jason is a good role model of how helping vulnerable and persecuted minorities can be a noble and selfless task, despite the risks and dangers associated with such action. In places where Christians are a minority faith group and are severely persecuted, it is because of people like Jason that they can feel some solidarity with each other and pray together. Even today in certain places, such worship is opposed as vehemently now as it was in the time of Paul's missionary preaching.

Let us pray for those who work hard, courageously, to protect and give shelter to those in our world persecuted for their faith, for example in Syria, in other parts of the middle East, in regions of Africa and indeed closer to home. Why not decide to pray each week for a certain part of the Christian world facing persecution, that the hearts of the oppressors might be turned to repentance?

COLLECT

God, who in generous mercy sent the Holy Spirit
    upon your Church in the burning fire of your love:
grant that your people may be fervent
in the fellowship of the gospel
that, always abiding in you,
they may be found steadfast in faith and active in service;
through Jesus Christ your Son our Lord,
who is alive and reigns with you,
in the unity of the Holy Spirit,
one God, now and for ever.

| *Reflection by* **Christopher Woods**

Thursday 13 September

Acts 17.16-end

'... some scoffed' (v.32)

Paul's missionary journey now finds him in Athens, where he acknowledges a great religious fervour. However, the object and focus of the Athenians' worship is 'an unknown God'. Paul explains to them that the God whom they must worship is the one revealed through the resurrection of Christ. He does this in the very public forum of the Areopagus, the rocky hill that was the seat of the ancient supreme court of Athens. As a population already devoted to religious belief, but who do not yet 'know' God as he has been revealed, some of the Athenians prove receptive to Paul's teaching, notably Dionysius and Damaris. However, not everyone is so receptive. Some 'scoffed' at Paul's preaching. Paul takes this in his stride; he does not let scoffers push him off course.

In our contemporary world, we are slowly beginning to realize that we may need to take a leaf out of Paul's book and not be put off by those who mock what we believe in. Often, scoffing is a symptom of misunderstanding or an unwillingness to meet someone else at their point of understanding. Scoffers can have minds closed to new ideas or to conversations that have the potential to transform. It is clear that Paul did not spend a vast amount of time trying to convince the scoffers. He allowed those who wanted to come to join him on his journey and he allowed the scoffers to stay behind.

The question for us is whether we expend energy trying to convince the scoffer to believe, or instead spend time nurturing the faith of those who are – even just a little bit – interested.

Lord God,
defend your Church from all false teaching
and give to your people knowledge of your truth,
that we may enjoy eternal life
in Jesus Christ our Lord.

COLLECT

Friday 14 September
Holy Cross Day

Psalms 2, 8, 146
Genesis 3.1-15
John 12.27-36a

John 12.27-36a

'Now my soul is troubled. And what should I say –
"Father, save me from this hour"?' (v.27)

It is simultaneously comforting and a little unsettling to read that Jesus questioned the ensuing events of the Passion. Perhaps he thought of finding a way to avoid his imminent death. It is unsettling because we have sanitized Jesus' passion, crucifixion and death in our spirituality. We are comforted because we know from his reaction that Jesus was human; he can and does stand in our shoes in the midst of our suffering. Similarly comforting but rather more unsettling is Jesus' acceptance of the fate that awaits him. He eschews the temptation to pursue an alternative option, and instead recognizes that he has no choice if he is to fulfil his vocation.

Our vocation is to do the same: to accept the most difficult path and realize that sometimes we have no real choice or – at the very least in our free world – we are to choose the hardest option. The message of the cross is precisely this. Yet so often we find ways of avoiding the tough call and instead remain in the safe zone of our lives and existences.

It is not so for many in the world, in places of religious persecution, where freedom of expression is not tolerated. They have no choice but to face the cross constructed for them. Torture, violence and death are their constructed crosses.

This leaves us with an uncomfortable reality: that salvation is built on an instrument of torture, but through this, God transforms this unspeakable suffering into unspeakable joy.

COLLECT

Almighty God,
who in the passion of your blessed Son
made an instrument of painful death
to be for us the means of life and peace:
grant us so to glory in the cross of Christ
that we may gladly suffer for his sake;
who is alive and reigns with you,
in the unity of the Holy Spirit,
one God, now and for ever.

254 | *Reflection by* **Christopher Woods**

Psalms 41, **42**, 43
I Kings 12.1-24
Acts 18.22 – 19.7

Saturday 15 September

Acts 18.22 – 19.7

'When Paul had laid his hands on them, the Holy Spirit came upon them' (19.6)

Paul acts with episcopal authority and apostolic faith to new Christian believers in Ephesus. We witness people who have been exposed by advocates of John the Baptist to some basic aspects of the Christian faith, but whose faith, education and experience are not yet mature. The most vital experience they lack is that of the Holy Spirit. However, through Paul's laying on of hands and teaching, they come to experience the fullness of God's Holy Spirit.

This is an example of how the early Church regularized a variety of independent streams of Christianity. Baptism very clearly in the name of the Lord Jesus followed by the laying on of hands are the litmus tests of apostolic Christianity as Paul understands it.

For the joy of faith to be fully alive in us, we too are invited to receive the Holy Spirit into our hearts. This is effected in many ways in the contemporary Church, most obviously in the form of the sacraments. Paul's laying on of hands might be understood to be an early form of the sacrament of confirmation, where the seal of the Spirit is conferred on the newly baptized.

The Church offers sacramental ministry as a free and open access to the Holy Spirit for each and every one of us who wishes to accept this gift. Let us rejoice in this and receive it happily.

God, who in generous mercy sent the Holy Spirit
upon your Church in the burning fire of your love:
grant that your people may be fervent
in the fellowship of the gospel
that, always abiding in you,
they may be found steadfast in faith and active in service;
through Jesus Christ your Son our Lord,
who is alive and reigns with you,
in the unity of the Holy Spirit,
one God, now and for ever.

COLLECT

Reflection by **Christopher Woods** | 255

Monday 17 September

Acts 19.8-20

*'A number of those who practised magic collected their books
and burned them publicly' (v.19)*

The conversion of many people from alternative spiritualities or ritual practices to the resurrection faith is celebrated clearly in the Acts of the Apostles. The fact that Luke, the author of Acts, remarks on the detail of the burning of books of converts who had practised magic is a proof that gestures of change of whatever size were important for the community in the transition to Christianity.

The books of magicians were clearly very expensive – their value was 'fifty thousand silver coins'; this was a marker of the sacrifice these new converts were making. Yet such sacrifice led to joy and more conversion. A public gesture of conversion to Christianity led to more widespread preaching of the 'word of the Lord' and to the deepening of the faith of new converts.

Of course, we must strike a note of caution: more recently, book burning has gained much more sinister overtones, from World War II anti-Semitism to the more recent destruction of historically valuable heritage material. Nowadays, public signs of Christian commitment may take less dramatic forms – an outdoor baptism, new Christians joining in a prayer walk or being invited to carry palm branches at the front of a Palm Sunday procession, for example. Such positive rituals can be important not only for individuals but also for the wider community of faith, building confidence, and encouraging and inviting others to seek a life of faith.

COLLECT

O Lord, we beseech you mercifully to hear the prayers
     of your people who call upon you;
and grant that they may both perceive and know
     what things they ought to do,
and also may have grace and power faithfully to fulfil them;
through Jesus Christ your Son our Lord,
who is alive and reigns with you,
in the unity of the Holy Spirit,
one God, now and for ever.

| *Reflection by* **Christopher Woods**

Psalms **48**, 52
1 Kings 13.11-end
Acts 19.21-end

Tuesday 18 September

Acts 19.21-end

'About that time no little disturbance broke out concerning the Way' (v.23)

Luke's attention to detail, as noted in the public gesture of the burning of the magicians' books, is made even more obvious in the great riot in the enormous theatre in Ephesus, with its capacity of over 20,000 seats. Here we see a clash between pagan culture and a new era of the faith in the 'good news of Jesus'. Paul's preaching clearly had a significant impact in Ephesus, directly challenging those who remained loyal and faithful to pagan idols and creating significant cultural tension.

We see such tensions and conflicts played out in many different ways in our own communities, in matters of religion, faith and world view. Religiously motivated attacks or riots may be rare, but they still happen, and they are frightening.

Where a community of faith experiences tension or hostility, it must be dealt with generously and sensitively. In today's Church life, as in previous generations, people may have very clear and decided views on matters of faith and order, but any Christian community needs to be able to reach consensus or compromise, seeking to find the most grace-filled methods of disagreement without becoming embroiled in personal bitterness.

It is easier said than done, but if we cannot do it as the body of Christ, then what hope is there for the world?

Lord of creation,
whose glory is around and within us:
open our eyes to your wonders,
that we may serve you with reverence
and know your peace at our lives' end,
through Jesus Christ our Lord.

COLLECT

Wednesday 19 September

Psalm 119.57-80
1 Kings 17
Acts 20.1-16

Acts 20.1-16

*'On the first day of the week, when we met to break bread,
Paul was holding discussion with them ...' (v.7)*

In today's portion of Acts we glimpse a description of typical early Church worship – a celebration of the resurrection. The first day of the week, being Sunday, would likely have begun on Saturday evening and continued through the night. We know that Paul preached and taught at length as the worshippers kept vigil to await the coming dawn. There is a humorous aside in this passage – that Paul's interminable talking was the cause of Eutychus' deep sleep! However, recognizing the terrible accident, Paul stops preaching and goes down to rescue the young man, declaring him alive, though he was thought to be dead.

Worship in this missional community was made up of elements very recognizable as a Christian Eucharist – with preaching and teaching, breaking of bread and healing. To explain why we meet on Sundays to worship and why the Eucharist is so central, we need look no further than the example of this early Church community, where the Jewish sabbath was extended to feature a distinctively Christian act of worship, one that called to mind Jesus' Last Supper.

The worship that we are invited to in this passage of Scripture is necessarily missional, *with* and *for* a new community of believers, who need encouragement, nurture and confidence. These are features needed in all communities of faith, so that we may be constantly outward looking.

COLLECT

O Lord, we beseech you mercifully to hear the prayers
of your people who call upon you;
and grant that they may both perceive and know
what things they ought to do,
and also may have grace and power faithfully to fulfil them;
through Jesus Christ your Son our Lord,
who is alive and reigns with you,
in the unity of the Holy Spirit,
one God, now and for ever.

| *Reflection by* **Christopher Woods**

Psalms 56, **57** (63*)
1 Kings 18.1-20
Acts 20.17-end

Thursday 20 September

Acts 20.17-end

'Keep watch over yourselves and over all the flock, of which the Holy Spirit has made you overseers' (v.28)

Paul is leaving his missionary community, and this departure is emotionally difficult. We read in detail about the pain Paul experiences, but even more about the pain and grief that the community feels.

However, Paul is determined to impart confidence and authority to the maturing community of faith he is leaving behind. He declares that they are 'overseers' (the same Greek word is translated into English as 'bishop'), that is to say responsible for the nurturing, teaching and proclamation of the apostolic faith of Christ. It is a daunting and challenging responsibility, as indicated by the reference to 'the blood' of Jesus that was needed for the foundation of the Church.

Paul warns the people in no uncertain terms of the dangers and threats that the Church in Ephesus will continue to face, but his assurances of solidarity – that he will also face similar threats and dangers wherever he continues his ministry – are equally important for us. When we leave behind a community of faith that we have helped to nurture and nourish, we assure those we leave behind of our continued prayers, and, despite the emotional grief and pain, we entrust them to God. We have confidence that they will continue to be stewards and apostles of the faith of Christ.

Lord of creation,
whose glory is around and within us:
open our eyes to your wonders,
that we may serve you with reverence
and know your peace at our lives' end,
through Jesus Christ our Lord.

COLLECT

Reflection by **Christopher Woods**   259

Friday 21 September
Matthew, Apostle and Evangelist

Psalms 49, 117
1 Kings 19.15-end
2 Timothy 3.14-end

2 Timothy 3.14-end

'All scripture is inspired by God and is useful for teaching, for reproof, for correction, and for training in righteousness' (v.16)

Verse 16 of 2 Timothy is well used and well known, quoted in a variety of contexts to imply a variety of meanings. What is clear is that the author of the second letter to Timothy is referring to the Jewish scriptures. That is not to say that we as Christians cannot infer the same weight of meaning to both the Old and New Testaments, but it is worth bearing in mind what is being referred to in the verse itself.

The clear message is that believers are to be committed to sound doctrine, to faithful reliance on the Scripture for guidance in matters of belief, religious practices and moral behaviour. Moreover, the verse affirms the importance of sacred Scripture in the equipping of Church leaders.

Scripture, however, should not be used to judge, belittle or demean one another. Rather, it is a sacred resource from which to build one another up in faith and confidence and to sustain a growing Christian community.

Those who were inspired to write Scripture have prayed, struggled and been faithful to the God who called them to follow him. Among them we count Matthew, apostle and evangelist, whom we celebrate today. Those of us who continue in this faith are charged to struggle to make sense of their ancient wisdom, to enliven and excite the faith of each fresh generation of believers.

COLLECT

O Almighty God,
whose blessed Son called Matthew the tax collector
to be an apostle and evangelist:
give us grace to forsake the selfish pursuit of gain
    and the possessive love of riches
that we may follow in the way of your Son Jesus Christ,
who is alive and reigns with you,
in the unity of the Holy Spirit,
one God, now and for ever.

Reflection by **Christopher Woods**

Psalm **68**
I Kings 19
Acts 21.17-36

Saturday 22 September

Acts 21.17-36

'When the seven days were almost completed, the Jews from Asia
... stirred up the whole crowd' (v.27)

It seems that Paul causes controversy wherever he goes. Or rather, what he preaches stirs within people a sense of resistance. This is because he is preaching something counter-cultural, a message that demands a radical change, both of heart and of practice. It is perhaps highly symbolic that he has now reached Jerusalem, the place he had challenged himself to travel to. The resistance to him here after seven days is vitriolic and intense, despite an initial warm reception and a recognition from his fellow pilgrims that many Jews had begun to believe the message of the gospel. This surely reminds us of the last week of Jesus' own life – first a triumphal entry into Jerusalem to cheering welcome from crowds, but leading only a few days later to highly charged and cruel rejection by a baying mob.

How often do we feel that the message we try to proclaim not only falls on deaf ears but is met with resistance and rejection? Is it safer to avoid the subject of faith and religion so as to avoid a heated argument? Yet Paul does not avoid these awkward encounters – some would say he walks into them. He accepts that they are necessary for the sake of spreading the gospel message.

Perhaps the next time we are confronted with a potentially awkward conversation about our faith, we might have a little of Paul's conviction and not be phased by the conflict.

O Lord, we beseech you mercifully to hear the prayers
of your people who call upon you;
and grant that they may both perceive and know
what things they ought to do,
and also may have grace and power faithfully to fulfil them;
through Jesus Christ your Son our Lord,
who is alive and reigns with you,
in the unity of the Holy Spirit,
one God, now and for ever.

COLLECT

Reflection by **Christopher Woods** | 261

Monday 24 September

Psalm **71**
I Kings 21
Acts 21.37 – 22.21

Acts 21.37 – 22.21

'...let me speak to the people' (21.39)

Having almost caused a riot in the temple in Jerusalem, Paul is arrested by the tribune. On his way to the barracks he asks to speak to the people. Allowed to do so, he makes the most of this opportunity. The story of his dazzling encounter with the living Lord Jesus and his subsequent dramatic conversation, first told by Luke in Acts 9, is retold from Paul's own mouth. The crowd are attentive, even spellbound.

Paul offers a masterclass in witnessing to our faith. First he lays out his credentials. His birth, nurture and education indicate his strong Jewish inheritance – he can be trusted. Second, he speaks his listeners' dialect – not just Hebrew, but almost certainly Aramaic. Next, he offers his testimony, demonstrating how Jesus has stopped him in his tracks and turned his life around. His account is honest, open and unvarnished. His encounter with Jesus has taken him from persecuting to worshipping: he is a changed man, and this transformation comes from divine intervention and is not of Paul's making. His account is clear, and the detail lends authenticity.

Finally, he leads his listeners to the startling revelation that the Messiah is found in Jesus, and is for everyone. They listen, they are with him - though for the time being, his commission to the gentiles is a step too far. Let's remind ourselves that God acts powerfully and people will listen when we dare to speak of Jesus.

COLLECT

Almighty God,
you have made us for yourself,
and our hearts are restless till they find their rest in you:
pour your love into our hearts and draw us to yourself,
and so bring us at last to your heavenly city
where we shall see you face to face;
through Jesus Christ your Son our Lord,
who is alive and reigns with you,
in the unity of the Holy Spirit,
one God, now and for ever.

| *Reflection by* **Catherine Williams**

Psalm **73**
I Kings 22.1-28
Acts 22.22 – 23.11

Tuesday 25 September

Acts 22.22 – 23.11

'Keep up your courage!' (23.11)

Paul's presence in Jerusalem continues to cause upset and mayhem: he is ushered off to the barracks to be interrogated and flogged. Now he throws into the mix his Roman citizenship – another credential that earns him respect, fear and, most importantly, better treatment from the tribune. Paul is brought before the Jewish council, where more insults are thrown and further misunderstandings occur. He has another opportunity to speak of his faith. This time he stresses the resurrection, knowing that it will divide the Pharisees and Sadducees, who believed very different things regarding the afterlife (Mark 12.18). Thus he skilfully turns the council against itself, recognizing that a divided house (Matthew 12.25) will be weaker in its pursuit of him.

Testifying to Jesus can be very demanding, requiring skill, wisdom and tenacity. Knowing when to speak, who to speak with and what to say, as well as rising to the occasion whenever God presents opportunity, however unpromising, requires courage, grit and grace. None of us, including Paul, witness to Jesus from our own strength. It's by the Holy Spirit working within us that we testify to Jesus as Lord (1 Corinthians 12.3). Paul's initial life-changing encounter with Jesus is supplemented by a vision in the barracks – to top up his courage and enable him to keep going so that he can witness in Rome. In the kingdom-work God calls us to, we can be assured that Christ will be before, alongside and behind, supplying confidence and courage for our calling.

Gracious God,
you call us to fullness of life:
deliver us from unbelief
and banish our anxieties
with the liberating love of Jesus Christ our Lord.

COLLECT

Wednesday 26 September

Acts 23.12-end

'I came with the guard and rescued him' (v.27)

Events can take extraordinary twists and turns when God is in the driving seat! Paul remains in great danger in Jerusalem, where a group of Jews take an extreme oath – not to eat or drink until they have killed him. God's providence arrives in the shape of Paul's nephew, who is able to warn Paul, tell his tale to the tribune and foil the plot. The story moves on apace and Paul is moved with half the garrison into the jurisdiction of governor Felix, in Caesarea. Thus Claudius Lysias, the tribune, rescues Paul from almost certain death and moves him with such a heavy guard that his passage is secure.

We are left with questions from Luke's brief narrative. Who are Paul's sister and nephew? Does Paul have more family? What happened to those who took the oath? Did they starve? Why send so many soldiers to deliver Paul?

In God's economy we are never really in control of events, and the details can be full of surprises, both delightful and concerning. God's purposes are worked out through those both with and without faith in Jesus. Good people, used by God, can show up in unexpected ways, and with exquisite timing. In contrast we can be so concerned with stamping out what we perceive to be heresy within our ranks that we miss the generous, gracious and exciting new work that God is doing to bring about the new creation in our midst.

COLLECT

Almighty God,
you have made us for yourself,
and our hearts are restless till they find their rest in you:
pour your love into our hearts and draw us to yourself,
and so bring us at last to your heavenly city
where we shall see you face to face;
through Jesus Christ your Son our Lord,
who is alive and reigns with you,
in the unity of the Holy Spirit,
one God, now and for ever.

| *Reflection by* **Catherine Williams**

Psalm **78.1-39***
2 Kings 1.2-17
Acts 24.1-23

Thursday 27 September

Acts 24.1-23

'It is about the resurrection...' (v.21)

Paul is given the opportunity to speak about his faith to higher and higher authorities and in increasingly formal settings. We meet him today making his case to the governor, high priest, elders and lawyers. The case brought against him is one of profaning the temple and causing civil unrest. It doesn't take Paul long to demonstrate that he has done nothing of the sort. He uses the case against him to share again his belief both in the specific recent resurrection of Jesus Christ, and the promised general resurrection of all. He shows the seamless link between 'the God of our ancestors', the law and the prophets, and the developing beliefs of 'the Way', founded on the death and resurrection of Jesus Christ. No amount of flattery from Tertullus towards Felix can bring the hearing to a satisfactory conclusion for the Jerusalem cohort. The case is adjourned.

If we are serious about sharing our Christian faith, then we must be open to all opportunities. God may call us to speak into a wide variety of contexts – some more challenging to our comfort than others. There will be those who are intent on bringing us down, picking holes in our witnessing, trying to make us look foolish. Whoever we witness to – whether powerful or not – we are called to speak in truth and with love of the hope that is in us (1 Peter 3.15).

Gracious God,
you call us to fullness of life:
deliver us from unbelief
and banish our anxieties
with the liberating love of Jesus Christ our Lord.

COLLECT

Friday 28 September

Psalm **55**
2 Kings 2.1-18
Acts 24.24 – 25.12

Acts 24.24 – 25.12

'After two years had passed ...' (24.27)

Paul is called to witness in Rome – the Lord told him in a vision, but it is taking ages to achieve. We sense that governor Felix is fascinated by his prisoner, and with his wife, Drusilla, takes time discussing 'the Way' with Paul. Here are echoes of the dialogue between John the Baptist and Herod, whose marital adventures were not dissimilar to those of Felix. Those who know that their lives are far from blameless can be equally excited and disturbed by the good news of Jesus, which pricks consciences. Paul must wait patiently: Felix is in no hurry to try his case again.

Two years pass and the new governor, Festus, is urged to resolve the matter, encouraging Paul to be tried in Jerusalem. Paul has spent long days devising his next steps. Here comes his ace: as a Roman citizen he can appeal to the very highest secular power. He asks to see the Emperor – at last he is on his way to Rome.

Sometimes we can be certain of what we are called to do, and yet everything seems to transpire against us. Remaining constant and focused when little is happening or when we are powerless to move things along can be draining and demoralizing. Playing the long game is a spiritual art in which nothing is wasted. What we learn through trusting in God, and remaining faithful and patient in adversity, is precious fuel for the journey ahead.

COLLECT | Almighty God,
you have made us for yourself,
and our hearts are restless till they find their rest in you:
pour your love into our hearts and draw us to yourself,
and so bring us at last to your heavenly city
where we shall see you face to face;
through Jesus Christ your Son our Lord,
who is alive and reigns with you,
in the unity of the Holy Spirit,
one God, now and for ever.

| *Reflection by* **Catherine Williams**

Psalms 34, 150
Tobit 12.6-end
or Daniel 12.1-4
Acts 12.1-11

Saturday 29 September
Michael and All Angels

Daniel 12.1-4

'Michael, the great prince, the protector of your people, shall arise'
(v.1)

Traditionally, in the UK, Michaelmas was the Quarter Day that signalled the end of the financial year – when all accounts were settled, and new servants and labourers hired. It was a time when the Church prayed to Michael and All Angels for protection during the coming longer nights when dark forces were thought to be abroad and evil lurking. The numerous encounters with angels in the Bible herald important events when heaven and earth meet, and belief in angels as guardians, protectors, messengers and deliverers runs deep in the spiritual psyche of many, not just those who profess faith.

Michael is the Archangel depicted as the messenger of God who protects and delivers God's suffering people. It is he who leads the armies of angels in their defeat of Satan during the war in heaven recorded in the apocalyptic book of Revelation (Revelation 12.7). Here in Daniel, too, the end times are being reviewed. Written during the Maccabean revolt (167–160 BC), the book of Daniel witnesses to those who remain faithful to God under persecution and great duress. Daniel points to the time when there will be a general resurrection prior to judgement so that justice can be done and those who have died a martyr's death can enter everlasting life. Wise ones will shine; those who lead others to faith will be like the stars. It's a vision of restoration and redemption, keeping hope alive and offering protection in dark times.

Everlasting God,
you have ordained and constituted
the ministries of angels and mortals in a wonderful order:
grant that as your holy angels always serve you in heaven,
so, at your command,
they may help and defend us on earth;
through Jesus Christ your Son our Lord,
who is alive and reigns with you,
in the unity of the Holy Spirit,
one God, now and for ever.

COLLECT

Reflection by **Catherine Williams** | 267

Monday 1 October

Acts 26.1-23

'... turn from darkness to light' (v.18)

God continues to line up dignitaries to whom Paul can witness. It's the turn of King Agrippa, who asks to hear Paul's case when he welcomes Festus, as governor. Paul has another opportunity to share his story, and we hear more of his dramatic conversion. Paul is keen to demonstrate how in his turning to Christ he is not being unfaithful to his and Agrippa's Jewish ancestry ('our religion') but rather finds its fulfilment therein. The resurrection that the Pharisees look to has been demonstrated by God in Jesus – the general has become particular in Jesus who is 'the first fruits of those who have died' (1 Corinthians 15.20). The longed-for new creation has broken in.

Paul also demonstrates his mission to the gentiles as a continuation of Israel's vocation to be a 'light to the nations' (Isaiah 49.6). Just as he has moved from being blinded to having his eyes opened, so Christ has called him to lead others from darkness to light, both in the Jewish community and further afield. God's light is for all people, irrespective of heritage. In this account Paul stresses his commissioning by the risen Christ to continue God's mission to save all.

This is our discipleship's mandate too. Who are those that we believe to be 'beyond the pale'? Where are the barriers to believing in and belonging to the kingdom? Where do we need to switch on the lights?

COLLECT

Almighty and everlasting God,
increase in us your gift of faith
that, forsaking what lies behind
and reaching out to that which is before,
we may run the way of your commandments
and win the crown of everlasting joy;
through Jesus Christ your Son our Lord,
who is alive and reigns with you,
in the unity of the Holy Spirit,
one God, now and for ever.

| *Reflection by* **Catherine Williams**

Psalms 87, **89.1-18**
2 Kings 6.1-23
Acts 26.24-end

Tuesday 2 October

Acts 26.24-end
'I know that you believe' (v.27)

Jesus told his disciples that they would be 'dragged before governors and kings' to witness to the gentiles (Matthew 10.18). Paul has been fulfilling that prophecy with aplomb. Though the authorities have been angered, frustrated, excited and enticed by his message, none of them have found him guilty of the charges against him. Passed from pillar to post, Paul has had opportunity to tell the good news of the resurrection of Jesus to numerous people, both secular and religious, leaders and those led. If he hadn't appealed to the Emperor, he would be free by now, but due to Jesus' commission Paul's sights are firmly fixed on Rome. God's calling rarely allows for the easy way out.

Few of us are called upon to witness to Christ before our monarch or head of state, though some are, and it's good to be open to God's surprises! But day to day, as Christian disciples, we are all the Lord's witnesses wherever we go – walking, talking, active expressions of Jesus Christ who dwells within us and makes himself known through us to those with whom we live, work, play and socialize. While most of us in the West won't be in physical danger because of our faith, it still takes courage and commitment to speak openly of Christ and to encourage with care and skill those who are seeking and long to believe. We are all called to witness to Christ.

God, our judge and saviour,
teach us to be open to your truth
and to trust in your love,
that we may live each day
with confidence in the salvation which is given
through Jesus Christ our Lord.

COLLECT

Wednesday 3 October

Psalm 119.105-128
2 Kings 9.1-16
Acts 27.1-26

Acts 27.1-26

'... keep up your courage ... for I have faith in God' (v.25)

Paul is finally on his way to Rome. Luke writes in great detail of the ports, cargoes, winds and sea conditions encountered so that we can all enter into the adventures taking place aboard ship. Paul is sailing at a dangerous time of year, after the Fast for the Day of Atonement, between autumn and winter when the seas in the Mediterranean can be perilous – as we know from numerous recent refugee tragedies in that region.

In Jewish mythology the sea was a symbol for danger, filled with dark powers and monsters. There are echoes in this passage of the voyage of Jonah, where many things have to be discarded in order for the ship to stay afloat, and all are at the mercy of the elements. Paul, like Jonah, is prophetic on this voyage, but, unlike Jonah, he is not running away from God, but fulfilling God's mission. He is able to reassure those on board. An angel has told him that everyone will be safe. Paul speaks the same words to his fellow travellers that Jesus spoke to him in prison: 'Keep up your courage!' (Acts 23.11). Passing on the words of Jesus restores hope, keeps vision alive and brings calm.

It's not that faith in God protects us from danger, but it does enable us to endure crises, exercise leadership in demanding situations and restore calm and confidence in those around us.

COLLECT

Almighty and everlasting God,
increase in us your gift of faith
that, forsaking what lies behind
and reaching out to that which is before,
we may run the way of your commandments
and win the crown of everlasting joy;
through Jesus Christ your Son our Lord,
who is alive and reigns with you,
in the unity of the Holy Spirit,
one God, now and for ever.

| *Reflection by* **Catherine Williams**

Thursday 4 October

Acts 27.27-end

'... all were brought safely to land' (v.44)

A fortnight into the storm and soundings taken suggest land is close by. Fearing rocks and possible disaster, the sailors try to escape, leaving the soldiers and prisoners to their fate. Paul knows a thing or two about being shipwrecked: it's happened to him at least three times before. He steps up into leadership and his example and encouragement to eat, build up strength and work together ensures that, even though the ship breaks up in the waters, everyone eventually lands safely and is saved. He is convinced that the Lord doesn't want anyone to be lost on this venture.

Luke's writing of the meal shared by those on board has eucharistic echoes, with bread being taken, blessed, broken and shared. Paul remarks that the food will help everyone survive and the Greek word used here is the same as that for 'salvation'. Paul shows an interesting balance of spirituality, natural authority and practical common sense in his leadership. Inspired by his faith in the God who saves and has promised deliverance for all, he is able to take charge in the face of setbacks, demonstrating resilience and compassion. All aboard, from the centurion and soldiers to the crew and the prisoners, listen and respond.

Christian leadership, shaped by faith and experience should enable all who are struggling in deep stormy waters to swim with or cling to the salvages of faith in order to make it safely to shore.

God, our judge and saviour,
teach us to be open to your truth
and to trust in your love,
that we may live each day
with confidence in the salvation which is given
through Jesus Christ our Lord.

COLLECT

Friday 5 October

Acts 28.1-16

'... a viper ... fastened itself on his hand' (v.3)

After all Paul has been through and survived, suddenly it looks as if a Maltese snake will curtail his mission to the gentiles once and for all. The snake, like the sea, is another classic symbol of evil, reaching all the way back to Eden. Paul shakes it off with hardly a thought. The new creation is breaking in wherever the disciples of Jesus stand firm, and nothing can halt it.

For the locals, Paul has become god-like, and even more so when he begins to cure their ailments, from the father of Publius down to the ordinary islanders. Honours abound. Wherever he goes and whatever circumstances occur, Paul is always first and foremost the Lord's servant. Nothing it seems can stop him speaking and acting for Christ. Luke is showing that the gospel of Jesus Christ is alive and active, reaching out to the ends of earth – unstoppable.

Winter over, Paul sets out on the final leg of his journey to Rome. He sails under the figurehead of the 'Twin Brothers', a symbol common in both Greek and Roman mythology, but also perhaps here reminding us again of Paul's mission to unite gentiles and Jews – children of the same heavenly father – into the one body of Christ. The confidence, commitment and tenacity shown by Paul and his companions throughout these chapters should inspire us afresh to hold onto and exercise with confidence God's call on our lives.

COLLECT | Almighty and everlasting God,
increase in us your gift of faith
that, forsaking what lies behind
and reaching out to that which is before,
we may run the way of your commandments
and win the crown of everlasting joy;
through Jesus Christ your Son our Lord,
who is alive and reigns with you,
in the unity of the Holy Spirit,
one God, now and for ever.

| *Reflection by* **Catherine Williams**

Psalms 96, **97**, 100
2 Kings 17.1-23
Acts 28.17-end

Saturday 6 October

Acts 28.17-end

'... teaching about the Lord Jesus Christ' (v.31)

He's made it! The Lord promised that Paul would testify in Rome and he is at the end of Acts doing exactly that. At the ascension Jesus told his disciples that they would be his witnesses 'to the ends of the earth' (Acts 1.8). It might be more accurate to say that Paul has reached the 'centre of the earth' – at least in political and secular terms – but his mission is accomplished. He spends his time meeting firstly with the Jews in Rome, trying to convince them that Jesus is the promised Messiah. As often happens with Christian witness, some believe and some don't – it was ever thus. Paul points out – as does Jesus in all four of the Gospels – Isaiah's prediction that Israel would fail to grasp the good news of God when they heard it (Isaiah 6.9-10). The message is for the gentiles too: 'they will listen'. For the next two years Paul preaches and teaches to the gentiles – and the rest, as they say, is history.

Did Paul testify to Emperor Nero? Luke is tantalizingly silent on the subject. Does it matter? Jesus' commission to Paul was to witness in Rome – it was Paul himself who appealed to the Emperor in order to reach Italy. Keeping our eyes fixed on fulfilling God's calling and not getting side-tracked by our own elaborate plans is the way of faithful discipleship to Christ.

COLLECT

God, our judge and saviour,
teach us to be open to your truth
and to trust in your love,
that we may live each day
with confidence in the salvation which is given
through Jesus Christ our Lord.

Reflection by **Catherine Williams** | 273

Monday 8 October

Psalms **98**, 99, 101
2 Kings 17.24-end
Philippians 1.1-11

Philippians 1.1-11

'And this is my prayer, that your love may overflow more and more' (v.9)

Aesop tells of a wren who hid in the feathers on the eagle's back, to win the competition to decide who was the king of birds. When the eagle had flown to the greatest height that he could, the wren flew just a little bit further.

This illustrates a paradox in the relation between comparatives and superlatives: 'betters' and 'bests'. The trouble with superlatives is that they suggest an end-point. And once such a point is imagined, we find ourselves thinking (like the wren) what a little bit beyond it might look like. The 'little bit more' makes the 'most' look like it has fallen short.

God is never an end-point. In God there is always more. Paul conjures up this mind-blowing abundance in this passage. He instructs his hearers to 'discern what is best', but 'what is best' (life with God) is known in the experience of a love that 'overflows more and more'. In such a love there is no satiation point and the delight never palls.

Even the eagle tires, and even the wren who goes that little bit higher would tire too if forced to keep going up. But God's perfection – God's 'bestness' – is not like that. As C. S. Lewis' children found as they moved into the 'real Narnia' at the end of *The Last Battle*, heaven has no borders and no limits: there is no end to going 'further up and further in!'.

COLLECT

O God, forasmuch as without you
we are not able to please you;
mercifully grant that your Holy Spirit
may in all things direct and rule our hearts;
through Jesus Christ your Son our Lord,
who is alive and reigns with you,
in the unity of the Holy Spirit,
one God, now and for ever.

Tuesday 9 October

Philippians 1.12-end

'I am hard pressed between the two' (v.23)

Complexity is troubling. Plurality disturbs. One all-too-easy way to deal with this is to narrow your focus, to close down alternatives, artificially to simplify your particular piece of world. Some politicians make their careers by promising they will do this; it can have huge appeal. But when people simplify their world in this way, they often deny themselves opportunities to go on new adventures of imagination and learning: to be challenged, surprised, and stretched in new directions. Living out of control can be the key to really living.

Paul is a model, here, of how not to seek control at all costs. He accepts unresolved alternatives. He exemplifies how to remain open to more than one pathway; to what he cannot control in advance. He takes some classic opposites ('to live' and 'to die') and subverts the opposition by interpreting one as 'gain' and the other as 'Christ', which are not opposites at all. In other words, he helps us to see that both life and death can be grace.

'Christ is proclaimed in every way, whether out of false motives or true' – 'whether I come and see you or am absent and hear about you, I will know that you are standing firm.' Paul proclaims that uncertainty does not have to be the enemy of confidence. It is not our job to make our story come out right by making a set of perfectly correct choices and closing down all the alternatives. A simplified world would be a shrunken world.

Faithful Lord,
whose steadfast love never ceases
and whose mercies never come to an end:
grant us the grace to trust you
and to receive the gifts of your love,
new every morning,
in Jesus Christ our Lord.

COLLECT

Wednesday 10 October

Psalms 110, **111**, 112
2 Kings 18.13-end
Philippians 2.1-13

Philippians 2.1-13

'... he emptied himself' (vv.6-7)

What is the 'name above every name' that Jesus is given? It is unlike any other name in the world's long history, for it is a name that has the power to unite the whole world in worship: before this name, every knee will bow. But this power, likewise, is unlike any power in the world's long history. It is the power of radical generosity.

The name that Jesus bears by virtue of his willingness to live and die as a gift to others is a name that cannot be pronounced or written. It is the name communicated to Moses in the burning bush, signified in the 'tetragrammaton' (YHWH) and replaced in speech by many Jews and Christians with the words 'the LORD'. The 'name of Jesus', in other words, is much more than simply 'Jesus'. It is the eternal name of God. And what Paul wants to show us here is that the eternal God is a radical, intoxicatingly generous giver.

Feminist thinkers have rightly warned against using the 'self-emptying' of Jesus as a warrant for legitimating human self-abasement. It is not so much abased humanity that is celebrated here as generous divinity. Christ's 'emptying of himself' was not a suspension of divinity but an enactment of it. Perfect in power, he didn't fight those around him for elbow room, for recognition, for a piece of the action. Perfect in love, he didn't need to promote his 'name', as we do, treating it as a possession, an asset or a tool.

How shall we respond? Paul's answer is simple: make like-minded communities whose heart is generosity.

COLLECT

O God, forasmuch as without you
we are not able to please you;
mercifully grant that your Holy Spirit
may in all things direct and rule our hearts;
through Jesus Christ your Son our Lord,
who is alive and reigns with you,
in the unity of the Holy Spirit,
one God, now and for ever.

| *Reflection by* **Ben Quash**

Psalms 113, **115**
2 Kings 19.1-19
Philippians 2.14-end

Thursday 11 October

Philippians 2.14-end

'...so that you may be blameless and innocent' (v.15)

How can you *become* 'blameless and innocent'? Once innocence has been lost, surely it is lost forever? There are grubby fingerprints all over our histories; our every action is to some extent tarnished by the compromises and failures of our past.

The German pastor and anti-Nazi dissident Dietrich Bonhoeffer made a distinction between 'simplicity' and 'purity'. Simplicity, he thought, could be learned and practised (as we might learn and practise temperance, for instance), whereas purity can only be received as a gift from God. 'In ourselves', he wrote, 'as we live and grow, we cannot any longer be "pure".'

But even in our fallen history there are moments in which – if only briefly – we can know a purity of intent. The compromised and double-minded Simon Peter found for a transient but glorious moment that he could walk on water when Jesus' command 'Come!' reached him across the waves. It wasn't something he had learned; it was more like a forgetting, a forgetting of all the doubts and fears that were his inherited baggage. His gaze was fixed on, and consumed by, a new object. Such tastes of a new innocence are the surfacing in time of a wholeness that lies ahead in eternity.

Self-forgetfulness and other-directedness are what Paul wants the Philippians to know. Taking delight in the delight of others is the motivation for gift-giving – for 'being poured out' – and is the basis for all success in human relationships. Peter asked Jesus to call him out of the boat – to give the purity he couldn't have taught himself. We do the same if we ask God to help us to love one another.

Faithful Lord,
whose steadfast love never ceases
and whose mercies never come to an end:
grant us the grace to trust you
and to receive the gifts of your love,
new every morning,
in Jesus Christ our Lord.

COLLECT

Reflection by **Ben Quash** | 277

Friday 12 October

Psalm **139**
2 Kings 19.20-36
Philippians 3.1 – 4.1

Philippians 3.1 – 4.1

'... our citizenship is in heaven, and it is from there that we are expecting a Saviour' (3.20)

My best friend when I was 12 had a huge collection of hats: hundreds of them, of all shapes and sizes. One of our favourite games (I am embarrassed to say) was to put on different sorts of exotic headgear and stroll around the tourist city where he lived, hoping narcissistically that passers-by might want to photograph us.

Paul asks us here to face the infinite mystery of *ourselves*. For we are not what we have made of ourselves. I wasn't fully any of the characters I pretended to be in those hat-wearing experiments. Nor, in later life, have I fully been any of the various social roles I have enacted. The who I *am* is hidden with Christ as a gracious gift of new creation, conceived by God before the foundation of the world, awaiting its fulfilment at the end of time, and only gradually, momentarily being disclosed in the Spirit-shaped company of the Church now.

We are most the *possessors* of ourselves when we are most the *recipients* of the deepest truth of ourselves, and this is not a truth that we make. I'm not saying that we play no part in developing our own identity; only that in all our active experiments, however energetic, there's always something bigger going on, in which we are asked to receive ourselves as a gift.

Christ who 'makes us his own' gives us warrant to hope that one day all the many hats we have tried on will be replaced by a crown of glory that never fades.

COLLECT

O God, forasmuch as without you
we are not able to please you;
mercifully grant that your Holy Spirit
may in all things direct and rule our hearts;
through Jesus Christ your Son our Lord,
who is alive and reigns with you,
in the unity of the Holy Spirit,
one God, now and for ever.

Reflection by **Ben Quash**

Psalms 120, **121**, 122
2 Kings 20
Philippians 4.2-end

Saturday 13 October

Philippians 4.2-end

'... if there is any excellence and if there is anything worthy of praise, think about these things' (v.8)

'You are what you eat.' This is true of what we contemplate too. People talk about 'eye candy', and it's hardly a wholesome long-term diet. The decisions we make every day about what we will dwell longest on, think most deeply about, chew over most thoroughly, are decisions that will have profound long-term effects on the sort of people we become.

Paul is not, of course, telling us only to contemplate attractive or consoling things. 'Pleasing' is accompanied by 'true', 'honourable', 'pure', and more – all of which may also be challenging to face.

During the period of the centenary of the First World War, St Paul's Cathedral in London is displaying the astonishingly lovely altar frontal woven by the trembling hands of 140 shell-shocked soldiers as part of their occupational therapy. They were trained up by members of the Royal School of Needlework and did the work in various hospitals around the country. Their eyes had seen barely imaginable horrors; their heads were colonized by unwanted memories. But quietly, steadily, stitch by stitch, they were helped to consider beauty again as well, and to become part of its transmission to others.

To contemplate their achievement is to understand a little more about what Paul might have been calling the Philippians to do – and us too. Not to look away from the world's violence and trauma, pretending it isn't there, but to look insistently for the deeper and more enduring 'excellences' that can nourish and heal it. The altars from which Christians feed remember brutality but proclaim love.

Faithful Lord,
whose steadfast love never ceases
and whose mercies never come to an end:
grant us the grace to trust you
and to receive the gifts of your love,
new every morning,
in Jesus Christ our Lord.

COLLECT

Monday 15 October

Psalms 123, 124, 125, **126**
2 Kings 21.1-18
1 Timothy 1.1-17

2 Kings 21.1-18

'I will wipe Jerusalem as one wipes a dish' (v.13)

The Books of Kings are among the great 'history books' of the Bible, and enshrine the principle that God can be found and known in the contours of human history when they are preserved, passed on and traced aright.

Manasseh wants to make history unreadable. He attacks it in two directions. First, he tries to eradicate the legacy of his father: 'he rebuilt the high places that Hezekiah his father had destroyed', we are told. Then he tries to erase the shoots of a future generation: we hear the chilling report that he burned his son.

To turn on both your forebears and your offspring with such violence suggests a paranoia reminiscent of those acts of cultural vandalism that religious and political extremists in every era – including our own – resort to when their insecure agendas feel threatened. Both the past and the future can stand in judgement on the present, and if you are afraid of such judgements, then you might want to shut both past and future down.

But it is only God, the great rememberer, who also has the power to 'wipe the dish' of history. 'Wiping' is a term (and an image) that finds new currency in our computer age. Like an infected hard drive, God's holy city is filled by Manasseh with profane clutter – idols and ceremonies whose profusion and noise he hopes will drown out the steady call of God's purpose. But it is *his* devices and desires that are the ones that will finally be 'wiped'.

COLLECT

God, the giver of life,
whose Holy Spirit wells up within your Church:
by the Spirit's gifts equip us to live the gospel of Christ
    and make us eager to do your will,
that we may share with the whole creation
    the joys of eternal life;
through Jesus Christ your Son our Lord,
who is alive and reigns with you,
in the unity of the Holy Spirit,
one God, now and for ever.

| *Reflection by* **Ben Quash**

Tuesday 16 October

2 Kings 22.1 – 23.3

'The king ... made a covenant before the Lord' (23.3)

Legend tells of how St Francis, in the small church of San Damiano, heard Christ tell him to 'rebuild my church', and took it literally. Placing stone upon stone, he restored the fabric of the building, only to realize there was deeper meaning to the call. He listened again: 'rebuild my church.' And so his life of missionary preaching for the spiritual renewal of Western Christendom began.

Josiah, remembered by Scripture as one of the holiest and most courageous of the kings of Judah, experiences something similar. He feels the imperative to use the tax revenues that have accumulated in his coffers to begin the work of restoring the fabric of the Jerusalem temple. But his stepping forth on this great enterprise delivers to him a further summons. The outer restoration is meaningless without an inner restoration: a restoration of the spiritual life of his people. In short, he finds God calling him a second time. The temple yields up a holy book containing the 'architect's plans' for the holy life God wants the entire nation to embrace.

The transformation that follows is huge. Josiah enters a new relationship with God and a new relationship with his people. They all re-covenant with one another, knowing that the restored wood and stone of the building that represents their highest calling means nothing without a restoration of their hearts and minds.

A restored exterior with no inner transformation is an empty façade. Josiah and Francis encourage us that such transformations can really happen.

God, our light and our salvation:
illuminate our lives,
that we may see your goodness in the land of the living,
and looking on your beauty
may be changed into the likeness of Jesus Christ our Lord.

COLLECT

Wednesday 17 October

2 Kings 23.4-25

'Let him rest; let no man move his bones' (v.18)

The word 'bonfire' refers back to the practice of burning bones. Such bone-fires were, for example, a central feature of those midsummer celebrations in medieval Christendom that centered on John the Baptist's feast day.

Perhaps such bonfires were especially appropriate then, because the pagan Roman Emperor Julian is said to have tried to dig up and incinerate John the Baptist's remains, threatened by the devotional cult that had grown up around him. The trouble was that John's prophetic hand, which touched Christ's head in baptism and pointed to him with the words 'Behold the Lamb of God!' (John 1.29), simply wouldn't burn.

Josiah here undertakes a spiritual clean-up operation on an industrial scale. He also institutes a Passover celebration that has not been seen since before the establishment of the monarchy. His renewed turn to the law is here accompanied by a very public act of respect for the ancient institution of prophecy. These are the two pillars of ancient Israel's relationship with God. They will one day be the twin witnesses to Christ's status, when Moses and Elijah appear either side of him on the Mount of the Transfiguration.

Julian couldn't eradicate the prophetic legacy of the Baptist, even though he wanted to. Josiah, by contrast, recognized that he must honour such men of God, so amid all his acts of destruction, he 'passed over' the tomb of the man of God who once told the truth. We too need to defer to what can't – and shouldn't – be tidied away for our own comfort and convenience.

COLLECT

God, the giver of life,
whose Holy Spirit wells up within your Church:
by the Spirit's gifts equip us to live the gospel of Christ
    and make us eager to do your will,
that we may share with the whole creation
    the joys of eternal life;
through Jesus Christ your Son our Lord,
who is alive and reigns with you,
in the unity of the Holy Spirit,
one God, now and for ever.

| *Reflection by* **Ben Quash**

Thursday 18 October
Luke the Evangelist

Isaiah 55

'... you that have no money, come, buy and eat!' (v.1)

The person who has no money is the one who is here called by God's prophet to 'buy'. The people who do have money can buy *nothing* of worth. This is the paradoxical logic of worshipping a God who created everything that there is *ex nihilo* – from nothing. Perhaps it is why the prophet's message about free grace is framed by a celebration of creation: the gratuitous abundance and beauty of the natural world.

Only when you know that nothing that you think is yours to bargain with is really *yours* will you be equipped to unlock God's storehouses and be nourished and refreshed from them.

God's creation of the universe from nothing means that we have nothing to bargain with. Everything has come from God. Knowing we have nothing to bargain with is not an endpoint, however, on account of which we sink back and give up. Knowing we have nothing to bargain with is a beginning: the beginning of a transformative spiritual journey in which we learn to be radical receivers, set in motion by our gratitude in a way that allows us to contribute to God's kingdom. Luke, who gave us the story of the prodigal son and who we celebrate today, knew this well.

'Just as I am, without one plea', as the hymn has it. 'Compassion' and 'pardon' are the bread and wine and milk that God offers us. All Isaiah asks us to do in order to purchase them is to 'return', admitting our empty-handedness. Only empty hands have room to receive. 'O Lamb of God, I come!'

COLLECT

Almighty God,
you called Luke the physician,
whose praise is in the gospel,
to be an evangelist and physician of the soul:
by the grace of the Spirit
and through the wholesome medicine of the gospel,
give your Church the same love and power to heal;
through Jesus Christ your Son our Lord,
who is alive and reigns with you,
in the unity of the Holy Spirit,
one God, now and for ever.

Reflection by **Ben Quash** | 283

Friday 19 October

Psalms 142, **144**
2 Kings 24.18 – 25.12
1 Timothy 5.1-16

2 Kings 24.18 – 25.12

'... the captain of the guard left some of the poorest people of the land to be vine-dressers and tillers of the soil' (25.12)

The Victorian intellectual Thomas Carlyle propagated the so-called 'great man' theory of history. Heroic individuals' deeds hold the key to what makes history happen. Who are the 'great men' in this passage?

Zedekiah of Judah tries to make his mark by rebelling against Nebuchadnezzar of Babylon. It is wildly prideful, and he brings the full might of his enemy's armies down not only on himself but also on his city and his people, who suffer terribly.

In this, he rejects the best example of his father, Josiah, who resisted the desire for this sort of grandstanding greatness. When Josiah went humbly to consult Huldah, the prophet, he seems to have been content for her to describe him as just 'a man' (an unusual and potentially provocative way to refer to a king). And he made himself subject to God's law – placing himself 'under' the higher authority of a sacred book – in a way that has been an inspiration to Christian monarchs for two thousand years. (Elizabeth II, in a famous speech on her 21st birthday, made a very Christian vow to be a 'servant' of her people and of God, a vow she has honoured ever since.)

Perhaps the real people who sustain human history are neither the losers nor victors of big fights like this one: neither Zedekiah nor Nebuchadnezzar. They are those without whom there could be no great men at all: those who quietly keep on dressing the vines and ploughing the fields, for the sake of generations as yet unborn. Wine and bread: signs of a better future.

COLLECT

God, the giver of life,
whose Holy Spirit wells up within your Church:
by the Spirit's gifts equip us to live the gospel of Christ
    and make us eager to do your will,
that we may share with the whole creation
    the joys of eternal life;
through Jesus Christ your Son our Lord,
who is alive and reigns with you,
in the unity of the Holy Spirit,
one God, now and for ever.

| *Reflection by* **Ben Quash**

Saturday 20 October

2 Kings 25.22-end

'So Jehoiachin put aside his prison clothes' (v.29)

The hospitality and mercy of a foreigner emerge here as the first sign of God's redemption in a situation that must have looked like the end of the road for the people of Judah – and there is a stark contrast with the behaviour that springs up among the people themselves. Like a 'failed state', the country is at the mercy of brutal roving militias, pulling it even further toward ruin.

The book of Lamentations, written at that time, captures the despair: 'The tongue of the infant sticks to the roof of its mouth for thirst; the children beg for food, but no one gives them anything' (Lamentations 4.4). The Judeans appointed to govern on Babylon's behalf are here the object of a vicious assassination by their fellow Judeans, led by a man who may have been a former military officer turned warlord. He seems to have murdered them while at a feast in Mizpah, violating their shared, deep customs of hospitality.

After a quarter of a century of waiting, there is a green shoot of hope. A new king takes the Babylonian throne and looks with kindness on the exiled king rotting in his jail, drawing him into the light, clothing him in decent attire, bringing him to his own table as an honoured guest.

These acts are several of what Christian tradition will one day call 'corporal works of mercy', and where mercy is shown to the king, mercy for the people can be hoped for. As so often in this long story, grace arrives from another shore, not from where we expected it.

God, our light and our salvation:
illuminate our lives,
that we may see your goodness in the land of the living,
and looking on your beauty
may be changed into the likeness of Jesus Christ our Lord.

COLLECT

Reflection by **Ben Quash** | 285

Monday 22 October

Exodus 22.21-27; 23.1-17

'... for you were aliens in the land of Egypt' (22.21, 23.9)

The root of the Hebrew word *torah*, usually translated as 'law', comes from the verb meaning to teach or instruct. The character of the commands given to Moses as teaching comes out very clearly in this short passage. In the case of 'aliens' (we might say migrants or refugees), of widows and orphans, and of those needing financial assistance, instruction as to what is to be done is informed by compressed sketches of why God's people are to act in this way and not another.

In all three cases, the teaching pivots on what might be termed moral empathy: recognizing the other person as one whose experience you can imagine and whose condition you could inhabit. This is simplest in the case of the 'resident aliens', for all the people of Israel have known what this is like; it belongs to their history. In the case of widows and orphans, they are compelled to picture their own wives and children bereaved and defenceless. In the case of the poor, they are asked to consider the daily dilemmas of those who are destitute. Finally, they are reminded that the Lord responds to the vulnerable and marginalized with compassion: they are asked to contemplate God's response if they fail to act with the justice and mercy expected.

The gift of the *torah* is to shape those who hear it, to form our minds and hearts and imaginations, so that we might run with eagerness and freedom the way of God's commandments.

COLLECT

Grant, we beseech you, merciful Lord,
to your faithful people pardon and peace,
that they may be cleansed from all their sins
and serve you with a quiet mind;
through Jesus Christ your Son our Lord,
who is alive and reigns with you,
in the unity of the Holy Spirit,
one God, now and for ever.

| *Reflection by* **Jeremy Worthen**

Tuesday 23 October

Exodus 29.38 – 30.16

'I will meet the Israelites there' (29.43)

The instructions about sacrifice are perhaps among the hardest parts of the Bible to find 'useful for teaching' (2 Timothy 3.16). There is plenty we might say about the principle of sacrifice, but the many details of the practice are more resistant to our reflections. It would be easy, then, to skip through these chapters and miss the point that verses 42–46 of chapter 29 mark a climactic point in the narrative. The establishment of continual daily sacrificial worship represents a fulfilment of God's promise even before the entry into the promised land. The primary purpose of God in delivering Israel is 'that I might dwell among them', not simply so that they might inhabit this rather than that piece of territory around the Eastern Mediterranean. And the promise becomes reality here at the tent of meeting in the wilderness, though still 'only a shadow of the good things to come' (Hebrews 10.1).

This dwelling of God with humanity takes place in time, punctuated with the daily rhythm of morning and evening. It rests on commitment and constancy, and on a willingness to hand over and give away. What is offered to God is simple food, not demonstrative extravagance for a hungry deity but the transformative sharing of our daily bread with the one from whom it comes. Such action opens a way for our sanctification, so the holiness of God can touch us, and the maker of heaven and earth can meet with us, speak with us. God with us.

Almighty God,
in whose service lies perfect freedom:
teach us to obey you
with loving hearts and steadfast wills;
through Jesus Christ our Lord.

COLLECT

Reflection by **Jeremy Worthen** | 287

Wednesday 24 October

Psalm 119.1-32
Judith 6.10 – 7.7 *or* Leviticus 8
2 Timothy 1.1-14

Leviticus 8

'For it will take seven days to ordain you' (v.33)

I remember once hearing that senior clergy at a certain cathedral held a yearly sweepstake on the likely length of the sermon at the ordination service. The duration of the whole exercise seemed excessive to them, but perhaps they should have been thankful that Anglican Churches do not take seven days to ordain their priests.

Of course, what we mean by 'priest' in the church is not identical with what is meant by 'priest' in this chapter, nor is the text describing an ordination as we understand it. No promises or prayers are mentioned, and instead of the laying on of hands, we have the placing of offerings to fill the hands of Aaron and his sons at verses 25–28, 'fill' being the root meaning of the word translated here as 'ordain'. Still, it is clear that this is the beginning of something new – for those at the centre of the ceremony, for Moses who presides over it and for the people they will serve.

As those called into 'a royal priesthood' (1 Peter 2.9), we might consider how the priesthood of Israel was inaugurated, at the foot of Mount Sinai. To begin with, it was not something to be invented or improvised, but rather about saying yes, faithfully and patiently, to the word God had spoken. It meant taking time, in the place of God's presence, God's meeting with humanity, and remaining there steadfastly in order to be changed. And it involved proximity to awesome, consuming holiness.

COLLECT

Grant, we beseech you, merciful Lord,
to your faithful people pardon and peace,
that they may be cleansed from all their sins
and serve you with a quiet mind;
through Jesus Christ your Son our Lord,
who is alive and reigns with you,
in the unity of the Holy Spirit,
one God, now and for ever.

| *Reflection by* **Jeremy Worthen**

Psalms 14, **15**, 16
Judith 7.19-end *or* Leviticus 9
2 Timothy 1.15 – 2.13

Leviticus 9

'Moses and Aaron entered the tent of meeting' (v.23)

The guidance for the consecration of Aaron and his sons as priests, along with other instructions about the regular practice of sacrificial worship, was given to Moses on the mountain in Exodus, before he descended to discover the people dancing around the golden calf that Aaron has made for them in his absence (Exodus 32). It is hard to imagine a more egregious failure: what more could Aaron have done for Moses to strip him of all responsibilities, or for God to strike him down? Yet here he is, taking on the duties of the priesthood, offering the sacrifices of the people, making atonement for himself and for them, and finally entering alongside Moses the tent of meeting, the holiest place where only Moses has been before.

We should not imagine that because God has called us to do the most remarkable things and to handle what is most holy, therefore we are remarkable, we are holy, of ourselves. Nor, however, should we be constantly fearful that it should not be us, that we should not be here. God has called, God has chosen and so, with contrition, humility and gratitude, we say yes. We approach the holiest place.

As he finishes the work of offering, Aaron blesses the people. Then as he and Moses leave the tent of meeting, they bless the people together, 'and the glory of the Lord appeared to all the people'. What is given to one is given for the sake of all.

Almighty God,
in whose service lies perfect freedom:
teach us to obey you
with loving hearts and steadfast wills;
through Jesus Christ our Lord.

COLLECT

Reflection by **Jeremy Worthen** | 289

Friday 26 October

Psalms 17, **19**
Judith 8.9-end *or* Leviticus 16.2-24
2 Timothy 2.14-end

Leviticus 16.2-24

'... sprinkling it upon the mercy-seat and before the mercy-seat' (v.15)

This is probably the best known chapter in Leviticus for Christians. Atonement – that's central for our thinking, even if it's not a word we use all the time. Theologians may disagree about the mechanics, but it's got something to do with sacrifice, with blood and with the putting away of sin, all of them present in Leviticus 16.

We might, however, find ourselves puzzling over various details, such as instructions to make atonement 'for the sanctuary' (v.16). Part of the challenge is the key word for the chapter in Hebrew, which can be variously translated as 'atone', 'expiate', 'cover' or 'propitiate'. The same root occurs in the name of the 'mercy-seat': the object that is placed over the ark, which is the site of God's manifestation, is more literally the 'place of atonement' (v.2). It's quite possible that Paul had this whole passage in mind when he wrote at Romans 3.25 that God intended Christ Jesus to be an 'atonement' by his blood, where the word can mean both 'place of atonement' (the 'mercy-seat' in our passage) or 'means of atonement'. For he is both of these for us: the place where we find the mercy of atonement, and the life offered up so that mercy may be poured out upon us.

Only at the place of atonement is God's glory revealed and God's face turned to sinful yet beloved humanity. God has provided the place and the sacrifice, the eternal Son, made flesh for our salvation.

COLLECT

Grant, we beseech you, merciful Lord,
to your faithful people pardon and peace,
that they may be cleansed from all their sins
and serve you with a quiet mind;
through Jesus Christ your Son our Lord,
who is alive and reigns with you,
in the unity of the Holy Spirit,
one God, now and for ever.

| *Reflection by* **Jeremy Worthen**

Saturday 27 October

Leviticus 17

'This shall be a statute for ever to them' (v.7)

Would it matter if Leviticus 17.1–9 was omitted from our Bibles? Historically interesting perhaps, but Christians don't make animal sacrifices, so they don't need to be told to bring them as an offering to the Lord; nor are they in any imminent danger of prostituting themselves to goat-demons. Can this really be 'a statute for ever'?

Perhaps part of the point here is that worship is the centring action of the people of God. The worship of God should join us together with the whole people of God, not draw us away from them to some other location or company, and it should be in accordance with God's word, not controlled by other demands or driven by our own lurking fantasies. Our worship should be, in a proper sense, public. In Leviticus, not everyone gets to enter every part of the tent of meeting, but everyone gets to know what happens in every part of the tent of meeting, and to have it explained to them: that's the point of the book. There are no secret actions, no private rituals.

The temptation to supplement the worship of the Church with some private practices of our own may be stronger than we think. In our most intensely solitary prayer, we are still called to pray in the name of Christ and therefore in communion with the body of Christ, not out of some imagined spiritual autonomy or more inclusive solidarity. There remains a statute for us here.

Almighty God,
in whose service lies perfect freedom:
teach us to obey you
with loving hearts and steadfast wills;
through Jesus Christ our Lord.

COLLECT

Reflection by **Jeremy Worthen** | 291

Monday 29 October

Leviticus 19.1-18, 30-end

'You shall be holy' (v.2)

It's easy to feel bewildered by a chapter like this, even though the lectionary has shielded us from perhaps the most bewildering elements. It can seem such a jumble: inspiring commands that could be mottoes for the Christian life (vv.2*b*, 18*b*); exhortations to virtuous behaviour to which we should aspire (vv.3, 10, 32, 34); basic moral teaching that underpins social order (vv.11, 13, 15, 35); and obscure instructions that don't appear remotely applicable (vv.5-8).

Yes, there is a miscellany of different kinds of command, but that's not to say there is no order or logic. We are being offered teaching about holiness, justice and love, and crucially we are being taught that these three are inseparable from one another: we don't get to choose between them. There is no 'mere' justice that does not stand with and seek the good of those around us, especially the most vulnerable. There is no loving 'attitude' that is not committed to seeking a society in which customs, laws and general behaviour alike all express what is right and what is good. Neither justice nor love can abide with contempt for the holy one, and there is no holiness on our part to respond that does not issue in a passion for justice in our world, and in a love that values each person we encounter 'as' ourselves, of immeasurable dignity and worth, a hearer with us of God's word.

COLLECT

Blessed Lord,
who caused all holy Scriptures to be written for our learning:
help us so to hear them,
to read, mark, learn and inwardly digest them
that, through patience, and the comfort of your holy word,
we may embrace and for ever hold fast
   the hope of everlasting life,
which you have given us in our Saviour Jesus Christ,
who is alive and reigns with you,
in the unity of the Holy Spirit,
one God, now and for ever.

| *Reflection by* **Jeremy Worthen**

Tuesday 30 October

Leviticus 23.1-22

'... a holy convocation; you shall do no work' (v.3)

Human life has its times and seasons. The call to be the holy people of the holy God is no cause to disdain them, or try to overcome them. But it does mean we need to set a kind of rhythm, a holy beat, that helps the varied music of our lives to be lifted up as unbroken praise to our maker.

This chapter sets out a weekly and then a yearly rhythm to shape the way God's people experience the recurring cycles of time. One specific element in that rhythm is the connection that keeps being made between a 'holy convocation' and refraining from all work (vv. 3, 7, 21). Presumably this is partly pragmatic: the community cannot assemble together unless people lay aside their normal occupations. But it is more than that too. There need to be times when our attention and our energy is given wholly to God, and not distracted by other demands.

There is perhaps a particular challenge here for those with responsibilities for worship and more generally for the business of the church. 'Convocations' on regular Sundays or on major festivals are hardly times when they can 'do no work', but there is danger in wholly divorcing times of rest from times of meeting with God's people around word and sacrament. Is it possible to be still and at rest in God's presence in the midst of the church's worship, without neglecting the responsibilities entrusted to us there?

COLLECT

Merciful God,
teach us to be faithful in change and uncertainty,
that trusting in your word
and obeying your will
we may enter the unfailing joy of Jesus Christ our Lord.

Reflection by **Jeremy Worthen** | 293

Wednesday 31 October

Psalm **34**
Judith 12 *or* Leviticus 23.23-end
Titus 1

Leviticus 23.23-end

'You shall live in booths for seven days' (v.42)

What does it mean when someone tells us something once, then moves on, then comes back and tells us the same thing again in a different way?

Instructions about the 'festival of booths' are given in verses 33–36. There follows a summary concluding the chapter's teaching about 'appointed festivals' (vv.37–38). But we then return to the festival of booths for a second time, and it's not just repetition. The passage spells out that the people must live in booths for the duration, and then links this to the deliverance from Egypt. In the chapter up to this point, the focus has been on offerings for sacrifice, but here it is on shared rituals that are not sacrificial – shared remembrance of what God has done and shared rejoicing in God's presence.

Finally, the Hebrew term for 'festival' is emphasized by a combination of verb and noun in verses 39 and 41; it has only appeared twice before in the chapter, and not in this way. Its origins aren't entirely clear, but it relates to the practice of pilgrimage – leaving home for a while to give time to the worship of God.

The round of the year needs to have space for more than offering what we 'owe' to God. There need to be times of journeying away from the familiar, to remember the deeper truths that our routines can come to obscure, and to be renewed in the joy of sharing in the unfolding adventure of God's deliverance.

COLLECT

Blessed Lord,
who caused all holy Scriptures to be written for our learning:
help us so to hear them,
to read, mark, learn and inwardly digest them
that, through patience, and the comfort of your holy word,
we may embrace and for ever hold fast
     the hope of everlasting life,
which you have given us in our Saviour Jesus Christ,
who is alive and reigns with you,
in the unity of the Holy Spirit,
one God, now and for ever.

| *Reflection by* **Jeremy Worthen**

Psalms 15, 84, 149
Isaiah 35.1-9
Luke 9.18-27

Thursday 1 November
All Saints' Day

Isaiah 35.1-9
'... the redeemed shall walk there' (v.9)

What do we see when we look around us? Do we see wilderness, desert, burning swamp? Or do we see abundant blossoming and springs of water?

The eyes of faith are perhaps bound to see both, adjacent to each other, and always the possibility of one turning into the other. And what changes dry land into abundant, burgeoning life is this: the presence of 'the Holy Way' for God's redeemed to walk on. It is in honour of their passing through that the 'wilderness and the dry land shall be glad', and 'the burning sand shall become a pool'. God acts to transfigure creation so that they shall 'see the glory of the Lord, the majesty of our God'.

On All Saints' Day, we give thanks for those who have seen God's glory on their way through the world, 'in whose heart are the highways to Zion' (Psalm 84.5). We give thanks for those in whom the grace of God has worked to undo the desolating energy of evil described in the previous chapter, where Edom's land becomes 'burning pitch' and 'the haunt of jackals' (Isaiah 34.9, 13), and to plant signs of abundant goodness on the earth. We give thanks for those in whose company we have come to know that if we travel this new and living way (Hebrews 10.20), then even in the midst of pain and emptiness, water still flows and fruit still grows to sustain us.

COLLECT

Almighty God,
you have knit together your elect
in one communion and fellowship
in the mystical body of your Son Christ our Lord:
grant us grace so to follow your blessed saints
in all virtuous and godly living
that we may come to those inexpressible joys
that you have prepared for those who truly love you;
through Jesus Christ your Son our Lord,
who is alive and reigns with you,
in the unity of the Holy Spirit,
one God, now and for ever.

Reflection by **Jeremy Worthen** | 295

Friday 2 November

Psalm **31**
Judith 15.1-13 *or* Leviticus 25.1-24
Titus 3

Leviticus 25.1-24

'... the land is mine' (v.23)

What gives us our sense of value? One part of the answer will be what we have done. But only part. The beginning and end must look to what we have been given.

The year of jubilee takes away from every Israelite the land they have acquired from others, and restores to every Israelite the land they were allotted with their family. It means going home, and knowing that home is a place that cannot be taken from you, whatever happens to you, because it is God's gift.

Because it is God's gift, it is your home, but not your possession, not your domain to do with what you will: 'with me you are but aliens and tenants'. The Hebrew root of the word for 'aliens' is a thread that runs through these first five books of the Bible, meaning to abide in a place that is not one's own. The gifts of God are truly given to us, but they remain *God's* gifts and cannot be received and held if we do not fear God, and will not let God be God.

The Hebrew for 'the land' also means 'the earth'. As Christians, we do not define our home in relation to a particular land, being 'exiles of the Dispersion' (1 Peter 1.1), yet we pray every day for the hallowing of God's name and the coming of God's kingdom here on earth. We cherish it as God's gift, and the place where God's glory would dwell.

COLLECT

Blessed Lord,
who caused all holy Scriptures to be written for our learning:
help us so to hear them,
to read, mark, learn and inwardly digest them
that, through patience, and the comfort of your holy word,
we may embrace and for ever hold fast
   the hope of everlasting life,
which you have given us in our Saviour Jesus Christ,
who is alive and reigns with you,
in the unity of the Holy Spirit,
one God, now and for ever.

| *Reflection by* **Jeremy Worthen**

Psalms 41, **42**, 43
Judith 15.14 – 16.end
or Numbers 6.1-5, 21-end
Philemon

Saturday 3 November

Numbers 6.1-5, 21-end

'So they shall put my name on the Israelites' (v.27)

It belongs to the calling of priests in the Old Testament to pray for God's blessing. Here, in verses 24–26, we have a solemn text for them to use, a threefold benediction, each line in two parts. One word occurs in all three, in the same emphatic place: the name of Israel's God, YHWH. For the power of the blessing is simply this: 'to put my name on the Israelites'.

In the New Testament, Jesus is our great high priest, who 'While he was blessing them … was carried up into heaven' (Luke 24.51), and who does not cease to intercede for us (Hebrews 7.25). In John 17, Jesus prays to the Father to keep those given to him 'in your name that you have given me, so that they may be one, as we are one' (John 17.11). This is the name the Son has made known to them, 'so that the love with which you have loved me may be in them, and I in them' (John 17.26).

The name of God has not changed. But Jesus reveals the giving of the divine name within the divine life, the eternal reality of the Trinity. We can still use the words of Numbers 6.24–26, but at the same time we pray the blessing of the Father, the Son and the Holy Spirit, that 'the love with which you have loved me may be in them', God's name upon us all.

Merciful God,
teach us to be faithful in change and uncertainty,
that trusting in your word
and obeying your will
we may enter the unfailing joy of Jesus Christ our Lord.

COLLECT

Monday 5 November

Psalms **2**, 146 *or* **44**
Daniel 1
Revelation 1

Revelation 1

'I was in the Spirit on the Lord's day' (v.10)

Patmos is beyond beautiful. It shines as a diamond in a deep blue sea under a cloudless sky (at least it did when I was there) and it's said to have 365 tiny churches and chapels. It's where John (probably not the apostle) wrote to seven churches at the end of the first century in a style that was part letter, part un-veiling (revelation), part prophecy. It's immensely powerful writing, both terrifying and reassuring, and it concerns the battle between God and Satan going on even then, even now.

The symbolism is rich to the point of bizarre, like the sword coming out of the mouth of Christ, but there's no doubt about the main figure John wants us to meet at the start – Jesus Christ, 'one like the Son of Man' (as in Daniel 7), who was dead and is now alive for ever, and who scares John to death before commanding him to write to the seven churches that he names. In the Bible the number seven is associated with completeness, so John was in effect writing to the whole Church.

The Son of Man has a lot to say to these churches in the next two chapters. It makes compelling reading, both positive and negative. If we were writing to our own church today I wonder what we would want to say?

COLLECT

Almighty and eternal God,
you have kindled the flame of love in the hearts of the saints:
grant to us the same faith and power of love,
that, as we rejoice in their triumphs,
we may be sustained by their example and fellowship;
through Jesus Christ your Son our Lord,
who is alive and reigns with you,
in the unity of the Holy Spirit,
one God, now and for ever.

298 | *Reflection by* **John Pritchard**

Psalms **5**, 147.1-12 *or* **48**, 52
Daniel 2.1-24
Revelation 2.1-11

Tuesday 6 November

Revelation 2.1-11

*'To everyone who conquers, I will give permission to eat
from the tree of life' (v.7)*

All the seven letters have the same basic shape: the name of the
church, some defining quality of Jesus, what the particular church has
been doing both well and badly, a promise 'to everyone who
conquers', and an encouragement to 'listen to the Spirit'. Each letter is
addressed to 'the angel' of the church, perhaps the leader who acts as
guardian, an angelic role. The encouragements and the charge sheets
make fascinating reading.

The church at Smyrna is facing imminent persecution of some form and
is promised the crown of life if it can remain faithful. The church at
Ephesus, however, while commended for its patient endurance, is
accused of abandoning its first love. Many Christians can identify with
this experience of losing their initial passion and wondering why
they've become dry, bored and unexpectant in their faith. There's much
that could be said about that, but the one thing Jesus says to this
church is that they should 'repent, and do the works you did at first'.
One answer to losing our first love can be to move on to new spiritual
resources, but equally it may be worth revisiting the works we did at
first, the basic disciplines and practices, and seeing if that familiar
ground can be re-owned, though in new ways.

The tree of life has many fruits, familiar and unfamiliar, but all of them
nourishing.

God of glory,
touch our lips with the fire of your Spirit,
that we with all creation
may rejoice to sing your praise;
through Jesus Christ our Lord.

COLLECT

Wednesday 7 November

Psalms **9**, 147.13-end
or **119.57-80**
Daniel 2.25-end
Revelation 2.12-end

Revelation 2.12-end

'To everyone who conquers I will give ...' (v.17)

The churches of Pergamum and Thyatira have in common their faithfulness, love, service and patient endurance, but they also have in common a temptation to idolatry – 'fornication' is the usual metaphor. In both cases Jesus gives them an Old Testament figure as a point of reference, Balaam for Pergamum and Jezebel for Thyatira. Neither allusion is encouraging. Nevertheless, if they make the right response, both churches are promised good things. Pergamum Christians will receive the hidden manna, the spiritual resources they need for a wilderness journey; they will also be given a white stone with their name on it as a sign of their unique identity in Christ. Christians in Thyatira will be given authority over the nations – no less – and the morning star, which, as Jesus himself has that title later in the book, probably refers to the level of intimacy they will have with him – he shares his very identity with them.

In both churches, then, the promise is of a particularly close relationship with Jesus. Some Christians find that idea elusive since their focus is more on the mystery of God than the person of Jesus. But here in Revelation the titles and references to Jesus Christ and to God often slide into each other. It doesn't matter where our main focus lies; what matters is to know that in whatever person of the Trinity we care to think most naturally, we are treasured, we are loved.

COLLECT

Almighty and eternal God,
you have kindled the flame of love in the hearts of the saints:
grant to us the same faith and power of love,
that, as we rejoice in their triumphs,
we may be sustained by their example and fellowship;
through Jesus Christ your Son our Lord,
who is alive and reigns with you,
in the unity of the Holy Spirit,
one God, now and for ever.

| *Reflection by* **John Pritchard**

Psalms 11, **15**, 148 *or* 56, **57** (63*)
Daniel 3.1-18
Revelation 3.1-13

Thursday 8 November

Revelation 3.1-13

'If you conquer ...' (vv.5,12)

The churches in Sardis and Philadelphia were in very different places. Sardis is told bluntly, 'you are dead', while Philadelphia is told 'you have but little power, and yet you have kept my word'. The church in Sardis is told in no uncertain terms to 'wake up', while the church in Philadelphia is told 'I will keep you from the hour of trial'. There's no danger of one-size-fits-all. But in one respect all the churches are similar; they are given a conditional promise – 'if you conquer'.

God's commitment to us and our wellbeing is never in doubt. What varies is how ready we are to appropriate that commitment, how ready we are to do our bit. We have to conquer our resistances to God's love or it will struggle to take effect, just as we have to take down the sun shades if we're to get a suntan. But the 'conquering' that Jesus refers to each time is an ambiguous concept when we remember that it was vulnerability that was the key to Jesus' victory on the cross. Sometimes we conquer through struggle; sometimes we conquer through absorbing the negatives and neutralizing them.

In a world where 'conquering' is often horribly abused, it's reassuring to be told that God's purposes for the universe (his 'conquering') are bound to be fulfilled; history just has to fill in the details.

COLLECT

God of glory,
touch our lips with the fire of your Spirit,
that we with all creation
may rejoice to sing your praise;
through Jesus Christ our Lord.

Friday 9 November

Psalms **16**, 149 *or* **51**, 54
Daniel 3.19-end
Revelation 3.14-end

Revelation 3.14-end

'I wish that you were either cold or hot' (v.15)

There seems to be nothing good to say about the church in Laodicea. To be told they were 'wretched, pitiable, poor, blind, and naked' wasn't encouraging. To be told Jesus would vomit them out of his mouth wasn't something to report at the AGM. John seems to have known this city and its church better than the other six, and his comments reflect considerable local knowledge about this smug, wealthy place with its black sheep (so famous that the promise is of white robes in contrast), eye salve and poor water (fit only to spit out, cf v.16) – all of which are alluded to here.

His main complaint, of course, is that the church is lukewarm, neither cold nor hot (there were hot and cold springs to the north and south), and Jesus' words convey real anger, the anger that comes from disappointment.

In our breast-beating periods of introspection, churches in the UK – and in the wider Anglican Communion – often apply that image to themselves, that we are lukewarm in our faith and mission. The Church of England has been called 'the bland leading the bland' and 'the Church that's dying of good taste'. The art is to distinguish between lukewarmness and modesty, between apathy and respectful sensitivity. What is less easy to see is the inner life of the individual Christian and the reality of the heart. Only we can tell whether our faith is cold, hot – or merely lukewarm.

COLLECT

Almighty and eternal God,
you have kindled the flame of love in the hearts of the saints:
grant to us the same faith and power of love,
that, as we rejoice in their triumphs,
we may be sustained by their example and fellowship;
through Jesus Christ your Son our Lord,
who is alive and reigns with you,
in the unity of the Holy Spirit,
one God, now and for ever.

| *Reflection by* **John Pritchard**

Psalms **18.31-end**, 150 *or* **68**
Daniel 4.1-18
Revelation 4

Saturday 10 November

Revelation 4

'... there in heaven stood a throne' (v.2)

As I write, there's just been another natural disaster, an earthquake with much loss of life. You can imagine the scene straight afterwards with its chaos and bewilderment. The cry at those scenes must have been 'Who's in charge here?' It's a question people often think of when things go wrong in the world. In the Revelation of John the answer is clear – 'the one seated on the throne'. We've just heard how the seven churches are having tough times, and now in this unveiling of the heavenly realm the churches catch an encouraging glimpse of the deeper reality behind their troubles: God is in charge and the heavenly liturgy goes on unchecked. The precious stones, the rainbow, the 24 elders in white robes and golden crowns, the thunder and lightning, the seven torches, the four living creatures – they all build up an atmosphere of awe and wonder, and would surely have given confidence to those little churches of perhaps no more than two or three dozen believers, clinging precariously to their new faith in a hostile culture.

All things come around, and many Christians in the West feel besieged in an unbelieving or hostile culture. But the true picture still lies before us. God is still God and the world still belongs to God. God is still 'in charge', though not as a celestial puppeteer. As the 20th-century Scottish philosopher John Macmurray wrote: 'False religion says "Fear not, trust in God and none of the things you fear will happen to you." Real religion says, "Fear not, the things you are afraid of may well happen to you – but they are nothing to be afraid of."'

God of glory,
touch our lips with the fire of your Spirit,
that we with all creation
may rejoice to sing your praise;
through Jesus Christ our Lord.

COLLECT

Monday 12 November

Revelation 5

'Who is worthy to open the scroll ...?' (v.2)

The scroll is clearly important. It must contain God's plan to defeat the destructive activity of the Beast (yet to appear). But who is worthy to open this scroll? John hears an elder say it's the Lion, the Root of David who is worthy, but what he *sees* is the Lamb who has been 'slaughtered'. The Lion won his victory, but through the sacrificial methods of the Lamb, the victim. From now on it's the Lion-Lamb we have to keep in mind. And now the build-up of praise begins, starting with the living creatures and the elders, growing through thousands of angels, and swelling finally to 'every creature in heaven and on earth and under the earth and in the sea'. The crescendo is enormous. Ultimately the elders fall down and worship, lost beyond words.

Is that reminiscent of worship at our church on Sunday morning? The problem with focusing on the accessibility of Jesus is that we can lose the scale of his divinity. Jesus, and even the God he called Father, can be reduced to proportions so manageable that his appearance wouldn't even get on the local news. Worship has to oscillate between the beautiful majesty of God and the astonishing availability of Jesus, the Lion-Lamb.

Do we realize how magnificent God is? Do we realize how humble God is?

COLLECT

Almighty Father,
whose will is to restore all things
in your beloved Son, the King of all:
govern the hearts and minds of those in authority,
and bring the families of the nations,
divided and torn apart by the ravages of sin,
to be subject to his just and gentle rule;
who is alive and reigns with you,
in the unity of the Holy Spirit,
one God, now and for ever.

| *Reflection by* **John Pritchard**

Tuesday 13 November

Revelation 6

'Then I saw the Lamb open one of the seven seals' (v.1)

This next scene in the throne of heaven comes as a bit of a shock. We've just has the wonderful sight of the whole of creation singing the praise of God and the Lion-Lamb. Surely we're all set for the dénouement, when God's rescue of the world will take place. Instead, we find four terrible horses released to do their worst, representing conquest, war, economic disaster and death. It seems that evil has to be exposed in its worst excesses before it can be confronted and dealt with. If the world's problems are to be healed, rather than merely patched up, the dark powers of evil have to be identified and faced full on.

It seems sometimes as if we lurch, in international affairs as well as in domestic life, from crisis to crisis, applying sticking plasters and soothing words, crying 'peace, peace, where there is no peace'. Ultimately we don't sort out our problems until we've gone deep enough to expose the root cause (think of a visit to the dentist!). It requires the kind of courage that five-year governments and anxious marriages are usually unwilling to do, but in the last resort this is the only path to healing. A score-draw with evil is a defeat.

God is calling the world to account; indeed the Lamb himself is angry (v.16). But this is the anger of Love against all that is unloving. Is that how our anger works?

God, our refuge and strength,
bring near the day when wars shall cease
and poverty and pain shall end,
that earth may know the peace of heaven
through Jesus Christ our Lord.

COLLECT

Reflection by **John Pritchard** | 305

Wednesday 14 November

Psalms 23, 25 or 77
Daniel 5.13-end
Revelation 7.1-4, 9-end

Revelation 7.1-4, 9-end

'These are they who have come out of the great ordeal' (v.14)

Just when we thought we'd made it to the seventh seal, there's a hold up. But it's for a good reason. Those who had been through the great ordeal, with their robes (curiously) bleached white by the blood of the Lamb, are to be sealed with God's guarantee of protection from the four mighty winds due to blow fiercely through land and sea as God's judgement takes hold. Their number is 144,000 – clearly a number symbolic of a vast crowd, and taken to represent the whole people of God, twelve times twelve times a thousand. God will shelter them as, with a wonderful role reversal, the Lamb becomes the (Good) Shepherd who will guide them to springs of living water, and, in anticipation of the final scene in Revelation, 'God will wipe away every tear from their eyes'.

Not a bad day's work. And it's important to hold in our minds that picture of God tenderly caring for his people. There are in Revelation images of God's transcendent power that can skew our perception of God's nature, but God's actions are always done in the name of a love that cannot bear to see this beautiful creation destroyed or God's people damaged. There are many images of God in scripture, and some confuse us, but the most profound description of all is that God is love, and the most accurate portrait is in the words of former Archbishop of Canterbury, Michael Ramsey: that 'God is Christlike and in him there is no unChristlikeness at all'. Hold on to that today.

COLLECT

Almighty Father,
whose will is to restore all things
in your beloved Son, the King of all:
govern the hearts and minds of those in authority,
and bring the families of the nations,
divided and torn apart by the ravages of sin,
to be subject to his just and gentle rule;
who is alive and reigns with you,
in the unity of the Holy Spirit,
one God, now and for ever.

| *Reflection by* **John Pritchard**

Thursday 15 November

Revelation 8

'Woe, woe, woe to the inhabitants of the earth' (v.13)

Horror stories have always been popular – until a horror happens to us. But today's reading must come close to capping them all. The seventh seal is opened and there's a forbidding, heart-stopping silence throughout heaven. What unimaginable terror is about to be revealed? It needs a divine liturgy with a censer filled with fire, releasing thunder, lightning, and an earthquake, to set the scene. And then the full horror is ready to explode. The first four angels blow trumpets that usher in unparalleled disaster on every aspect of the world. The most horrendous disaster movie seems like a child's bedtime story in comparison. And then we have to hold our breath yet again, for a solitary eagle gives off an even more chilling cry, 'Woe, woe, woe to the inhabitants of the earth'.

This isn't so much a prediction as a symbolic account of the chaos that occurs when the world abandons God. Every aspect of life nose dives. It's a hard message for secular society to hear and hard for believers to articulate, not wanting to appear sanctimonious. But when civilizations lose their divine moorings and start to worship and serve the creature rather than the Creator (Romans 1.25), the dogs of chaos are bound to be released into the world. That at least is the claim of John in Revelation. To what extent do you share that analysis? And, if there is truth in there, how might we respond, even today?

God, our refuge and strength,
bring near the day when wars shall cease
and poverty and pain shall end,
that earth may know the peace of heaven
through Jesus Christ our Lord.

COLLECT

Reflection by **John Pritchard** | 307

Friday 16 November

Revelation 9.1-12

'He opened the shaft of the bottomless pit' (v.2)

How much more horrific can this picture become? We now have an awesome image of a bottomless pit, a place of destruction and chaos that seems rather like what in astrophysics is called anti-matter. From it emerges an army of battle-hardened, heavy-armoured, man-torturing insects with the task of making life hell for everyone not marked with the seal of God on their foreheads. For five terrible months, until people longed for death.

If this seems somewhat remote on a Friday morning in November we might remember that John used this vivid symbolism not only as a vision of the end-times but also as contemporary commentary to name and shame the might of Rome. Alert readers at the time might have begun to pick up the references, such as the name of the king of these terrible insects – Apollyon might echo the name of the Roman God Apollo. Prophecy doesn't so much foretell the future as explain the significance of the present. But as the present is pregnant with the future, the prophet needs to be heard.

We have to ask what elements of this prophetic, apocalyptic writing should be heeded, by whom, and in what way. We also have to ask whether we have truly, deeply heard the words of Jesus echoing through the New Testament, 'Do not be afraid'.

COLLECT

Almighty Father,
whose will is to restore all things
in your beloved Son, the King of all:
govern the hearts and minds of those in authority,
and bring the families of the nations,
divided and torn apart by the ravages of sin,
to be subject to his just and gentle rule;
who is alive and reigns with you,
in the unity of the Holy Spirit,
one God, now and for ever.

| *Reflection by* **John Pritchard**

Psalms **33** *or* **76**, 79
Daniel 7.15-end
Revelation 9.13-end

Saturday 17 November

Revelation 9.13-end

'The rest of humankind ... did not repent' (v.20)

The sixth angel now steps forward and releases the four angels who apparently had been held ready for this precise time ('the hour, the day, the month ...'). As the next load of misery comes rolling down the track like a tribe of killers from the depths of Mordor, we might be inclined to 'look away now' or to return to more comfortable parts of the New Testament. Two hundred million murderous troops riding on horses that have fire, smoke and sulphur coming out of their mouths, set on killing a third of humankind with plague, makes an unpleasant vision, whether its hearers take it almost literally or as spiritual symbolism. And still the rest of humankind refuses to repent.

John always scales up the drama in order to clarify the issues. The forces that lead to destruction have to be recognized in order to be dealt with. This applies even in our own experience. Until we've recognized the deep-rootedness of our own death-dealing habits, we won't be inclined to face them. But if we feel close to despair at our refusal or inability to repent either personally or at the global level, we might remember what Desmond Tutu once said to a discouraged congregation. 'Don't worry,' he said, 'I've read to the end of the book. We win.' This is the confidence that John brought to the writing of the Book of Revelation – and offers to us.

God, our refuge and strength,
bring near the day when wars shall cease
and poverty and pain shall end,
that earth may know the peace of heaven
through Jesus Christ our Lord.

COLLECT

Reflection by **John Pritchard** | 309

Monday 19 November

Revelation 10

'There will be no more delay' (v.6)

This chapter, like much of the rest of the book of Revelation, is a patchwork of prophecies recycled by the author, the visionary John, from Old Testament books, particularly Daniel, Zechariah and Ezekiel. These have been artfully woven together to speak to a time of desperation in the life of the early Church, when persecution created a huge longing for the final redemption promised by Jesus. The temptation in reading Revelation is to attempt to assign a precise meaning to each and every image. But the book is intended to conceal as much as it reveals and we can never know precisely what John meant.

What we can appreciate is the certainty of divine judgement and final redemption. The sweetness and bitterness of the scroll reflects the two sides of the message. John eats the scroll to identify himself with the strange and terrifying message that he carries for the Church. We too, are called not just to proclaim the Word of God; to be effective witnesses, we need to 'eat' the Scriptures; incorporating them into our very being so that we ourselves are transformed by the words we reflect on. Or, as Thomas Cranmer, compiler of the Book of Common Prayer, put it in his Collect on Scripture set for the Second Sunday in Advent: 'Grant that we may ... hear them, read, mark, learn and inwardly digest them, that ... we may embrace and ever hold fast the blessed hope of everlasting life'.

COLLECT

Heavenly Father,
whose blessed Son was revealed
    to destroy the works of the devil
and to make us the children of God and heirs of eternal life:
grant that we, having this hope,
may purify ourselves even as he is pure;
that when he shall appear in power and great glory
we may be made like him in his eternal and glorious kingdom;
where he is alive and reigns with you,
in the unity of the Holy Spirit,
one God, now and for ever.

| *Reflection by* **Angela Tilby**

Tuesday 20 November

Revelation 11.1-14

'I will grant my two witnesses authority' (v.3)

The key point here is that the purpose that God announces through his witnesses cannot fail. John is commanded to measure the temple of God, suggesting that this prophecy is directed against Jews who have rejected Jesus, rather than against the gentiles. The 'witnesses' are prophets: possibly Moses and Elijah. They stand for the consistency of God's word against all who would destroy or wilfully misinterpret it. They are inside the great city, which here clearly means Jerusalem, where 'their Lord was crucified'. But Jerusalem has refused God, and is so identified with the sinful city of Sodom, or with oppressive Egypt. The prophets' message is intolerable to those who hear it. While they are speaking they have supernatural powers to defend themselves. But even prophets are vulnerable, and when they are finished, they are killed by the beast that emerges from the pit. But this is not the end; they are then resurrected and raised to heaven.

The violence and vehemence of the vision is difficult for us to assimilate, but think of those Christians, and others of minority faiths around the world who have seen their places of worship destroyed, their homes bombed or set on fire, and their families under constant threat. Holding on to faith in such circumstances is extremely challenging, but what is more important than our faith is that God holds on to us and can never be defeated.

Heavenly Lord,
you long for the world's salvation:
stir us from apathy,
restrain us from excess
and revive in us new hope
that all creation will one day be healed
in Jesus Christ our Lord.

COLLECT

Reflection by **Angela Tilby** | 311

Wednesday 21 November

Psalms **56**, 57 *or* **119.105-128**
Daniel 9.1-19
Revelation 11.15-end

Revelation 11.15-end

'He will reign for ever and ever' (v.15)

The trumpet blast of the seventh angel brings the beginnings of resolution for those who are still overwhelmed by the sufferings of persecution. The trumpet gives way to 'loud voices' echoing out of heaven and announcing God's final victory; the beginning of the Messiah's reign. The voices sing the triumphant words that Handel set in the famous 'Hallelujah' chorus of his oratorio *Messiah*. The song of the 24 elders suggests that resistance to God's will is ultimately self-defeating. All things work together to bring about his victory. Voice precedes vision as God's temple in heaven is opened and the Ark of the covenant is revealed within. The Ark is the guarantee of God's abiding relationship with his people; his living presence in our midst.

In scriptural thinking, hearing comes before seeing. It is by hearing and assimilating the word of God that we are prepared for the vision of God; by trust and obedience that we discover God present among us. The challenge to us is not to take God's presence for granted, but to discipline ourselves by prayer, study and worship so that we are more and more able to receive what he has to give us. The fullness of the reign of God lies ahead in the fullness of time, but it begins in the human heart, today.

COLLECT

Heavenly Father,
whose blessed Son was revealed
    to destroy the works of the devil
and to make us the children of God and heirs of eternal life:
grant that we, having this hope,
may purify ourselves even as he is pure;
that when he shall appear in power and great glory
we may be made like him in his eternal and glorious kingdom;
where he is alive and reigns with you,
in the unity of the Holy Spirit,
one God, now and for ever.

| *Reflection by* **Angela Tilby**

Thursday 22 November

Revelation 12

'The great dragon was thrown down' (v.9)

This chapter has given rise to many strange and exotic interpretations. The woman clothed by the sun was originally identified as the Church, whose task it is continually to bear forth Christ to the world. Later commentators saw the woman as a type of the Virgin Mary. She is often portrayed in Catholic iconography crowned with the stars and with the moon at her feet. The two interpretations are not incompatible since Mary has from ancient times been regarded as a symbol of the Church. Just as Mary bore Jesus into the world, so we, as his Church, bear his life into our society and culture.

We should expect opposition. The male child who is born from heaven provokes war both in heaven and on earth. The war in heaven supports the idea of a pre-cosmic fall of angels, hinted at elsewhere in Scripture (Isaiah 14.12-26; Ezekiel 28.13-17). Here, however, the war suggests the final conflict between God and the forces of darkness. The casting down of the dragon from heaven is a vivid reminder that there is no ambivalence in God; if the spirit of inquisition and accusation is part of our vision of who God is, it needs to go!

Jesus himself had a vision of Satan's defeat after the return of the missionaries sent out to proclaim the kingdom (Luke 10.18). However terrible our circumstances on earth, our God reigns.

Heavenly Lord,
you long for the world's salvation:
stir us from apathy,
restrain us from excess
and revive in us new hope
that all creation will one day be healed
in Jesus Christ our Lord.

COLLECT

Friday 23 November

Psalms **63**, 65 *or* **88** (95)
Daniel 10.1 – 11.1
Revelation 13.1-10

Revelation 13.1-10

'... a call for the endurance and faith of the saints' (v.10)

The reign of God is challenged by events on earth. The beast that rises from the sea stood in the mind of the seer, John, and his readers for the Roman Empire. The blasphemies of the beast are the emperors' claims to semi-divine status, a status that was reinforced by the visual imagery of the emperor in every town and city, and his head on the coinage. The emperors controlled the media, just as those in power often do in authoritarian states today.

No interpretation of Revelation is fixed, however; at the Reformation, Protestant commentators identified the beast with aspects of Catholicism. The point for us is that earthly authority tends to over-reach itself. The lust for power and domination is dehumanizing. It not only harms those whom it oppresses; it damages itself. The beast receives 'a mortal wound'. The authority of the beast is derived from the dragon, who, though defeated in heaven, still has power to create mayhem on earth. The beast has real power to demand submission, even worship, and controls the means of communication.

In the face of this overwhelming challenge to the reign of God, the faithful cannot hope to conquer by the power of resistance and persuasion. They must simply accept what happens to them, and endure.

COLLECT

Heavenly Father,
whose blessed Son was revealed
    to destroy the works of the devil
and to make us the children of God and heirs of eternal life:
grant that we, having this hope,
may purify ourselves even as he is pure;
that when he shall appear in power and great glory
we may be made like him in his eternal and glorious kingdom;
where he is alive and reigns with you,
in the unity of the Holy Spirit,
one God, now and for ever.

| *Reflection by* **Angela Tilby**

Psalms **78.1-39** *or* 96, **97**, 100
Daniel 12
Revelation 13.11-end

Saturday 24 November

Revelation 13.11-end

'... it deceives the inhabitants of earth' (v.14)

The identity of the second beast, with its ominous number 666, has been the subject of lively speculation from the beginning of the Christian era. Historical identifications include emperors, in particular Nero, and later, certain popes. Modern interpretations include the EU, the United States and global capitalism. The early Church Father Irenaeus thought that the second beast represented all the apostasies against God since the foundation of the world.

We do not need to identify the beast with any specific person to recognize the fact that human beings can easily be deceived by those determined to dominate. For us today, the mark of the beast could indicate any enslavement to 'the system' – the opposite of the liberating sign of the cross conferred in Christian baptism. It is characteristic of the beast to impose conformity and insist on replication, as in the re-animation of the first beast and the worship of its image.

The beast always seeks to wipe out originality and creativity. We owe it to our leaders in Church and state to support them in our prayers and to challenge them whenever it appears that the pursuit of power has become an end in itself. On the eve of Christ the King, we should remember that God's reign is known in the humility of the servant king, not in power that is self-seeking and ultimately self-deluding.

COLLECT

Heavenly Lord,
you long for the world's salvation:
stir us from apathy,
restrain us from excess
and revive in us new hope
that all creation will one day be healed
in Jesus Christ our Lord.

Reflection by **Angela Tilby**   315

Monday 26 November

Psalms 92, **96** *or* **98**, 99, 101
Isaiah 40.1-11
Revelation 14.1-13

Revelation 14.1-13

'Fear God and give him glory' (v.7)

Suddenly the vision changes; the Lamb appears on Mount Zion. His appearance reveals in all its clarity the sharp division between those who have chosen to be faithful to Christ and those who have worshipped the beast. The 'two ways' of life and death are a familiar theme in scripture and in much Jewish and early Christian writing, but here they are set out in the starkest contrast. Salvation is not limited to the celibate martyrs who have already been redeemed. An angel brings the good news to those still on the earth, offering them the chance to recognize and respond to the true God. The invitation is quickly followed by further judgement as the downfall of 'Babylon' is announced. This is the persecuting Roman state that has so callously shed the blood of God's saints. The writer sees no glimmer of hope for those who have worshipped the beast.

Yet, in spite of this grim prophecy, a note of universalism is present. The eternal gospel of verse 6 is still offered to everyone on earth. Those who are facing death can be assured that they are not forgotten. They will rest from their labours, their trials over. The words of verse 13 have become familiar by being frequently used at funerals. The narrow vision of the Book of Revelation opens up to something universal in the experience of the Church.

COLLECT

Eternal Father,
whose Son Jesus Christ ascended to the throne of heaven
    that he might rule over all things as Lord and King:
keep the Church in the unity of the Spirit
and in the bond of peace,
and bring the whole created order to worship at his feet;
who is alive and reigns with you,
in the unity of the Holy Spirit,
one God, now and for ever.

| *Reflection by* **Angela Tilby**

Psalms **97**, 98, 100 *or* **106*** (*or* 103)
Isaiah 40.12-26
Revelation 14.14 – 15.end

Tuesday 27 November

Revelation 14.14 – 15.end

'Great and amazing are your deeds, Lord God, the Almighty!'
(15.3)

Two images of judgement dominate this passage: the harvesting of the earth and the seven bowls of the wrath of God. Between the two is a vision of the redeemed beside a sea of glass, mingled with fire. The scriptural allusions here come from the Exodus story. The song of the redeemed echoes that of the Israelites who have crossed the Red Sea, except that it contains the universal hope that all nations will come to worship the true God.

The problem for many of us in reflecting on this passage is the dominating theme of God's wrath. We could see this as a response to the history of bloodshed that has accompanied the human journey from time immemorial and still scars our world. God is not withdrawn from the horror of the world, but enters into it, experiencing it to the full through the suffering of Christ and his saints.

Vindictive as the theology of Revelation may seem, there is a countertheme of universal redemption. The wrath of God is not ultimate, but has an end. It may even, though with difficulty, be seen as therapeutic, for how can humanity be saved unless we are honest about our capacity for violence against our neighbours and ourselves? In all of this, the fire that cuts through the glassy sea recalls the Spirit, bringing life out of human chaos.

God the Father,
help us to hear the call of Christ the King
and to follow in his service,
whose kingdom has no end;
for he reigns with you and the Holy Spirit,
one God, one glory.

COLLECT

Wednesday 28 November

Psalms 110, 111, **112**
or 110, **111**, 112
Isaiah 40.27 – 41.7
Revelation 16.1-11

Revelation 16.1-11

'You are just, O Holy One' (v.5)

The plagues poured out from the seven bowls of wrath remind us of the plagues of Egypt. Here, though, they are not intended to persuade Pharaoh to release God's people, but rather to demonstrate to the whole inhabited earth the extent of human wrongdoing. However, like the plagues of Egypt, they do not bring about a change of heart. Wounded as they are, the victims of the plagues do not repent but continue to curse God. It is as though the elements of creation have turned against humanity; the sea and the rivers turn to blood, the sun to scorching heat, and a deep darkness gathers over the kingdom of the beast. The justice of this judgement is underscored by the voice of the angel of the waters and the voice of the altar.

Although the detail of Revelation can be obscure and confusing, people have always resonated with its message of divine vengeance, perhaps because, in our hearts we long for justice and believe we deserve it. This is why, even in our age, we can see parallels between, for example, the damage human beings have done to our environment on earth, and the consequences this may yet have on our lives. The apocalyptic spirit is part of the human imagination and it is one way in which the living God speaks to us, warning us to change direction before it is too late.

C O L L E C T

Eternal Father,
whose Son Jesus Christ ascended to the throne of heaven
that he might rule over all things as Lord and King:
keep the Church in the unity of the Spirit
and in the bond of peace,
and bring the whole created order to worship at his feet;
who is alive and reigns with you,
in the unity of the Holy Spirit,
one God, now and for ever.

| *Reflection by* **Angela Tilby**

Psalms **125**, 126, 127, 128
or 113, **115**
Isaiah 41.8-20
Revelation 16.12-end

Thursday 29 November

Revelation 16.12-end

'Blessed is the one who stays awake and is clothed' (v.15)

The sixth and seventh angels complete the outpouring of God's wrath.
The consequence is the total break up of the physical geography and
geology of the earth: the life-giving Euphrates dries up; the bowl flung
into the air makes the mountains and islands vanish. The whole
landscape is thus made strange and unfamiliar.

All this is the backdrop for the spirits of evil to make ready for the last
and final battle at Armageddon, a location intended to recall Megiddo,
where the righteous king Joshua met his fate. The demonic spirits
preparing for battle are lying spirits, luring the bulk of humanity to
destruction while the faithful remember the warnings of Jesus about
the suddenness of his return (Matthew 24.43-4; 1 Thessalonians 5.2).
They remain alert, clothed in holiness.

Armageddon has, of course, been a symbol of a final dramatic conflict
through the whole of the Christian era. It has also come into modern
times as an allusion to all-out global war – World War III to many of our
contemporaries. It is not impossible that humanity might perish in a
final nuclear conflagration, but it is doubtful that John foresaw this.
His concern is, as always, the vindication of God's purpose and the
certainty of judgment and redemption. This is what we hold on to in
times of global threat.

God the Father,
help us to hear the call of Christ the King
and to follow in his service,
whose kingdom has no end;
for he reigns with you and the Holy Spirit,
one God, one glory.

COLLECT

Friday 30 November
Andrew the Apostle

Psalms 47, 147.1-12
Ezekiel 47.1-12
or Ecclesiasticus 14.20-end
John 12.20-32

Ezekiel 47.1-12

'... everything will live where the river goes' (v.9)

According to the Gospels, St Andrew was one of the first disciples to be called, a fisherman. Legend credits him with bringing the gospel to Georgia and other regions around the Black Sea.

Today's reading points to the life-giving power of God that gushes out from the temple sanctuary, bringing fertility to the land and life to the waters. The mission of the apostles is to bring life: knowledge of the living God, dignity to the human person, energy and purpose to the human community. The Christian life is about much more than religion, though at its heart is the thirst for holiness. The energy of God's life is unstoppable. The water flows from the sanctuary whether or not it is adequately channelled by human beings; it is 'deep enough to swim in', and eventually so deep that it cannot be crossed. The gospel is for everyone; the fish produced by the river are 'of a great many kinds'. This passage has perhaps influenced the account of the fishing miracle in John's Gospel (John 21.11) and suggests that God desires his image to be brought to fulfilment in many and diverse ways.

Apostles are missionaries, and we share their calling to be caught up in the living stream of God's love for the world. We can never control or determine the path of that stream, but we can – and should – go with its flow.

COLLECT

Almighty God,
who gave such grace to your apostle Saint Andrew
that he readily obeyed the call of your Son Jesus Christ
  and brought his brother with him:
call us by your holy word,
and give us grace to follow you without delay
  and to tell the good news of your kingdom;
through Jesus Christ your Son our Lord,
who is alive and reigns with you,
in the unity of the Holy Spirit,
one God, now and for ever.

| *Reflection by* **Angela Tilby**

Psalms **145** *or* 120, **121**, 122
Isaiah 42.10-17
Revelation 18

Saturday 1 December

Revelation 18

'Come out of her, my people' (v.4)

This great denunciation of 'Babylon', Rome, foresees the destruction of
the great city as though it were happening at the present moment.
Rome is guilty of the blood of the martyrs; her basic sin is idolatry,
which includes the worship of the emperor. The destruction is total.
All the wealth that has flooded into the city from other parts of the
empire is finished. In fact, of course, John's prophecy and vision were
unfulfilled. Rome did not fall in the early Christian era. Even more
surprisingly, with the conversion of Constantine, Christianity became
the faith of the Roman Empire.

There are two points at which the prophecy of Rome's downfall has
something to say to us. The first is to note that the denunciation
includes judgements that Jesus himself made against Jerusalem;
compare verse 24 with Matthew 23.34-37a ('Jerusalem, Jerusalem,
the city that kills the prophets and stones those who are sent to it!',
v.37). A city that kills God's prophets is always going to come under
God's judgement.

The second point is that there is a call to God's people to detach
themselves from the corruption of the city, including its tendency to
worship wealth and power. Christians should always be alert to the
temptation to covetousness and avarice. Prosperous cities can be built
on brutal injustice, and the Christian community of Rome is warned, as
we are, not to be seduced by the city's false glamour.

COLLECT

Eternal Father,
whose Son Jesus Christ ascended to the throne of heaven
that he might rule over all things as Lord and King:
keep the Church in the unity of the Spirit
and in the bond of peace,
and bring the whole created order to worship at his feet;
who is alive and reigns with you,
in the unity of the Holy Spirit,
one God, now and for ever.

Seasonal Prayers of Thanksgiving

Advent

Blessed are you, Sovereign God of all,
to you be praise and glory for ever.
In your tender compassion
the dawn from on high is breaking upon us
to dispel the lingering shadows of night.
As we look for your coming among us this day,
open our eyes to behold your presence
and strengthen our hands to do your will,
that the world may rejoice and give you praise.
Blessed be God, Father, Son and Holy Spirit.
Blessed be God for ever.

Christmas Season

Blessed are you, Sovereign God,
creator of heaven and earth,
to you be praise and glory for ever.
As your living Word, eternal in heaven,
assumed the frailty of our mortal flesh,
may the light of your love be born in us
to fill our hearts with joy as we sing:
Blessed be God, Father, Son and Holy Spirit.
Blessed be God for ever.

Epiphany

Blessed are you, Sovereign God,
king of the nations,
to you be praise and glory for ever.
From the rising of the sun to its setting
your name is proclaimed in all the world.
As the Sun of Righteousness dawns in our hearts
anoint our lips with the seal of your Spirit
that we may witness to your gospel
and sing your praise in all the earth.
Blessed be God, Father, Son and Holy Spirit.
Blessed be God for ever.

Blessed are you, Lord God of our salvation,
to you be glory and praise for ever.
In the darkness of our sin you have shone in our hearts
to give the light of the knowledge of the glory of God
in the face of Jesus Christ.
Open our eyes to acknowledge your presence,
that freed from the misery of sin and shame
we may grow into your likeness from glory to glory.
Blessed be God, Father, Son and Holy Spirit.
Blessed be God for ever.

Blessed are you, Lord God of our salvation,
to you be praise and glory for ever.
As a man of sorrows and acquainted with grief
your only Son was lifted up
that he might draw the whole world to himself.
May we walk this day in the way of the cross
and always be ready to share its weight,
declaring your love for all the world.
Blessed be God, Father, Son and Holy Spirit.
Blessed be God for ever.

Blessed are you, Sovereign Lord,
the God and Father of our Lord Jesus Christ,
to you be glory and praise for ever.
From the deep waters of death
you brought your people to new birth
by raising your Son to life in triumph.
Through him dark death has been destroyed
and radiant life is everywhere restored.
As you call us out of darkness into his marvellous light
may our lives reflect his glory
and our lips repeat the endless song.
Blessed be God, Father, Son and Holy Spirit.
Blessed be God for ever.

Ascension Day

Blessed are you, Lord of heaven and earth,
to you be glory and praise for ever.
From the darkness of death you have raised your Christ
to the right hand of your majesty on high.
The pioneer of our faith, his passion accomplished,
has opened for us the way to heaven
and sends on us the promised Spirit.
May we be ready to follow the Way
and so be brought to the glory of his presence
where songs of triumph for ever sound:
Blessed be God, Father, Son and Holy Spirit.
Blessed be God for ever.

---

*From the day after Ascension Day
until the Day of Pentecost*

Blessed are you, creator God,
to you be praise and glory for ever.
As your Spirit moved over the face of the waters
bringing light and life to your creation,
pour out your Spirit on us today
that we may walk as children of light
and by your grace reveal your presence.
Blessed be God, Father, Son and Holy Spirit.
Blessed be God for ever.

---

*From All Saints until the day before
the First Sunday of Advent*

Blessed are you, Sovereign God,
ruler and judge of all,
to you be praise and glory for ever.
In the darkness of this age that is passing away
may the light of your presence which the saints enjoy
surround our steps as we journey on.
May we reflect your glory this day
and so be made ready to see your face
in the heavenly city where night shall be no more.
Blessed be God, Father, Son and Holy Spirit.
Blessed be God for ever.

The Lord's Prayer and The Grace

Our Father in heaven,
hallowed be your name,
your kingdom come,
your will be done,
on earth as in heaven.
Give us today our daily bread.
Forgive us our sins
as we forgive those who sin against us.
Lead us not into temptation
but deliver us from evil.
For the kingdom, the power,
and the glory are yours
now and for ever.
Amen.

(or)

Our Father, who art in heaven,
hallowed be thy name;
thy kingdom come;
thy will be done;
on earth as it is in heaven.
Give us this day our daily bread.
And forgive us our trespasses,
as we forgive those who trespass against us.
And lead us not into temptation;
but deliver us from evil.
For thine is the kingdom,
the power and the glory,
for ever and ever.
Amen.

The grace of our Lord Jesus Christ,
and the love of God,
and the fellowship of the Holy Spirit,
be with us all evermore.
Amen.

An Order for Night Prayer (Compline)

The Lord almighty grant us a quiet night and a perfect end.
Amen.

Our help is in the name of the Lord
who made heaven and earth.

A period of silence for reflection on the past day may follow.

The following or other suitable words of penitence may be used

**Most merciful God,
we confess to you,
before the whole company of heaven and one another,
that we have sinned in thought, word and deed
and in what we have failed to do.
Forgive us our sins,
heal us by your Spirit
and raise us to new life in Christ. Amen.**

O God, make speed to save us.
O Lord, make haste to help us.

**Glory to the Father and to the Son
and to the Holy Spirit;
as it was in the beginning is now
and shall be for ever. Amen.
Alleluia.**

The following or another suitable hymn may be sung

Before the ending of the day,
Creator of the world, we pray
That you, with steadfast love, would keep
Your watch around us while we sleep.

From evil dreams defend our sight,
From fears and terrors of the night;
Tread underfoot our deadly foe
That we no sinful thought may know.

O Father, that we ask be done
Through Jesus Christ, your only Son;
And Holy Spirit, by whose breath
Our souls are raised to life from death.

The Word of God

Psalmody

One or more of Psalms 4, 91 or 134 may be used.

Psalm 134

1   Come, bless the Lord, all you servants of the Lord, ♦
   you that by night stand in the house of the Lord.

2   Lift up your hands towards the sanctuary ♦
   and bless the Lord.

3   The Lord who made heaven and earth ♦
   give you blessing out of Zion.

Glory to the Father and to the Son
and to the Holy Spirit;
as it was in the beginning is now
and shall be for ever. Amen.

Scripture Reading

One of the following short lessons or another suitable
passage is read

You, O Lord, are in the midst of us and we are called by
your name; leave us not, O Lord our God.

Jeremiah 14.9

(or)

Be sober, be vigilant, because your adversary the devil is
prowling round like a roaring lion, seeking for someone
to devour. Resist him, strong in the faith.

1 Peter 5.8,9

(or)

The servants of the Lamb shall see the face of God, whose
name will be on their foreheads. There will be no more night:
they will not need the light of a lamp or the light of the sun,
for God will be their light, and they will reign for ever and
ever.

Revelation 22.4,5

The following responsory may be said

Into your hands, O Lord, I commend my spirit.
Into your hands, O Lord, I commend my spirit.
For you have redeemed me, Lord God of truth.
I commend my spirit.
Glory to the Father and to the Son
and to the Holy Spirit.
Into your hands, O Lord, I commend my spirit.

Or, in Easter

Into your hands, O Lord, I commend my spirit.
Alleluia, alleluia.
Into your hands, O Lord, I commend my spirit.
Alleluia, alleluia.
For you have redeemed me, Lord God of truth.
Alleluia, alleluia.
Glory to the Father and to the Son
and to the Holy Spirit.
Into your hands, O Lord, I commend my spirit.
Alleluia, alleluia.

Keep me as the apple of your eye.
Hide me under the shadow of your wings.

Gospel Canticle

Nunc Dimittis (The Song of Simeon)

Save us, O Lord, while waking,
and guard us while sleeping,
that awake we may watch with Christ
and asleep may rest in peace.

1   Now, Lord, you let your servant go in peace:
    your word has been fulfilled.

2   My own eyes have seen the salvation
    which you have prepared in the sight of every people;

3   A light to reveal you to the nations
    and the glory of your people Israel.

Luke 2.29-32

Glory to the Father and to the Son
and to the Holy Spirit;
as it was in the beginning is now
and shall be for ever. Amen.

Save us, O Lord, while waking,
and guard us while sleeping,
that awake we may watch with Christ
and asleep may rest in peace.

Prayers

Intercessions and thanksgivings may be offered here.

The Collect

Visit this place, O Lord, we pray,
and drive far from it the snares of the enemy;
may your holy angels dwell with us and guard us in peace,
and may your blessing be always upon us;
through Jesus Christ our Lord.
Amen.

The Lord's Prayer (see p. 325) may be said.

The Conclusion

In peace we will lie down and sleep;
for you alone, Lord, make us dwell in safety.

Abide with us, Lord Jesus,
for the night is at hand and the day is now past.

As the night watch looks for the morning,
so do we look for you, O Christ.

[Come with the dawning of the day
and make yourself known in the breaking of the bread.]

The Lord bless us and watch over us;
the Lord make his face shine upon us and be gracious to us;
the Lord look kindly on us and give us peace.
Amen.

REFLECTIONS FOR SUNDAYS (YEAR B)

Reflections for Sundays offers over 250 reflections on the Principal Readings for every Sunday and major Holy Day in Year B, from the same experienced team of writers that have made *Reflections for Daily Prayer* so successful. For each Sunday and major Holy Day, they provide:

- full lectionary details for the Principal Service
- a reflection on each Old Testament reading (both Continuous and Related)
- a reflection on the Epistle
- a reflection on the Gospel.

This book also contains a substantial introduction to the Gospels of Mark and John, written by Paula Gooder.

£14.99 • 288 pages
ISBN 978 1 78140 030 2

Also available in Kindle and epub formats

REFLECTIONS ON THE PSALMS

£14.99 • 192 pages
ISBN 978 0 7151 4490 9

Reflections on the Psalms provides original and insightful meditations on each of the Bible's 150 Psalms.

Each reflection is accompanied by its corresponding Psalm refrain and prayer from the *Common Worship Psalter*, making this a valuable resource for personal or devotional use.

Specially written introductions by Paula Gooder and Steven Croft explore the Psalms and the Bible and the Psalms in the life of the Church.

These two shortened editions of *Reflections* are ideal for group or church use during Advent and Lent, or for anyone seeking a daily devotional guide to these most holy seasons of the Christian year.

They are also ideal tasters for those wanting to begin a regular pattern of prayer and reading.

REFLECTIONS FOR **ADVENT 2017**

Monday 27 November – Saturday 23 December 2017

Authors:
Christopher Cocksworth
Paula Gooder
Malcolm Guite

Please note this book reproduces the material for Advent found in the volume you are now holding.

£2.99 • 48 pages
ISBN 978 1 78140 024 1
Available August 2017

REFLECTIONS FOR **LENT 2018**

Wednesday 14 February – Saturday 31 March 2018

Authors:
Gillian Cooper
Martyn Percy
Jane Williams
Jeremy Worthen

Please note this book reproduces the material for Lent and Holy Week found in the volume you are now holding.

£4.99 • 64 pages
ISBN 978 1 78140 027 2
Available November 2017

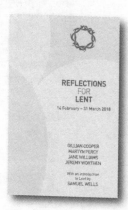

REFLECTIONS FOR DAILY PRAYER
App

Make Bible study and reflection a part of your routine wherever you go with the Reflections for Daily Prayer App for Apple and Android devices.

Download the app for free from the App Store (Apple devices) or Google Play (Android devices) and receive a week's worth of reflections free. Then purchase a monthly, three-monthly or annual subscription to receive up-to-date content.

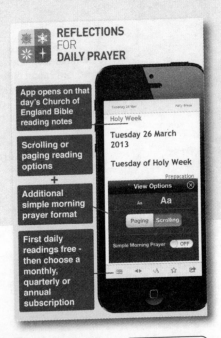

RESOURCES FOR DAILY PRAYER

Common Worship: Daily Prayer

The official daily office of the Church of England,
Common Worship: Daily Prayer is a rich collection of
devotional material that will enable those
wanting to enrich their quiet times to develop
a regular pattern of prayer. It includes:

- Prayer During the Day
- Forms of Penitence
- Morning and Evening Prayer
- Night Prayer (Compline)
- Collects and Refrains
- Canticles
- Complete Psalter

896 pages • with 6 ribbons • 202 x 125mm

Hardback	978 0 7151 2199 3	**£22.50**
Soft cased	978 0 7151 2178 8	**£27.50**
Bonded leather	978 0 7151 2277 8	**£50.00**

Time to Pray

This compact, soft-case volume offers two simple,
shorter offices from *Common Worship: Daily Prayer*.
It is an ideal introduction to a more structured personal
devotional time, or can be used as a lighter, portable
daily office for those on the move.

Time to Pray includes:

- Prayer During the Day
  (for every day of the week)
- Night Prayer
- Selected Psalms

£12.99 • 112 pages • Soft case
ISBN 978 0 7151 2122 1

Order now at www.chpublishing.co.uk
or via **Norwich Books and Music**
Telephone **(01603) 785923**
E-mail **orders@norwichbooksandmusic.co.uk**